Exploring
The Mysteries of Life

30 years research

by
Nellie B. Cain

740 Hubbard St., N.E.
Grand Rapids, Mich. 49505

Illustrated by Martha Gras and Tim Boxell

With loving gratitude and acknowledgement to my husband, Edward H. Cain, without whose constant inspiration and incalculable help throughout the years this book could not have been written.

DEDICATION

As I am compiling the material which will comprise this book I am enjoying the solitude and beauty of our delightful "retreat" among the pine trees beside a beautiful spring-fed trout stream in Western Michigan. The Cosmic Masters have made this place available to us for the furtherance of their work on the earth plane. We are told that it is on intersecting lines of Cosmic Energy with which they girded the earth eons ago, so that such places could be used as "grounding points" for their love and energy to be focused in the earth dimension as it is needed. As each New Age begins, it requires an outpouring from them to help lift the vibrations and the consciousness of mankind. All who come here are aware of more than the physical beauty of the place; they also feel the wonderful vibrations here. We were told that we must make it available to those who are in need of relaxation, solitude, and respite from the hectic world. We feel very fortunate to have been chosen to help the Masters in their work and have therefore dedicated this place to them. I also hereby lovingly dedicate this book to them, for it is only through their great Love, Wisdom, and unending Patience, that it has been received and recorded.

The Author

TABLE OF CONTENTS

EXPLORING THE MYSTERIES OF LIFE

30 Years Research

PREFACE

My husband and I have had the wonderful experience of sharing thirty years of intensive study into many facets of the occult and mystical aspects of life. This has resulted in many exciting and enlightening experiences that have run the gamut from the phenomenal level of spirit manifestation to sublime "mystical revelation" of great magnitude. This has so transformed our lives and has been so soul-rewarding that we feel it should be shared with our fellow travelers on "The Path." We do this in the full knowledge that each individual walks his own Pathway and that no two people have, or need, exactly the same experiences. However, since the sharing by others has often helped us, perhaps our sharing can, in turn, help others to gain a broader understanding of man's Divine Destiny.

Since many of these experiences have been of a very personal nature, I trust the reader will forgive the use of the first person and will realize that this is not used for personal acclaim or aggrandizement, but merely as a more convenient means of conveying the great truths we have been privileged to find and now humbly wish to share.

My husband, Edward H. Cain, Jr., had the rare privilege of being the son of an outstanding Spiritualist medium, so he was raised in that atmosphere during all of his early years. However, in his youth he turned from it, partly because of the stigma attached to the occult at that time, and partly because he could see no good in it. Although he had little interest, he always accepted the fact of the continuity of life after death and of communication with those who had made the transition, and he often told me of the things that had transpired in the seances he had attended in their home. I had been raised in an orthodox Methodist home so it all seemed very far-fetched to me. While I did not doubt his sincerity, at that time I thought he was both gullible and had been hood-winked, but I later found, through his father and many other fine mediums, that these things are not only possible but do happen, and that there is a vast reservoir of Infinite Intelligence and information to be tapped in the "invisible world" if we will open our minds and hearts to it. The past thirty years of our lives have been dedicated to the exploration of this reservoir, and in that exploration we have received reams of material from those who work upon its various levels. Our experiences encompass communication with departed loved ones, with our personal guides and guardian angels, and with the Ascended Masters of the White Brotherhood who act as the Cosmic Guardians of the entire human race, as well as many personal mystical experiences and revelations. These I shall attempt to relate in the sequence in which they were received, thus showing what is possible for those who are sincere and dedicated Seekers of Truth.

We were very fortunate to have had the mediumship of my father-in-law as a springboard for our interest and our pursuit into the deeper aspects of Universal Law and Truth. So, in grateful acknowledgement to him and his great talent, and for "rending the veil" for me and many others, and because I think the reader will find his mediumship interesting and enlightening, I shall devote the first chapter of this book to relating a few of the many manifestations he had in psychic phenomena.

Part 1

Chapter 1

Mediumship of Edward H. Cain

Edward Cain, Sr. was first introduced to spirit manifestation in a rather startling way. He was about twenty-
one years old and had recently married. He and his wife
were living with his widowed mother, his father having
passed on when he was much younger. His wife had been
raised by parents who had attended seances, so she was
partially acquainted with the phenomena of Spiritualism and
with the code used to communicate through rappings on a
table or an object, but she had never discussed this with
her husband or her mother-in-law. One day she had been
shopping and was returning home. Mr. Cain, seeing her
coming down the street prankishly decided to frighten her
as she entered the house, so he stepped behind the door and
awaited her arrival. His deceased father's picture hung on
the wall near where he was standing, and just as she entered there were loud rappings on the picture. The raps were
so loud they were heard by his mother, who was working
in the kitchen. She entered the living room, wondering
what it was all about. Mrs. Cain recognized it as being
spirit raps but was reluctant to speak of it. However, since
the rapping persisted, she finally asked if "spirit" was doing the rapping, and received three raps in return, meaning
"Yes." She then asked if it was Mr. Cain's father and again
received three raps. Mr. Cain's mother, being very skeptical, remarked that it would have to be proven to be her

husband before she could believe it, so she asked if he could tell her where his sister Sarah was. Many years prior to this time, the father, with his parents and brothers and sisters, had moved to America from Ireland. The family had become scattered and had lost contact with each other. Through the years they had all moved from their original settlement site in Oswego, New York, to various parts of this country. No one knew the whereabouts of Sarah, for she had never written to any of her family after she had married and left home. In answer to the question regarding Sarah's whereabouts, they also received an affirmative reply. They then said they would go through the alphabet and the numerals and the spirit was to rap when they came to the right ones. They received the number and name of a street in Indianapolis, Indiana. They sent a letter to Sarah at that address and received a prompt reply from her asking how they had found where she was living.

They later had a similar experience in locating another relative in San Francisco, California. In this instance they were given the name of the street, as well as the city, but were told that the relative would be found living in a red house at the top of a hill, which proved to be true.

Of course, this experience excited them and led them to start what they called a "developing circle." They, along with a group of their interested friends, "sat" in a circle twice a week with a trumpet, such as is used by mediums, to develop Mr. Cain's mediumship. Strangely, while the original raps had come involuntarily on the picture, it was about six months before they received anything through the trumpet. Then they began receiving raps on the trumpet, and in a short time it would levitate and various voices began speaking through it. Mr. Cain soon began to "sit" in a cabinet, which is a small enclosure made of black curtains, and full spirit forms would emerge from the cabinet and identify themselves, by voice, to the audience. Many times, rather than emerging from the cabinet, the forms would build outside the cabinet, first appearing like a vapor arising from the floor, and gradually gaining full height and taking on the shape of a human being. When leaving, they would simply disintegrate in full view of the audience.

Voices coming through the trumpet would often speak in foreign languages and carry on a complete conversation with someone in the circle. Mr. Cain could speak nothing but the English language, so this was very evidential to many people. When my husband was about sixteen years old he witnessed an instance of a conversation spoken entirely in the Dutch language coming through the trumpet in the daylight. One afternoon an elderly Dutch couple came to the Cain home. The old gentleman was very deaf and could speak only Dutch. The lady spoke very broken English, but was able to tell Mr. Cain that they had come because her husband was being incessantly bothered by some force they could not identify. Although he was deaf, he could hear voices, he had been slapped and pushed down on several occasions, his pillow had been torn open during the night and feathers strewn about, and many other disturbing and unaccountable things had taken place. He had gone to the doctor but had been told it was either his nerves or his imagination. Now they were hoping to find a satisfactory answer to his dilemma. As they had entered the house, Mr. Cain, who often had extended vision, had seen a third party with them who seemed to be carrying a legal document. After the lady had told of her husband's experiences, Mr. Cain held the small end of the trumpet to her ear, with the large end resting in his hand. Soon a voice, speaking in Dutch, could be heard, with which she carried on a long conversation, she too speaking in Dutch. She would often pause to relay what the voice was saying to her husband, who used an old-fashioned ear trumpet to enable him to hear. The voice identified itself as the brother of her husband. He told that at the death of their father, in Holland, a sum of money had been left which he had promised to share with the brother in America, but he had used it all himself. Now that he was on the other side of life, he realized his mistake and his spiritual progress was impeded because of it. He had been bothering his brother to get him to go to someone where contact could be made so he could confess his guilt and be forgiven.

Another phase of mediumship that developed was called "hand seances." Mr. Cain and two other people would sit in a well lighted room in front of a curtain which would be stretched across a corner where there were no windows or doors. They would hold each other's hands, probably to generate strength, but also proving that he was not faking the phenomena. Several hands would appear through the curtain at the same time. At times, some would be lacking fingers, or be otherwise identifiable. Those in the audience would go up and shake the hands, which often felt warm, and would return their grasp. Sometimes the materialized hands would pat the faces, or heads, of those who were sitting in front of the curtain. Many times a guitar was handed over the curtain and was played and then handed back again.

An instance of materialization in full light once occurred. Mr. Cain had gone into the cabinet, which was in a corner of the dining room, to sit for his development. His wife and mother were in the kitchen doing the dishes. In a short time they were startled to see a tall Hindu standing in the doorway between the two rooms. Mr. Cain was a short man, but this figure was well over six feet tall. He was dressed in full Hindu garb with a turban and tunic, and was of swarthy complexion. The ladies talked to him. Although he did not speak, he would nod or shake his head to answer them. Mrs. Cain asked if he could give them some memento of his visit. He reached down and tore a piece from his tunic and gave it to her. The fabric was the texture of burlap. She placed it in the Bible and later showed it to their group. A few days later, she was going to show it again, but it had dematerialized. When the Hindu left he also dematerialized from where he had been standing, not returning to the cabinet.

At one seance a lady was present who had never been there before and who was unknown to the others who were present. The trumpet moved to her and the voice coming from it stated that it was her mother. She replied that this could not be true because her mother was alive and resid-

ing in Germany. With her doubt, the trumpet fell to the
floor but was soon raised again. A new voice then gave
his name and identified himself as having been her French
teacher in Germany. This, she said, was valid. The voice
told her that it had been her mother's voice, for the mother
had just passed on, and that there was a five page letter
in the mail informing her of her mother's death. A week
later she returned with the five page letter, confirming
what had come through to her.

Probably the most awesome of all the manifestations
the Cain's had was a phenomenon which I doubt has ever
occurred in any other seance room. They often had the
materialized form of a Catholic Sister who gave her name
as Bridgett Doran. This evening when she appeared, she
carried a cross which sparkled with small lights, as did
her habit. She asked the group if they would like to see a
demonstration of the power of spirit beyond anything they
had ever seen, or were ever likely to see again. Of course,
they replied in the affirmative. She told them to repeat the
Lord's Prayer and sing hymns and she would do her best.
In about twenty minutes she emerged from the cabinet
carrying Mr. Cain by the coat collar. He was very limp
and in a deep trance. She asked for a chair and placed
him in it. Then she stood behind the chair and kept passing her hands through the air just above him. She talked
for several minutes, explaining that the law of gravity can
be overcome by using the higher laws of Spirit. When she
finished talking she again raised the medium by the collar
and carried him back into the cabinet. In all of our research,
we have heard of no other instance in which a materialized
form was able to carry the medium about.

The Cains were often subjected to the usual skepticism.
During one seance, an unbeliever grabbed a materialized
form. Of course, he had nothing, but Mr. Cain, who was
in the cabinet, fell unconscious to the floor. He had to be
carried out of doors into the fresh air, where he was in
great agony. It was several days before he was well again.
Apparently the sudden return of the "vital force" was more
than the physical body could accept.

Many times he "sat" under test conditions to prove his

mediumship. He was often placed in a chair, bound and gagged, his hands and feet placed in pans of flour, and mosquito netting tacked all around him. Forms still appeared on each occasion and identified themselves to the different ones present.

I must confess, I was very skeptical when I first heard these stories. However, after my interest was aroused and my husband's interest rekindled, as is related in the next chapter, I was privileged to witness a great deal of Mr. Cain's outstanding mediumship. We had many seances with him in our home, where I knew there were no props or fakery. Many times books were taken from the bookcase and placed in the laps of those in the circle. Pictures would be taken from the wall and handed to the sitters. Hands would materialize and pat people on the face or knees. On two different occasions my glasses were removed from my face and placed on the face of my sister, who was across the room from me. The trumpet would move all about the room, sometimes tapping the ceiling or various objects, and often moved gently over our shoulders and heads, or up and down the buttons on our clothing, but at no time did it ever hurt or bump into anyone. It would often stop before different individuals and the voices would speak from it, identifying themselves as loved ones or guides. This all took place in a completely darkened room with all in the circle holding hands. I often sat beside the medium and held his hand, so I was firmly convinced of his sincerity and ability.

I consider myself fortunate indeed to have had the opportunity for this firsthand, irrefutable proof of the continuity of life after so-called death. I am grateful also for the proof of communication with those in the other dimensions, for this opened new and wonderful doors which have led us into experiences and understanding far beyond our fondest dreams.

Part 1

Chapter 2

Contact with Invisible Helpers

Our interest in, and understanding of, the mystical and occult aspects of life were of such a gradual nature and in such an orderly fashion that we could not have foreseen their magnitude and beauty. Neither did we appreciate what was happening until we could view our unfoldment in retrospect. As we look back we are amazed, very humble, and grateful for all that has happened.

My first introduction to these things came one evening when my half sister, who is fourteen years my junior, and her friend came to visit us. They brought an ouija board with which they started to play. They were laughingly asking silly, girlish questions and receiving equally silly answers until my husband suggested that they try to find out whom they were contacting. I was surprised to see the name of my father spelled out. He had died when I was five years old. My sister had known very little about him or his family, so I began asking questions which I was sure only he could answer. Many irrefutable answers came, which were proof to me that it was actually he. My interest was aroused, so I suggested that they leave the ouija board for a few days and let us experiment with it. Since I was very skeptical and wanted no part of being fooled, we tested in every conceivable manner. We would operate the board while we were both blindfolded and have someone read the answers. Being afraid of subconsciously pushing it, I would ask questions while two other people held the board. I still received many answers from loved ones which no one else could possibly have known. Some answers gave dates of family events which I did not know, but was able to verify later. Many deceased relatives came and unmistakably identified themselves.

To give me further proof, my husband asked his father to have a seance for us and for some of our friends. Although he had not held seances for many years, he graciously came to our home many times, with the previously mentioned remarkable results.

Soon after our introduction to the ouija board the name of "Harmon" was spelled out. We asked for his message and received the reply that he was my Guardian Angel. He said he had been with me from the time I had been fourteen years old and was constantly helping me. I was told to call upon him at any time, and he would attempt to guide and instruct us.

One would have to have known us prior to this time to appreciate the full measure of help which this blessed Being brought us. Our affairs and marriage were in a very unhappy state. In fact, we were on the verge of a divorce. Harmon came on the board and gave us many beautiful lectures and much good advice. He soon stated that he had brought another helper who had been assigned to guide and assist my husband. Through the advice and counsel of these two dear friends, our lives were completely transformed, and we were led into many wonderful new experiences. Through their lessons we were brought to an awareness of spiritual values and a new understanding of how to straighten out our lives. When we would ask questions of a material nature they would always reply, "We are not concerned with your material welfare. We are concerned only with your spiritual progression. Put that in first place in your lives and everything else will take care of itself." We have found this to be very true. We were often severely chided, but always with their great love. Harmon always made his presence known by brushing lightly over the top of my hair. He became a very real Presence in our lives, and we owe him a great deal.

After some time of contact through the ouija board, we were amazed one evening, as we sat at the board, I had a sensation of fainting and lost awareness of what was going on in the room. I was dumbfounded, upon awakening, to find that I had been talking at great length and had presented a message from Harmon. From that time, we seldom received anything on the Ouija board, for apparently they preferred the short cut. It was not long before my husband was also receiving in this manner. Our interest attracted our friends and relatives, and we soon started having regular meetings to study and receive from the "unseen." We investigated many branches of metaphysics and the occult, and learned a great deal.

Harmon continued to come and gave us beautiful bits of philosophy to instill in our minds the necessary qualities for spiritual advancement. He often told us that we were being prepared for greater things which were to come, things beyond our greatest expectations. This was hard for us to accept or understand, for we knew so little about the higher aspects of Universal Law at that time. Our hearts were made heavy when, after about fifteen years of his devoted love and counsel, he made this announcement, "It is with deep regret that I must leave you. You have progressed to a point where higher teachers are taking over. I will come occasionally to note your progress, for my love for you remains. I have finished the task set before me and I must now go on to further the labors of the Masters with some other struggling Soul."

We had a feeling of great loss and expressed our gratitude for all that he had done for us. He replied, "Remember, you are likened to your very lives. When you are children you must play with simple things, and as you gradually mature, the simple things give way for greater things; so is your life. Remember, always have the simplicity of a child. Only then can you gain the wisdom of the Masters."

We expressed regret at his leaving and asked about those who would take his place. He replied, "I shall never forget you, although my work with you is finished. Have no fear, yours will be the best of teachers."

We asked if this was for what he had been preparing

us. In his great humility he replied, "I only pointed the way for greater things, and now with the blessings of God and the eternal love of the Masters, I bid you farewell."

We wept, as at the loss of a dear friend, but he has continued to come from time to time as he promised. My prayer is that we may fulfill all that he had hoped for us.

Gems of Truth from the Masters

Part 1

Chapter 3

Gems of Truth from the Masters

At the time of our first contact with the new teachers they introduced themselves in the following manner:

"I come to you in Love. My name is Tao-Tsing; that will be my identification to you. It means God's Follower. There are many who will serve you, for this is as a school in which there are many teachers to bring different lessons. You will be taught the Laws of the Universe from the standpoint of the Masters.

"We are a group of souls who have banded together to aid in awakening mankind, that he might come to know his true relationship with God and thereby recognize every man as his brother and treat him as such. The Universal Brotherhood of Mankind under God is our aim. To bring this about, man must learn many lessons. We shall endeavor to bring some of these lessons to you that you might be helped in your spiritual progression and, in turn, help others. It is our prayer for you that you will come to know God so intimately that you will be completely immersed in the realization of the Divine Presence and the oneness of all life. It will be the most real thing in your life and the only thing of lasting value. We are God's servants, ready to help you in any way we can. Bless you."

"My name is Kermit. I am also one of the teachers in the White Brotherhood. I shall endeavor to teach you the true meaning of Brotherhood as we understand it, and attempt to live it. We are most eager to help you. We have learned that there can be no true happiness until you feel your Oneness with the Divine Creator. When you know the completeness of living Divinely every hour of every day, you will reach the sublime heights for which your Soul is yearning. Accept our love and teachings and together we will accomplish great things. Blessings to you."

"I also come to you in the Spirit of Brotherly Love. You will know me as Moco. I am to be your gatekeeper and teacher. We have many lessons to bring to you, some of which will be symbolic in nature, that they might create for you a mental picture and thus become established in your consciousness. It is our joy and privilege to come to you. We ask only that you be sincere and diligent in your search for spiritual unfoldment and that you be ready and willing to give to others that which will be freely given to you. Love is the Key. Bless you."

During this period of our unfoldment, a new method of "receiving" developed. Instead of being in total trance, I began to "see" with the third eye. At first I saw only a blue light before my eyes. Gradually, as I learned to concentrate on the light, pictures began to appear in the light. It was as if I were looking at a television screen. Sometimes I seemed to be merely an observer, at other times I seemed to become a participant in what was being shown. As I would start to tell what I was seeing, and concentrate completely upon it, the picture would unfold and the words would come fluently, giving its symbology. When the message was over, I could not have repeated the words, but the picture seemed to have been etched into my mind, and I was aware of its spiritual significance.

The following messages from the Far-Eastern teachers were received in the above manner. They were published in 1965 under the title *Gems of Truth from the Masters*. They are exactly as they came, in the words of the Masters. While simple, they are still profound, and they helped to transform our lives. I hope the reader will find them equally enlightening and helpful.

Included here, and also in a separate chapter, are some of the poems which came through inspiration. They literally "wrote themselves," for there was no thought or effort on my part. I merely put them down on paper.

Man and God

Mankind is on a glorious and promising journey which is gradually bringing him into ever new and exciting experiences, where he is learning more about Himself and the Universe. Ultimately this will culminate in the Universal Brotherhood of Mankind, but it is a long, slow process and will come only by each individual becoming aware of his own True Nature and of his place in the Divine scheme of things.

The first great step is for man to become aware of, and accept the fact of, his own Divine Origin and Nature. Within each Soul there has always been a yearning for some contact or identification with that which man has felt to be his Source of life and power. He has always realized that some great power and intelligence created and runs the universe and he has envisioned and paid homage to this power according to his own limited understanding.

Primitive man worshipped the things of nature: the sun, the rain and the fire because this was the limit of his environment and experience. The sun gave him light which made him feel more secure from wild beasts. The rain and the sun made his food grow. The fire kept him warm. Therefore, these were the things which he worshipped.

As tribal life came into existence and it became necessary to preserve the tribe, their God became a protector and also a wrathful and vengeful God who destroyed the enemy.

At other times God has been thought of as a dictating, punishing ruler who reigned with an iron hand and dealt out favor or punishment according to his whims.

Lacking something tangible, man has often made symbols or idols to characterize that which he worshipped, then gradually degenerated into worshipping the idol itself.

As society has developed, its concept of God has changed. As Man has become more concerned about his fellowman his idea of God has come to be that of a benign and loving Father.

Man has always envisioned his God according to his own needs, desires and understanding. With an expanding awareness of the Universe and its many facets and laws, man now stands at the threshold of a new and greater concept of that which he has called "God." He will also have a new concept of his own relationship to God, to his fellowman and to the Universe.

Man has thought of God as a Being, or with physical form, not realizing that when God created man "in His image," it is the Spirit of man which is in His image, for God is SPIRIT. God is not "Him." God is Creative Spirit, all encompassing and everywhere present. All of creation is the body of God. As the hand or foot is a portion of the body and the life within the body is in each member, so is God within all of that which is in existence.

Thus, God INDWELLS all of creation and is the Life, Power, Intelligence and Substance of ALL that exists, from the atom to the Universe. The same creative and sustaining Spirit is manifesting through all forms, whether they be in the mineral, vegetable, human or etheric kingdoms. The form is merely the vehicle which Spirit uses as a means through which to express.

With this concept of God man must necessarily arrive at a new concept of himself. No longer will he think of himself as a worm of the dust, but he will recognize the dignity and stature of his Divine Self. Becoming consciously aware of the Oneness of all life, man will then change his attitudes toward his fellowmen. This will result in the establishment of true Brotherhood.

This will be a very gradual change, for old habits and concepts are not easily replaced. Each individual must work diligently and realize that the change must come about WITHIN HIMSELF before it can become a universal reality. It is necessary for everyone to learn and to apply Universal Laws in a very personal way. Our lessons will be presented with this objective.

Many analogies will be presented to help establish a picture in the mind; as these become a part of the Consciousness they will outpicture in one's life. If the student will accept these ideas and relate them to himself he will find that he will become much happier, more at peace with himself and his world, and he will become a mighty force in the promotion of Universal Brotherhood and Peace.

Brotherhood

Much has been said concerning the Brotherhood of Man, but the conditions of the world today would indicate that, while man has an intellectual knowledge of its necessity, it is most certainly not universally practiced. Brotherhood goes deeper than something one might talk about or understand with the mind. It is something which must be FELT. Something which transforms the very Soul.

As you become consciously aware of your Oneness with the Divine, you cannot help but feel your Oneness with all of Creation. You will know that all of Mankind is bound together in Divine Sonship. It does not matter what color their skin may be, what religion they may have, what race they belong to or what creed they may profess. They are one of God's creations, the same as you are. The same Spirit which is within you is within them, and you can no longer ignore your kinship.

When you can come to this realization and really FEEL it, your complete area of human relationships will undergo a change. You will find love and tolerance replacing hatred and criticism. Suspicion and inharmony will disappear and faith and understanding will take their place. When you feel your ONENESS with your fellowman you cannot look upon him with apathy and be unconcerned about him; you will feel that it is a part of your very self to which something adverse is happening. In love and understanding you will then feel impelled to help and serve as the need requires. Love is always felt by the recipient and it always draws forth a response. It is as a magnet drawing all Souls together. As you express love you release a great power which welds the band of Brotherhood together.

True Brotherhood is not something to talk about or

think about occasionally, and then become so enmeshed in material thoughts, emotions and trivialities that it is given no more attention. It cannot be put on and off as a cloak. It is something which must be put into practice in ALL human relationships. It must be the code by which life is lived! When this is achieved in each heart a new day of Peace, Love, Understanding and Brotherhood will have dawned.

Love and then LIVE YOUR LOVE!

Mankind as a Clock

Mankind could be likened to a clock. Each person would be as a separate wheel or cog within the case, which could be thought of as the Band of Brotherhood. Each part must be in its specific place, doing its specific work, in the proper relationship to every other part. All are perfectly balanced and secured. God could be thought of as the mainspring which is energizing every moving part. Without the power released by the mainspring the clock would be a useless and inert object, but as each part is set in motion through the power it receives, it performs perfectly and becomes a thing of usefulness and value.

So it is with mankind. All serve their place in the world, all are motivated by the same great power, all within the Band of Brotherhood. As they all function in perfect rhythm and harmony, energized by God, they achieve a valuable and useful purpose. When they become separated from each other and from the mainspring through wars or misunderstanding, they cease to function as a unit and are as useless and valueless, in the Divine Plan, as a broken and disassembled clock.

May you be the perfect cog, utilizing Divine power in establishing balance and harmony within the Band of Brotherhood!

A Strand of Beads

As each bead must depend upon the string to form a necklace, so is mankind strung together upon the string called God. God is the connecting thread between all persons, running through each one, securing them all together. One bead alone is of little value or beauty. It is only as each bead is securely established upon the string that a jewel of great beauty is wrought.

God's plan for humanity is that each Soul be firmly fixed upon Him and all bound together in brotherly love, but many are not aware of this. They are as a broken strand of beads. As beads slip off the string they scatter in every direction, there is no "wholeness" left; there are only disassembled pieces, bearing no relationship to each other and serving no purpose. This is what happens when each individual pursues his own selfish desires, with no thought of his Divine nature or his fellowman. He becomes a lost bead. He enjoys no fellowship with his brothers, he feels alone and separate from God and he is destined not to experience the joy of true fulfillment, which comes only through serving others.

Recognize the lòving Divine Presence which is binding all men together. All must work together as a part of the great "whole," for each one is dependent upon the other. No Soul stands alone. All are important to each other and equally important in the Divine Plan. With this realization mankind will create a jewel which is priceless. The beautiful STRAND of BROTHERHOOD!

Treasure

The mighty kings of empires great,
  Rich treasures have acquired,
And piled high their treasure chests,
  With jewels they have desired.

With their vast wealth their coffers burst,
  And yet, for more they always thirst.
They deck themselves with crowns and rings,
  Rich robes and countless other things.

With pomp and show and glory vain,
The earthly kings will always reign.

The Heavenly king's vast treasure chest
    I looked into one night,
Its brilliance was so wondrous
    I scarce could stand the light.

Diamonds and rubies I thought I'd see,
    But what a surprise was in store for me,
For a single strand of pearls rare,
    Was the only thing He had in there.

"How can this be?" was my question lame,
Then within my ear the answer came.

Each Soul is a pearl, I understood,
    In the precious strand of Brotherhood,
And the thread on which they all are strung,
    Is *Love* for each and every one.

One simple jewel this King requires,
    The only treasure He desires,
But how much greater is its worth
    Than all the riches of this earth!

You are as the Diamond

If one were to visit a diamond mine, they probably would see nothing but ordinary earth, for diamonds in their rough state bear little resemblance to the brilliant gems which are seen in store windows or adorning someone's finger. They must be found, cut and polished before they become gems of beauty and value.

If the chemical properties of which a diamond is composed were analyzed, they would be of little worth individually, but the slow hand of God working with these elements has molded them into the diamond. Thus it is with you. Through the steady molding and changing by God's hand, you have become what you are. God has made of you a Gem of Life. Now you must take this diamond in the rough and fashion it into a thing of beauty and brilliance.

Each person is the diamond cutter of his own life. He alone determines what facets he will cut upon his stone. Each experience will cut a new facet, each action and reaction will determine its brilliance, value and beauty. As the perfection of the cutting determines the value of the diamond, the value of your life is determined by what you cut into it. There are many facets which you might cut. Are you cutting the facets of love, understanding, tolerance, faithfulness, integrity, beauty, awareness, charity, gratitude and hope into your diamond? Or are you cutting the facets of hate, greed, intolerance, inharmony, distrust, fear, avarice, lust, unfaithfulness, anger and misunderstanding? It is well to ask yourself what facets you are cutting as you go through life, *for the diamond will radiate exactly what has been cut into it.*

A diamond is smoothed and polished by rubbing one diamond against another. This is what is happening to you in your daily relationships with your fellowmen. You are constantly rubbing the diamond of your life against the diamonds of their lives, and a smoothing and polishing process is taking place. Greater beauty and luster comes forth from your life as you allow your rough edges to be smoothed off as you come into contact and understanding with your fellowmen. This is life. This is why you were placed upon the earth with fellow human beings, that you might each be buffed and smoothed and beautified, that your spiritual brilliance might be brought forth.

When the diamond is perfected, it is placed in a setting so that its beauty might be further enhanced and displayed. Your "setting" is the Brotherhood of Man. There you will give forth beauty and light as you become the perfect reflector of Divine Love.

Your Life as the Life of the Caterpillar

Your life, your understanding and the Consciousness

which you hope to attain could be likened to the Life of the caterpillar.

Consider the species of caterpillar which will someday blossom forth into the beautiful butterfly. As a caterpillar, he leads a very limited existence. His realm is merely to crawl around in a very limited way. He has no conception of what his future is to be; he is just a caterpillar. But, there is a power within the caterpillar which understands and knows the pattern which he is to follow. The intelligence which is working within him teaches him to instinctively do what is necessary to bring about his evolution. So, without knowing why, he limits himself even more by spinning around himself a cocoon or chrysalis. Here he is not even able to crawl about, but he has not questioned the motivation. He has obeyed the voice within and done as he was bidden.

This is what is happening to you. You are placed in this world; you do not know why. You do not always understand the purpose of your being here or where you are going. You spin your little world around you, like a cocoon, and you are very limited in your life and understanding. Situations seem to bind you tightly and you question the reason. During all of this process, God has a pattern for you to fulfill and is working through you to perfect His creation. Subconsciously you are learning the lessons you must know, and gaining the strength you must have before blossoming forth. Within the cocoon, growth has been taking place, and the wings are taking shape in preparation for their flight.

Finally the time comes when you feel the urge, as the caterpillar does, to break free from the cocoon which you have spun about yourself. You no longer want to experience the limitation which is all about you. You feel that you must go forth into greater light, greater understanding, and to something more beautiful. You know that beyond these limits is something to which you must go forward, something which you must attain. God is impelling you to fulfill His pattern for you. So you beat your wings against the Cocoon of Limitation and break free into the Light of Understanding.

As the caterpillar first emerges from his chrysalis, he does not have much strength. He is cold and wet, and the world looks very strange to him. But soon the sunlight shines upon him and dries his wings, and we see the beautiful creature which he has become. Soon he is soaring to unknown heights, heights of which he never could have dreamed. He is FREE. He can look down upon his discarded chrysalis and know that he will never be bound to it again.

So it is with the human Soul. When you gain the light of spiritual understanding, when you grow the wings of Spiritual Unfoldment and Enlightenment, you will soar into a beautiful new existence. You will be FREE to explore God's vast universe, FREE from ALL limitation, going forth in beauty and perfection with the wings which have been provided for you.

Obey the still small voice within you and come into the beautiful new life which spreads out in every direction for you.

THE BUTTERFLY

A butterfly goes winging by
    With gossamer wings so fine,
One knows this could not come to be
    Without some Plan Divine.

How could this fragile beauty,
    With freedom in its wings,
Have come from out a chrysalis
    So binding by its rings?

God made the chrysalis to bind,
    That in it could be found
The strength and growth to thus prepare
    The fly to be unbound.

And so it is with human trials
And burdens which we question,
'Tis but a chrysalis to give us strength
For greater exploration.

When we are strong enough to soar
To loftier heights and wisdom,
God takes the chrysalis away
And gives us wings and freedom.

You as the Sea

Life has often been referred to as a Sea with humanity adrift upon it. Think for awhile of *yourself* as the sea.

Consider the depths of the sea, the violence and power of the sea, its richness with all that it contains, and the purpose to which it is put.

As one looks out over the sea, he is not conscious of its great depths, for he sees only the surface. This is also true of you. As people look at you, they are not aware of what is within the depths of your soul, and it is most probable that you have never plumbed those depths yourself. Perhaps you have been content to go along seeing merely that which lies upon the surface of yourself, never striving to know what is deep down within. Within the depths of the sea is its vast wealth of mineral, plant and marine life. No one knows to what great benefits for humankind this all may be converted someday. Within you also is great wealth. The depths of your soul is as unexplored as the bottom of the sea. No one knows to what degree your potentialities may be converted for the advancement of mankind. As the sea is teeming with life, so are you teeming with thoughts and ideas, but you must lower your nets and bring them up where they can be used. Great spiritual values are within you. You must send down the "divers" of Desire and Persistence to bring the treasure up.

The vast power of the sea could never be estimated. Nothing can stop the ebb and flow of the tides as the sea obeys the magnetic power of the planets in their perfect order in accord with the Divine Laws of the Universe. Unlimited and untold power can also be yours when you harmonize your life with the Divine.

Often the surface of the sea is troubled by great storms. This also can happen in your life. Deep below, however, the sea is tranquil. So go deeply within to find tranquility when the storms of life come to you. Regardless of how violent the storm may be, it is always followed by the calm, and peace will always return to your life. Who knows what the storms may bring forth? Perhaps they will be of such intensity that they will bring up some of that which has been lying dormant at the bottom of the sea. So out of the storms of life will come greater knowledge, more understanding and richer potentialities than you have ever known, all to be utilized to enrich your life and the lives of those whom you touch.

The sea is the means whereby goods and ideas are transported by ships to other peoples and lands. You must be the sea which brings to others love, knowledge, understanding and enlightenment.

So do not always think of yourself as being *upon* the Sea of Life, but sometimes think of yourself as *being* that Sea. Search your soul, go deep within the depths of yourself and bring forth that which is there to be used to God's glory and for the benefit of all humanity.

Your Life as the Rose

As the rose grows in the garden, it lets itself be motivated from within by the life and power of God. It puts up no resistance but lets God have full sway of its life to fulfill its perfect Divine pattern. At first it is a tiny bud which might be thought of as your present stage of enlightenment and understanding—merely a promise of that which is to come. But as time goes on, the rose begins to unfold. When it reaches its maturity a thing of great beauty has come into manifestation. It is a lovely, full-blown rose, a masterpiece divinely created.

So it will be with your life if you will allow your Divine Pattern to be brought forth in you. By using the truths that will be revealed to you, your life can become as the full-blown rose. When you reach that stage of maturity, you will then give off the perfume of God's love and understanding to all the world. For it is only the full-blown rose which gives off its perfume for the world to enjoy, and it is only those who have come into the understanding of Divine truths who are able to give off the Perfume of Truth.

As the rose gives freely to anyone who will partake of its fragrance, so you will be willing to give freely of the perfume of Truth which has been given to you. When you come to the full realization of your Divine nature and your Oneness with the Divine, you cannot help but give it off. It will emanate from you as freely as the perfume emanates from the rose. As surely as the rose would be unable to stifle its perfume, you will be unable to stifle the Truth when it has become an integral part of you.

When you become so closely aligned with God that you understand His truths, they cannot help but radiate from you. God is then working through you, revealing Himself to and through you, God radiating from you. You are His instrument through which His perfume is being released to the world.

Let God work through you as perfectly and with as little resistance as he does through the rose. It is only then that perfection can be brought about, only then will you be the full bloom of God's love.

Climbing the Mountain of Divinity

Perhaps the way of spiritual progression seems hard, and you might wonder if you will ever be able to make much progress. It might seem that you are standing in a valley at the foot of a great mountain. Everything looks beautiful and green. The valley is fertile and all of your needs seem to be well satisfied. You look at the mountain, which seems cold and bare and high, and you can see no point in trying to climb up its rugged face. You can stay snug and satisfied in the valley, so why make the tortuous climb? It seems silly and a waste of time and effort.

Those who have climbed mountains realize a wonderful sense of satisfaction in having achieved the climb. There seems to be within those who endeavor to climb the heights an irresistible something which compels them to make the climb—a challenge to reach the highest pinnacle. There is also an irresistible something in you. It is the Divine within which is calling you to scale the heights until you reach the highest pinnacle, your Oneness with God. As the mountain climber is never satisfied until he has climbed to the highest point, neither will your soul be satisfied until you reach the spiritual heights.

As you start your climb, it may seem that you are making very slow progress, but as you turn and look back to where you have been, you realize that you have come a long way. If you analyze your life, it might seem that you still have far to go, but you will find yourself much higher up the mountain than you were last year or even last month. You will look back and think, "Would I be satisfied to go back to the understanding which I once had? As I have climbed the mountain, my view has become broader, and I am able to see much beauty that I was not able to see in the valley. New and beautiful vistas now lie before me." So with each upward step, tortuous though it may be, you are able to look out and, from a new perspective, see things which you had not realized existed. They had been there all of the time, but in your limited vision from the valley, you had not been able to see them.

There is another aspect of mountain climbing to consider. The wise climber never starts his mountain journey without acquiring the tools which he must use in his ascent. He realizes the importance of taking his rope and his ax. You too must have the necessary implements if you successfully climb the Mountain of Divinity. Your "rope" is your faith in God. Your "ax" is earnest desire.

As the mountain climber throws his rope over the rocks above and pulls himself up, you can use your faith in God. It is the safety measure which will keep you from falling

back down the mountain. Many times as a climber progresses up the side of the mountain, he would fall onto the
treacherous rocks below if it were not for his rope. Your
rope, your security, your safety, is the knowledge of your
Oneness with God and your faith in the fulfillment of God's
plan for you.

With the ax of Earnest Desire you can hew the rocks
away which would halt your progress. Surer footing is
assured by frequent use of your "ax."

Be very careful in your climb, for if you step upon the
rocks of hatred, fear, intolerance or misunderstanding you
will start an avalanche which will sweep you to the depths
below.

As in mountain climbing, so it is in life. One never
climbs alone. In sharing and climbing together, with the
Rope of God binding men together in brotherly love, you
will reach the top.

When you have tasted the thrill and exhilaration which
comes from the climbing, when you have known the grandeur and felt the ecstasy of reaching the heights, you will
be satisfied with nothing less than reaching the very summit.
This you may not accomplish in your limited earth span,
but as you go on through Infinity, your horizons will be
ever broadened as you climb higher and higher.

Set your sights on the mountain top and know the joy
of an expanding Consciousness as you make your climb.

Experiencing the Presence of God

Oftentimes students who are relatively new in their search
for the Truth of life will be so thrilled by their new dis-
coveries that they chase madly to and fro trying to find
books or teachers who can add to their knowledge. This is
fine up to a point, and the work of authors and teachers
should not be discredited, but you should be cautioned a-
gainst pursuing only these sources of enlightenment. While
they all have their place and are necessary in your unfoldment, any book can only be a record of the ideas or experiences of someone else, and any teacher can only impart

knowledge to you as he understands it. There are so many diverse ideas being propagated that this can be very confusing. Each may be right in his ideas or convictions, but what he believes is only right for *him* at his particular level of unfoldment. *You* are an entirely different Being, at your own level of understanding. God has His own special pattern for you to fulfill, and it is not like any other in the Universe. So what may seem Truth to one is not necessarily Truth for another, and what might seem Truth at one time in your life may be later discarded in the light of greater understanding.

You could search for a lifetime and still be dissatisfied with the second hand knowledge you receive from outside yourself. The Spirit of God within *you* is your only "Perfect Teacher," and you must learn to tap this source of enlightenment.

This is best done by the practice of silence and meditation. Turn your thoughts away from worldly clamor and din and take time to be still and *realize* the Presence of God. Think of God as the very core of your Being, the wisdom, the power and the expression of *all* that you are. Experience God's living Presence IN YOU. In this quietness you will find the inspiration and strength you are seeking. You will be taught by Divine revelation the Truths which you are capable of understanding. Any knowledge which you gain in this way is truly YOURS to keep forever, for a true spiritual revelation sears itself upon the soul of the one who receives it. This is WISDOM; all else is intellectual.

As you are taught by the Spirit, you will be brought to the full flower of spiritual attainment. Therefore be very sure to spend sufficient time EXPERIENCING the Presence of God. Where could you make a better investment? Time spent in the accumulation of material wealth can bring no lasting peace or happiness. Time spent in acquiring spiritual understanding brings eternal rewards.

The Silent Place

How oft the hungry soul cries out
    To be at One with God,
Desolate, bereft, alone,
    Along life's path we plod.
We seek Him in the chapel,
    We query of the sage.
We search in vain to find Him,
    Upon the printed page.

Our quest may take us far and wide,
    Through struggle and through din,
While we seek to find Him far away,
    Instead of deep *within*.
When we enter in the Silent Place,
    And close that sacred door,
We will feel His blessed Presence,
    As we never have before.

A mighty surge of power,
    Great joy and peace Divine,
An abiding sense of Oneness,
    Security sublime.
These are the priceless treasures,
    For which the soul has sought,
The Father's "Pearl of Great Price,"
    Which never could be bought.

But is His precious *gift* to those
    Who enter through this door,
And here we will abide in love
    And peace forevermore,
When we have come at last to know
    That God is not apart
But is the very *life* of us,
    And dwells within our Heart.

Love as the Springtime

The foundation of the Brotherhood of Man is built with

the stones of Faith and Understanding and Tolerance. The cement which binds them all together is Love. This is the most necessary requirement and the one cohesive force in the Universe.

The Soul without Love is as barren as the earth in the wintertime. When winter comes to the earth, the leaves shrivel and die. There are no blossoms and no fruit, and the soil does not produce. The earth stands cold and barren with the bleak winds blowing over it. Such is the life without Love—cold, desolate, barren. But as the springtime awakens the earth, so will Love awaken the human Soul.

As spring brings forth the blossoms, the green grass, buds and leaves, the earth comes alive, and so it is with the heart that is touched with Love. Life takes on purpose and meaning, beauty and productiveness, and the barrenness is wiped away. As the earth bursts forth in all of its glory and beauty, so does the Soul which accepts and expresses Love.

The earth gives of its fruitfulness to all who would pick or gather its abundance. The loving Soul also gives freely to ALL regardless of race, color or creed. The heart that is full of Love can no more help giving of that Love than the earth can help giving forth when it is touched by the wand of spring, for that is its Divine nature and function.

Open your heart and feel the budding new life which will come as you learn to love, for only as you give Love can you be expressing your true purpose. Only when each Soul comes into the glory of the Springtime of Love will Brotherhood become an accomplished fact. DO IT, do not just talk or think about it. When you actually *practice* Love, there is no room for anger, criticism, or impatience in your relationships with your fellowmen. If you *really* love, these things are wiped away as surely as the winter disappears when the springtime comes.

The Power of Love

Love is the greatest power in the universe. Without it there would be nothing. It is the creating, unifying, and sustaining life principle by which all things have their existence.

It is most important that you realize the necessity of expressing Love, not only for the benefit of those to whom it is expressed, but for your own sake as well. There is no other thing from which you can benefit as greatly as the expressing of Love. Love brings you in tune with the Infinite; it is your connecting link with the Divine.

The great commandment, "Love thy neighbor as thyself," is more powerful than one might think. There is very little which man would not do for himself, if he only understood and applied this commandment he would find that in so doing he would be doing himself the greater kindness. Not understanding this, he often foregoes his opportunity to enrich his own life. He who loves is reaping a much greater harvest than he who is loved. In loving, you are the channel through which the Divine is flowing. For Love is of God, and there is no other way to become ONE with God but through Love. As you express Love, you become the channel through which and into which ALL GOOD is flowing. Within the Divine are all things, and when you become the channel for all things, the power of God truly becomes yours.

Be very careful that you keep the channel clear, for it is as a life-giving stream running through a field. Perhaps a bit of debris falls into the stream and is not cleared away. This in turn collects more debris until the stream is choked and clogged, and a dam of debris dissipates the stream. The debris which you must guard against is criticism, anger, hatred, fear, worry, injustice and intolerance. Man has allowed all of these things to dam his stream, consequently he does not enjoy the purity and vitality which could be his. Behind the dam, trying to break through, are all of the constructive things of life—faith, tolerance, justice, patience and sympathy, which are borne on the Stream of Love.

Keep your channel clear so that the Divine Stream of Life, Love and Intelligence might flow through you unimpaired.

The Octagon of Brotherhood

Brotherhood is often referred to as the Circle of Brotherhood, for it must encompass all souls. To be a circle it must be unbroken. Therefore, as long as one soul is left outside, the circle is not complete. Your task and ours is to love and teach mankind until All are within the circle in perfect harmony and love.

For the purpose of this lesson let us think of an eight-sided circle, or octagon. We will name each side of the octagon with a quality which must be expressed toward all mankind and by all mankind if Brotherhood is to be brought about.

The first side we will call Charity. If you possess charity, it brings about a desire to give wherever there is need. Charity would see that your brother is at all times provided for in a material way. If you have charity, you cannot see suffering or lack without alleviating it to the best of your ability. Charity also means that you will be charitable to all of your brothers' short-comings.

On the next side we will place Faith. If you express faith in your fellowman, he will endeavor to live up to that faith. He in turn will have faith in his fellowman, and thus the circle widens. Faith is one of the most powerful forces in the world. If you have faith in your fellowman, you can literally change his life; without such faith he cannot feel like a worthwhile individual. There are no limits to which a human will go to live up to the faith which is placed in him. In a reverse manner, lack of faith can actually destroy his ambition, integrity and faith in himself. Certainly if you would help promote Brotherhood, you must have faith in your fellowman.

The next side of the octagon will be Forgiveness, and this is of tremendous importance. If you harbor animosity in your hearts and do not forgive, it is as a stone wall which you are placing around yourself and around him for whom you hold malice. Forgiveness is a very potent and powerful force. Someone can be at cross-purposes with you and you with them, but all that is necessary to straighten it out is to feel and express forgiveness. Even though it is not expressed, it may still be felt by the other party. However, it is much better to humble yourself to express forgiveness, for then you too reap the full harvest of your forgiving. If you can become humble enough to say, "I forgive you," you have taken a great stride in your own progression, and you have also brought about a condition through which harmony and love can be expressed.

Kindness would be the next side of the octagon. Have your ever thought about what happens when you express kindess to your fellowman, as opposed to harshness or bitterness? Have you noticed the wonderful reaction to kindness? The doorway to Brotherhood is opened with kindness. This is one of the lessons which Jesus tried to teach. "Be ye kind, one to another," he said. This is one of the most important qualities in promoting Brotherhood.

Sympathy must also be put in the circle. Holding out the loving hand of sympathy when someone is being buffeted and battered by the storms of life is a most advantageous time to work for Brotherhood. It is then that people are receptive, for their defenses are down when they are in need of sympathy. Finding you ready to help gives them the opportunity to see Brotherhood in action and they become eager to become a part of it.

Understanding would be the next facet of the octagon. If you take the time to try to understand your fellowman your attitudes toward him will be very different. If you can understand why he behaves as he does, why he thinks as he does, what the forces are that are motivating him, you will be much more tolerant. You can overlook the petty annoyances and give him love and understanding in spite of his shortcomings. Then how easy it would be to bring about a feeling of Brotherhood, for every soul is yearning to be understood.

Patience is the next side and what a lack of it there is in the world. It is one of the greatest positive powers which could be cultivated in man's life. With patience you are able to go along with your brother and let him work out his life in his own way. You know that the time will come when he will come into a better understanding and that growth cannot be forced. Patience will show the way of Brotherhood to all.

The last side of the octagon is Love, and truly this is the greatest of all. If you have love, you will have all of the other attributes. If you really love your brother, you will have patience, forgiveness, understanding, charity, faith, sympathy and kindness. All of these things will come as the by-product of love.

These are the eight qualities which you must have and which you must express toward ALL of your fellowmen if you are to be effective in helping promote Brotherhood. This means to EACH and EVERY one with whom you have any contact. For you cannot say, *"This* man is my brother, but *that* man does not think as I do, so he is not my brother." If you are brother to one, you are brother to ALL. You are all Sons of God, and no one is exempt from that circle. Each person is the child of God to exactly the same degree that you are a child of God. Each person is as important to God as you are. If you really FEEL that relationship, each person must be as important to YOU as you are to yourself. This is true Brotherhood, and this is the way it must be brought about. These are the things you must express. This is the way you must LIVE. We are hoping that you will learn this lesson and that you will make it the most important thing in your lives. We are dedicated to this task. We pray that you will be also. Widen your circle of Love to encompass all men everywhere!

Marriage

Those of you who have taken your marriage vows have some understanding of what constitutes a perfect marriage, and you wear the ring which is symbolic of marriage.

Pause and analyze your marriage and think of what you have brought into it. In the perfect marriage, the main requisite is love. Though a couple comes from diverse backgrounds, through their love for each other they blend their lives and build a life together. When you have sufficient love for each other, all things can be worked out within the marriage. No matter what situations arise, love will smooth the way. To a perfect marriage you must also bring unselfishness, a willingness to forget Self and to give of yourself, and a willingness to harmonize every difference of opinion and concede when necessary. As a marriage grows, there is a unification and blending together until you become so harmonized and modified that you almost think and act as one individual. This is a True Marriage. Symbolic of this union is the Circle, the ring.

Have you ever thought of humanity in this respect? If you would live in true Brotherhood, you would "Marry" humanity as truly as you marry your mate. The same requirements are present for this marriage as for your individual marriage. You must be willing to overlook the shortcomings of your brother as you would your mate. You must give freely of your love and service and be willing to harmonize and blend your lives together. This is the True Marriage of Humanity. This marriage also is symbolized by a ring, the Circle of Brotherhood. You should wear this ring as obviously and as joyously as you wear the ring of your individual marriage. A good marriage requires much work, patience, sacrifice and love and this is true of the larger marriage also. It will not be easy. You may feel that you have reached fulfillment through your personal marriage, but you will find the rewards and fulfillment of Marriage to Humanity far greater, for it brings you another step closer to your Divine fulfillment.

Give freely of your time, knowledge and love, and enter into the Holy bonds of wedlock with humanity; thus will you be fulfilled!

The Master Sculptor Hews a Statue

Your life could be likened to the fine statue which the sculptor makes. You are as the large block of rough marble. The sculptor is God.

No sculptor ever begins his creation without first having a pattern in mind, an image which he holds in his mind's eye. With that image in mind, he selects the piece of marble which will be the best for the beautiful pattern he has conceived. So it is with your life. God has a picture in mind, and He has selected you as the material upon which He will work to bring into existence the work of art which He envisions.

So the sculptor takes his block of cold rough marble which has nothing of beauty except in a rough unfinished way and sets about to shape it to his will, always holding in mind the image of what it will be when finished. He chips off a piece here and a piece there until he shapes the block into the rough pattern of what it will become. God, the Master Sculptor, is shaping your life, bringing about situations which you cannot always understand, hewing off a piece here and there and you wonder why. It often hurts to have this done. We can imagine the marble wondering, "Why am I being broken apart, why am I being chipped at and being put through all of this torture?" It cannot know what is in the mind of the sculptor. It must stand and take the hammering which it receives. You may not see the reason for the problems which come your way and the trials you must bear, for you cannot know what God has in mind for you.

The time finally comes when the sculptor starts putting in all of the fine lines which bring expression and life and beauty into His creation. Each experience etches those lines into your character, into your soul and your consciousness. You then come into a fuller expression of your Divine Nature. So do not rebel when things come your way which you cannot understand, but recognize the fact that you are being sculptored into a beautiful work of art. Realize that each trial and tribulation, each thing which seems like a set-back, each hurt which comes to you is merely putting in all of those fine lines which are making of you a thing of beauty which will forever portray God's handiwork.

God's Divine Plan is molding you into His Perfect Creation. As you look back over your life, you will see that those things which seemed so hard and were such trials and burdens were really adding to your Spiritual Beauty. As you go forward in your Soul's progression, you become more finely etched until you will become God's Masterpiece.

The Fence of Negative Thoughts

Many people are building a fence around themselves by

their negative thinking. A fence represents that which shuts one off from the world. It shuts the world out from those who are within, and it prohibits those who are within from getting outside. This fence is very restricting and becomes increasingly constricting. It is of a very special construction, for each of the bars is named. They are Hatred, Jealousy, Anger, Fear, Worry, Egotism and all of the things of a negative nature in which mankind indulges. Each time one allows himself to indulge in any of these, he builds his fence higher until, in time, he can become completely surrounded by it. Nothing of a positive nature can then penetrate, and he becomes his own prisoner.

Are you building this type of fence around yourself? Are you constantly disliking someone, are you fearful, or worried, or critical of others? Are you building your ego so high that it becomes a fence which is holding you within its bounds? All of these things are confining and restricting to you, and when the fence has become high and tight and secure around you, it becomes your PRISON.

It not only shuts out positive thoughts from your mind, but it creates such a barrier that other people have no desire to be near you. It becomes a restricting power which is so repellent to others that they will make no effort to penetrate it. You have all had experience with this type of person and were so repelled that you hesitated to have any further contact with them. Are *you* being careful not to have this happen to you? You would not deliberately shut yourself off from mankind in an actual prison behind high prison walls, and if society placed you there you would feel that a grave injustice had been done. But, you are doing that very thing to yourself when you allow all of these negative things to take root in your life, for then you are as imprisoned as if you were behind prison walls.

If you have erected this type of fence around yourself, there is only one way through it, and that is the Gateway of Love. That gate will always swing open and allow you to come out of your prison into the light and sunshine of God's lovely world to enjoy all of the beauty, companionship and harmonious relationships which are there for you. But it is only when you find the Gate and open it that you will be free. The Gate may be hard to find because lack of use may have allowed much thorny underbrush to obscure it. You must clear the pathway and come out. Outside of the fence the Brotherhood of Man awaits you. Here you will find and lend a helping hand. Here you may walk in unity, understanding and love. This is our wish for you and what we want to teach you. We stand ready to help you open the Gate. We are beckoning to you, and our hands are stretched through the Gateway to help you walk through!

The Rainbow

The Brotherhood of Man might be thought of as a rainbow with each individual as one of its hues. Each color does not stand distinct and apart in a rainbow, but each sheds a part of itself to intermingle with the one beside it. There is a delicate shading of each color into the other. This is as Brotherhood must be. With each of you standing close to the other, harmonizing, blending and giving a part of yourself to your brother, you create a thing of great beauty.

The rainbow can also be considered from a different point of view. Seldom is the rainbow seen until the storm is over. Each of you go through many storms and disturbances of life, but it is only after the storms have expended themselves that the sun appears and peace and calm returns. Love is the Sun which will dispel your clouds. Love shining in your life will help to bring about the Rainbow of Brotherhood. As surely as the sun dispels the storm, so will Love dispel any misunderstandings which you might have with your brother.

Blend and harmonize with your fellowman, let the light of Love shine through you and take your place in the Rainbow of Life.

Spiritual Unfoldment as an Assembly Line

Spiritual knowledge and understanding could be likened to an assembly line. It must be considered as an unfolding process because it comes only through gradual growth. It is not something which comes ready-made or which one can receive as a gift. We, as your teachers, cannot GIVE it to you. It would be so easy if you could receive it as a gift from us with our love and blessings, and that is what we would love to do as we watch mankind struggling in blindness and ignorance. But it cannot be done that way. It is the pathway which each Soul must walk by himself, and it must come to each Soul as an individual experience, for it is only to the measure that you will strive for yourself that you will achieve understanding and growth. It is an ACHIEVEMENT, not a gift. Perhaps this process could be better understood by using your modern technique, the assembly line, as an example.

Having purchased a beautiful new auto, you step into it and drive blithely along the highway. This is what you might like to be able to do with spiritual understanding—to buy the finished product, a beautiful shining knowledge of TRUTH, and drive down the Highway of Life with no thought of what had gone into the making of the vehicle. But just as the auto had to be assembled, so must you grow in understanding. If it were not for the assembly line there would be no auto; your life is the assembly line for your spiritual vehicle.

As you progress along this spiritual assembly line each operation adds something which will be within the finished product. Each experience which you have, each little bit of truth and understanding which becomes a part of you is added to that which you already have. At first your automobile would not be recognizable, for it would be only a few parts placed together. However, as it progresses along the assembly line other parts are constantly being added and it begins to assume its shape. As bits of truth, understanding and knowledge of Divine Law take shape in your consciousness, your vehicle finally stands ready to be taken upon your highway, The Highway of Eternal Life.

Consider this question; Would you be satisfied with an unfinished automobile? Would you accept an auto which had not gone to the end of the assembly line? Would you drive down the highway with merely the chassis? I think not. You would want your auto to have a beautiful paint job, tires to make it roll easily, windshield wipers to help you safely through the storm, glass enclosures and a top to protect you from the weather—in short, all of the things to streamline your vehicle so that it might travel more swiftly and comfortably. All of these features which enhance your automobile can be recognized as those things which are necessary for your spiritual vehicle. Love, faith and understanding will provide a beautiful and efficient vehicle for you.

However, there is still something lacking. How far will you travel in this beautiful automobile if you do not place within it the proper fuel? Your fuel is the POWER OF GOD. You might have all of the spiritual understanding and knowledge possible; you can be all ready with a highly developed, highly polished spiritual vehicle, but how far can you go without fuel? Your car would not move one inch, and you cannot make spiritual progression without recognizing and utilizing the Power of God. It is the *only* Power, the only fuel which can propel your spiritual vehicle. Intellectual understanding of Divine principles is not enough. You must FEEL the dynamic power of God. Never lose sight of this fact. Be willing and ready to refuel with that power. If you were to run out of gasoline for your auto, how quickly would you go to a station and refuel? How often do you turn to the Power of God to refuel your spiritual vehicle?

You *need* the Power of God. You cannot proceed without it. So constantly tap that power at the station of Prayer and Meditation. Keep your motor clean and well fueled, and may God Bless you on your journey.

The Symphony of Life

Picture in your mind's eye a blank piece of paper, then mentally make upon it some scattered musical notes. In this relationship they have no meaning, they are merely a jumble of black notations and stems, discordant and inharmonious. But place them upon a staff and they immediately become meaningful. Separately they have no quality or harmony, but as they are fixed upon the staff they form octaves and harmonic chords. They relate to each other and become the basis of all the harmonies and symphonies which can be played.

This is as the life of each Soul. Each is as an individual note with no purpose until it is established upon the Staff of Life. The five lines of this staff are these: Awareness of Oneness with God, Desire for Spiritual Progression, Love of Fellowmen, Faith, and Gratitude.

God, the Great Conductor, takes these notes, and in a series of resonant chords, binding us together, plays our pianissimos, our crescendos and our diminuendos in the beautiful Symphony of Life. Each Soul is a spiritual tone, and all have a part to play in God's Great Symphony.

God as the Fulcrum

There is a technical term which should be considered, as it can be very meaningful to one who is seeking spiritual progression. It is called a fulcrum.

A fulcrum is a wedge or point of leverage upon which one balances a lever when moving an object. By placing one end of the lever under the object and getting the proper balance upon the fulcrum, a slight pressure upon the other end of the lever will move an object which would be impossible to move without such a device. The fulcrum balances the weight of the object and the strength of the person operating the lever. Man is able to lift enormous weights in this way.

Think of GOD as the FULCRUM of your LIFE!

You have often experienced the frustration of trying to accomplish something "in your own strength." But if you become perfectly balanced upon the Fulcrum of God you will be able to accomplish the most difficult tasks with very little effort on your part. It will provide the extra power which is necessary in every difficult situation. The Master Jesus was aware of this great inner source of power for he often stated, "It is not I but the Father within, who doeth the works." With God as your Fulcrum and using the Lever of Love, there is no obstacle too great for you to overcome!

Tapestry Woven by Man's Thoughts

Vibrations intermingle from all aspects of Man's nature to weave the Tapestry of the cloak he wears. Think of the spiritual vibrations as the warp of the tapestry, or the basic foundation upon which the pattern is woven. Then think of the mental and emotional vibrations as the interweaving threads which form the pattern. The pattern will only be as lovely as the thoughts and emotions that are woven into it. The warp is not the finished product. The fine pattern is woven by the individual, and he alone determines what kind of design he will weave.

It is Man's free will that determines whether he will weave a thing of beauty or a dull, drab, uninspiring pattern. Too many dark, unloving, selfish threads, will produce this kind of pattern, but the threads of Love, Service, and Light will make a pattern that is lovely to behold and to wear. Man has only that which he has woven to protect him from the cold of the world. He weaves his own cloak, and he must wear it, be it beautiful or ugly.

Be Light-filled. Weave your cloak of the threads of Loving Service and it will protect you like a coat of armor throughout the ages.

Dungeons

The Masters view humanity with sadness, for there is so much selfishness and vanity and so little love and brotherhood.

This is analogous to a great castle built upon a feudal estate. The castle, with its high pinnacles and towers, was built for the enjoyment and use of the Lord and Master of the estate. Little thought was given to the arduous tasks which were expected of the serfs who labored to build the castle and worked in the fields. Their situation was very poor indeed. But it was only by the labor and efforts of those who were the servants that the castle was built and the fields were harvested. The landowner literally took the life's blood of the serfs that he might have a stately mansion and hold a position of authority in the community.

Many cultures and economies are operating in a similar way today. Many people erect elegant show-places and amass great fortunes with no thought of the ills and privations which have been inflicted upon those of a lower economic and social level as they have been exploited.

The beautiful castle was often a place of drunkenness and revelry as the Lord and Master and his cohorts engaged in all kinds of debauchery. Unfortunately, this has changed but little. Those who presumably are the upper strata of society, and should be doing the most for the upliftment of mankind, are trying to fill the spiritual void in their lives with materiality and revelry.

In each castle, was a dungeon. This was never seen by the visitors and, for the most part, was ignored by the Master. But its filth and purpose were a disgrace which could never be entirely disregarded. Those who could not pay their debts, or who incurred the displeasure of the Master, were cast into the dungeon and left to starve and wither away. So, in spite of the elegance of the castle, in its foundation was a festering core of filth, ignorance and inhumanity. Society and individuals today have their dungeons. It is easy to erect a facade of righteousness and build a castle for outward appearances, but what is within the inner chambers of the heart and soul? Many try to cover their hatred, jealousy and intolerance with a mantle of respectability but it is still festering and weakening their spiritual foundation. If these things were not in the dungeons of the individuals they would not be so evident in society, so it is the task of each person to open the dungeon of his soul and heart and expose it to the purifying warmth and sunshine of Love. Only then will Brotherhood and Peace reign in the world.

The Keys to the Kingdom

In your own hands, YOU hold the keys to the Kingdom of Heaven! Heaven is a state of Divine Consciousness and you can enter there with the proper Keys.

You hold the Keys to Heaven! Think what this means for you. If someone were to say to you, "Here, I am giv-

ing you the keys, and the Kingdom of Heaven is yours,"
would you not feel that you had received a priceless gift?
But it is not that easy. Someone else cannot do it for you.
However, we can say that with your knowledge and understanding you have the keys, but YOU must open the door.
The keys which unlock the door are Faith, Love, Hope
and Service.

Faith is born through knowledge and understanding.
When one recognizes his own Divine Nature, he then has
faith in God, faith in himself and faith in his fellowman.
He knows that his Divine Destiny will be fulfilled.

Love is born through faith, for when one has faith in
God and feels secure in the abiding Presence of God, he
then has love for God, love for his fellowmen and love for
himself. When you know your true worth you must love
yourself, not in a vain and boastful way but in recognition
of your Divine Origin and Nature.

When you become aware of your Oneness with God and
with all of humanity, there is hope for a better world to
come. You can envision the Brotherhood of Mankind becoming a reality through man's love for his fellowman.

Service is the Master Key, for when you give service you
are demonstrating each of the other factors of faith, hope
and love.

These are the Keys to the Kingdom, and only through
their use will the door be opened by you. All too often this
knowledge is merely intellectual and is not put into practice. It might be well to question whether you are merely
carrying your keys in your pocket or using them to open
the door.

Are you conscious every moment of the day that you are
ONE with God? This Divine Power is not something which
you must reach *Out* for and someday hope to gain, it is
here NOW, within you. You can never be separated from it.
Do you recognize the Reality of your own Being? You are
God's Creation, and as an expression of God you therefore are Divine.

If you were truly conscious of this Reality, would you
allow yourself to express the things which come forth from
your mouths, from your minds, from your lives? If you

were holding your Divine Image in mind you would censor some of the words which come from your lips and some of the thoughts which you project. For once you have spoken the unkind word or thought the evil thought, it can never be withdrawn; it is free to circulate in the ether to do its damage wherever it comes in contact with a receptive soul. When you fully understand that you are constantly "broadcasting" you will realize what a powerful force for good or evil you really are. Your thoughts and words are working for the detriment or upliftment of humanity. You can destroy as readily as you can build for God's Kingdom. So recognize yourself as a Divine Expression and allow only that which is Divine to be expressed through you.

You will then be using your keys, the door will open, and the Kingdom will be YOURS.

Fuel and Fire

In a symbolic way your lives could be likened to the fuel and the fire. Think first of an empty hearth. Can you conceive of anything less useful than a hearth upon which no fire is laid or burning? The empty hearth is a symbol of the barrenness and the emptiness in the life of one who has no spiritual desire. Barren and cold is such a life, and it gives forth nothing of beauty or warmth. But this is not true of those who have a spiritual fire burning upon the hearth of their hearts. You have kindled your fire and you are indeed fortunate, but you must keep it burning brightly.

Your fuel was laid bit by bit until you gathered enough to start a flame. This was done as you gathered bits of spiritual understanding, but the mere gathering was not sufficient. Until the "brand" of true spiritual desire was applied to it, it did not become ignited. Many fires are laid upon many hearths, and many brands are touched, but not all fires burst into brilliant flame. This could happen if there were no draft through the chimney; oftentimes there is a damper within the chimney which is obstructing the draft and smothering the flame. When this happens, the fire does not burn, and the room becomes filled with gases and smoke. If your fire is to burn brightly, you must open the damper which is your EGO and allow the pure draft of LOVE to pull out all of the impurities and keep your fire aglow.

Fuel comes in many forms, and if you examine the history of each type of fuel, you find that they have all been years in the making. Coal, gas and oil have been millions of years in the process, wood also has gone through a long period of growth. You, like the fuel, have been a long time in your progression. Now the time has come for the Spark of God to be applied to you as the brand is applied to the fuel. When the Spark of God is applied to your life, the same thing happens that happens to the fuel—a great combustion takes place and a complete change comes about. You will no longer be a compressed inert object, but you will burst forth into a glowing flame to do the job for which you were created. The fuel is not fulfilling its purpose until it is ignited, and your life serves little purpose until you allow yourselves to be used to bring light and warmth to humanity.

Perhaps you have thought that fire consumes the fuel, but this is not true. Fire does not consume, it merely transmutes the fuel from one element into another. As the fuel burns, it gives off heat, power, gases and light. As your Spiritual Fire burns, you too are being transmuted from the physical aspects of the world into the spiritual and more etheric expression of love, compassion, power and spiritual glow.

Perhaps your flame will be feeble at first, just as the first chips used to kindle the fire burn feebly. As you progress in understanding and desire, you will be placing a longer burning fuel upon your hearth where others may be warmed and enlightened. In turn their fires may become kindled and they too will pass the light along. This is analogous to the practice in olden days of carrying fire from one home to another and keeping the fire alive. With each Soul catching the spark and passing it on, Brotherhood will come to pass, and the Glory of God will light the world.

Man as a Tree

As the tree, so is the life of man.

Within each seed is sealed the Divine Pattern of that which it is to become, with all of the potentialities for its fulfillment inherent within itself. Man has the Pattern of the Divine sealed within him, and he must bring it into fruition. This is as inescapable as it would be for an acorn to become anything other than an oak tree. It is man's destiny, but just as the seed must be watered and nurtured, so must man's Divine Nature be brought into full expression by the proper conditions for that growth.

When observing a seed, it would be impossible to foresee that which it could become unless one had already seen a fruitful tree. When beholding an unenlightened man, it is impossible to foresee what he could become unless one already knew of those who have attained the stature of Divinity. As we think of the Christed Ones, we know the potential heights which are man's to achieve. With this recognition comes the resolution to fulfill our Divine Pattern.

As the seed is placed in fertile soil and allows itself to be nourished by that which God provides, it begins to expand. It accepts food from the soil, light from the sun and absorbs the rain which falls upon it. It goes through its process of growth unquestioningly. God has also placed man in the proper environment for his unfoldment and likewise nourishes and nurtures him, but man must accept and assimilate that which God provides if he would grow.

Just as the tree must do its part by reaching out for nourishment, so must man send out his roots in search of truth and understanding. Only as the tree sends out strong roots will it be able to withstand the storms. Likewise, man is only as strong in times of stress as the roots which he has established. If he has the strong roots of love, faith, integrity, charity and understanding he can withstand any storms which might come, but if his roots are few and shallow he will surely fall. A tree with a strong root system is able to absorb more and more nourishment, and it grows increasingly larger and stronger. Strong spiritual roots also help man to grow in Divine stature.

The taller a tree becomes, the more it is able to sway

with the breeze. Its arc is in direct proportion to its height. This is also true of man. As he grows in spiritual understanding, he is more flexible and better able to adapt to whatever storms may come and he is always able to come back to a stalwart upright position. Buffeted though he may be, he will never be defeated.

Unless a tree is crowded or misdirected, it will grow in lovely balance and symmetry. God's Perfect Plan for man will also unfold him in balance and symmetrical order if he will heed the still small voice within. However, just as many trees are misshapen and distorted, so are many lives because of the interference and influence of others upon them. No one has the right to overshadow another lest it distort or hamper his growth. Each must be allowed to fulfill his own pattern in his own way.

When the tree has matured sufficiently, it starts to blossom and finally bears fruit. This too has its parallel in the evolving consciousness of man. As man becomes aware of his Divine Nature and attempts to cultivate it, he sees a transformation taking place within himself. No longer is he dormant and fruitless, but he is aware of new life and activity taking place. New thoughts and concepts start budding, and they soon burst into full bloom. From the blossoms comes the fruit of the tree, and a spiritual life is the fruit of spiritual ideas and concepts.

This is the Universal Law of Life; first the seed, then the stalk, then the bud and blossoms, then the fruit which must mature and ripen, and finally the harvest.

When the blossoms of Love and Understanding have bloomed in the hearts of men, the harvest of Peace, Harmony and Brotherhood will be garnered. For no other purpose was man created, for no other purpose has God sown!

A Prayer

Lord, may my life forever be
Strong and steadfast as a tree.
Straight and stalwart may I stand,
Deeply rooted in Thy land.

To Thee my face I'll ever lift,
And know that Life's Thy greatest gift.
And, as the breeze the branches sway,
May I let Spirit have its way.

The Tree of Humanity

At twilight some evening, have you not seen a tree silhouetted against a darkening sky? As the darkness deepened, the tree had no dimensions except height and width—it had apparently lost its depth in the darkness. You were unaware of the birds or animals which might have been in the tree. It seemed more like a picture than a reality.

As morning came, it revealed the true aspects of the tree. You saw its depth, color and its beauty as it stood in the bright sunlight. How different than it had seemed in the darkness of the night.

Thus it is when man stands in the "Light of God." His life has color and activity and a new dimension. His true nature and relationship to his fellowman is revealed by the Light.

Mankind resembles the tree in still another manner. Humanity could be likened to the trunk with each branch being a particular race, each twig being a segment of its race and each leaf an individual soul. Flowing through the trunk and branches and the veins of each leaf is the same God life, each part dependent upon the other to bring it life and sustenance. To be separated from the tree is to be cut off from the vital Source of Life, for it is only in unification that man can be spiritually fed and sustained.

When all of mankind comes to the realization that he is but a leaf upon a branch and that all are sustained, vitalized and created by the same Source of Life, he will understand that each part is of equal importance in comprising the Whole. Then he will endeavor to allow no more dissension among cults, races and creeds than there is among the leaves upon a tree.

This is Rich Understanding, True Wisdom, the Perfect Life!

The Spider Web

You could be likened to the spider who spins his own web for his abode.

This you are doing as truly and with as much precision as the spider. He proceeds along a definite pattern and projects *from himself* the essence of that abode. This you also do with each thought which precedes each action in your life. The spider sends out a little bridge of himself over which he then travels. You are sending "thought bridges" before yourself over which you will also travel to fulfill the pattern of the thought. Thus you are constantly spinning your thought web which becomes the place where you must live. You alone determine the perfection and quality of the web. Will you spin it with kind and loving thoughts or will you spin a web of fear and despair? Will you spin your web in the dark cellar of doubt and inharmony or in the sunlight of Love where its gossamer loveliness will catch and reflect the Light of God? The choice is yours.

Think also of those who will be caught in your web. As the fly is inevitably caught in the spider's web, so will you trap and envelop your family and friends in your thought web. Your thoughts exert a tremendous influence upon those about you. Do not be guilty of trapping others in a web of despair and inharmony, but rather spin a web of happiness, light and love which will have the tensile strength to support all those who are within it.

Make your web a thing of beauty which will reflect the Beauty of God so others will wish to be caught in it and that you might enjoy its peace and security.

Man Encased in a Shell as the Turtle

For too long, man has encased himself in a shell of misunderstanding and fear. This could be thought of as the shell of a turtle. Man has pulled himself into this shell thinking he would be protected by it. In reality it has only impeded his spiritual progress. When the turtle is fearful, he retreats into his shell. As long as he stays there he remains stationary and makes no progress. Even when he comes out and tries to go forward he must drag his heavy shell with him wherever he goes.

Man must learn that there is little progress as long as he is content to be encased in fear, misunderstanding, hatred, intolerance or any encumbering shell. Only as he bursts out of these shells will he be free.

Perhaps the shell which hinders most people is the concept that man is an earthly creature and therefore confined to crawling in the dust. They must come to recognize that the True Man is the spiritual man. He has all the qualities of Spirit inherent within him which can lift him into realms of consciousness and understanding far beyond the limitations of the earth. When this is realized, mankind will come out of his shell and move forward, for he will understand his true relationship to God and to his fellowmen.

By identifying himself as a Spiritual Being, the whole realm of spiritual ideas becomes his to explore. He has emerged from his shell and is free to go, unhampered, into a new world of experience and expression. The shell of fear is left far behind, for there can be no fear where there is the realization of the Indwelling Presence of God.

May you be unencumbered souls who travel swiftly along the Pathway of Spiritual Fulfillment.

The Wheel

The human race is as the spokes of a wheel. The various spokes symbolize the different races, creeds, diverse groups and individuals who seem so far apart in their relationships with each other.

Consider how they have been assembled together to comprise the wheel. No spoke by itself could serve any purpose. Only as it becomes a part of the Whole does it become useful. In the event that one spoke becomes damaged or missing, the entire structure of the wheel is weakened. This is also true of mankind—if each individual, group or race does not assume its proper relationship with fellow human beings, the structure of God's Divine Plan for man is weakened.

With the spokes representing Humanity, think of the hub

as being God. Emanating from the Hub of God are all of his people, and all are held together by the outer rim which is the Brotherhood of Man. Together, within the Band of Brotherhood, each has his rightful place and function. It is interesting to note that the closer the spokes draw together, the closer they are to the hub. How true this is of man. The closer he draws in love and understanding to his fellowman, the nearer he is to the Divine where all are centered.

Ask yourselves where you are upon this wheel. Are you divergent from your brothers, at the outer rim, or are you near the hub where you feel a greater love and kinship for all of God's children? Every thought of intolerance, hatred, bitterness, criticism or jealousy places your farther out on the spoke. Love draws you to the center.

Do your part to make a perfect wheel which will help to carry the burdens of the world.

Thoughts as the Reverberations of a Gong

Thoughts are as the striking of a gong. When a gong is struck a series of vibrations are set into motion. They go out into the ether in an ever-widening circle much the same as when a stone is dropped into the water and starts a series of ripples. The sound vibrations travel until they reach an obstacle, and then they rebound or echo back. This reverberation is often much greater than the original sound because it is amplified by each object which it reaches.

This same principle is involved as you send thought waves into the ether. Thoughts are also a series of vibrations, and they emanate from you in a widening circle. As they touch the mind of another, they not only affect him, but they are bounced back to the sender. As an infinite number of minds are touched by your thoughts, consider the tremendous reverberations which are taking place. This activity in the ether is known as the Race Mind, it is the conglomeration of thoughts being broadcast by humanity.

Man is so constituted that he is not only sending out thought waves and patterns, but he is also a receiving apparatus and is sensitive to the thought frequencies of others. Think what a tremendous responsibility you have to your fellowman as your thoughts go from you! Are you sending kind and loving thoughts which will help to lift others or are you sending evil, unkind thoughts which will add to man's degradation? It is alarming to know how evil thoughts are picked up and acted upon by sensitive individuals.

Humanity in general is emitting very ungodly thought patterns. It is the responsibility of those who understand this law to counteract these negative patterns by broadcasting high spiritual vibrations. As you do this you not only help others, but you also help yourself. "As ye sow, so shall ye reap." You cannot escape the echo of your voice, and likewise you cannot escape the return of your thoughts, bounced back and amplified.

Just as your voice emanates from you in various frequencies or tones, so are your thoughts at various frequencies. You have the ability to control and modulate your voice to make it pleasant and harmonious. You must also learn to control your thoughts so that they might be equally acceptable.

Think about this when you are tempted to indulge in unkind or unholy thoughts. Would you wish to receive the same as you are sending out? That is the law—there is no escape! So send out nothing but love and receive harmony, peace and happiness in return.

Spiritual Progression as a Highway

Spiritual progression is as the building of a new highway. There is much to be done before it becomes complete. The high places must be leveled off and the low places filled in. The marshy spots must be reinforced and bridges built. It takes much time, patience and work before the smooth surface can be laid, but when it is completed it becomes "The Way" over which many can proceed to their destination.

As each person does the necessary work he not only has prepared his own "Way," but he also becomes "The Way" whereby others might also be brought more quickly to their spiritual fulfillment.

Make yours an "Expressway!"

You Are a Collector of Precious Jewels

As you go through life, think of yourself as a collector of precious jewels. Each bit of understanding which you gain, each new spiritual quality you achieve would be as another jewel to add to your collection. There are so many precious jewels that it would be impossible to enumerate them. Each person must search and find them for himself in his own way. There is the Jewel of Love, the Jewel of Understanding, the Jewels of Patience and of Faith. Everything which is Godlike could be considered a precious jewel.

A collector must find or pay for a jewel before it becomes his, and this is not always easy. However, the more effort he must expend in getting it, the greater is his appreciation for it. This is true as you collect your spiritual jewels. Often they are buried deeply or come at a great price, but does the collector ever say they were not worth the digging or the price?

The most brilliant and priceless jewel which you can add to your collection is the jewel of knowing your Oneness with God.

Collect God's precious gems, display them in your heart and they will be yours forever.

A Spiritual Bridge

Over the stream of life's circumstances you must erect a spiritual bridge if you are to avoid the dangers of the stream, for there are many rapids, whirlpools and currents which can sweep you downstream if you become immersed in them.

As in the construction of any bridge, much engineering must be done to insure its strength and safety. It is therefore necessary that you study the stream and its dangers and build your bridge to withstand them. You will have to combat the whirlpool of Ego, the rapids of Anger, the currents of Fear and Injustice and many more. To withstand these forces, your bridge must be moored in God and built with the steel girders of Love, Faith, Patience and Prayer.

It must be strong enough to withstand a flash flood, for situations can sometimes reach alarming proportions. It must also be built to endure time; you are not building for today alone. Each girder which goes into your bridge can strengthen it so that it can serve you eternally.

Build well, using only the best of materials, and when your bridge is completed you can cross swiftly and safely over any inharmony, injustice, misunderstanding or trial.

Crossing the River of Life

This wondrous River we call Life
Is eternal in its flow,
And many crossings we may make
As the eons come and go.

Perchance our paths may lead us
To a treacherous crossing place,
Where rapids swift and foam and rocks
Are the dangers we must face.

The maelstrom may engulf us,
Over high falls we may go,
To find that we are battered
On the rocks which lie below.

How easy to be swept downstream,
Or eddy with the pool,
But some time we'll awake to know
That we have been a fool.

Each struggling crossing which we make
Will serve to help us know
That there must be a better way
To span the River's flow.

We then will seek the quiet place,
Above the torrent's rage,
In care and strife and anguish
No more will we engage.

For we will find serenity
And peace and quiet there,
When we learn to cross the River
On the bridge of Love and Prayer.

The Spiral of Life

The Pathway of Spiritual Attainment is as a spiral up which man must toil to attain Perfection. All of mankind is making this climb. Many are farther advanced than others, but few have reached the top.

By the perfecting of each individual, the Brotherhood of Man will be established. This is our purpose in coming to you and teaching you. Banded together in the ties of love and faith, mortals and immortals, working hand in hand will promote Universal Brotherhood throughout God's Infinite Universe.

All souls must be taught the spiritual laws of life. All are learning as they climb that which is often called the Ladder of Life. On the lower rungs man is climbing above the rungs of fear, hatred, intolerance, anger, misunderstanding and frustration as he reaches for the higher rungs of love, tolerance, faith, peace and brotherhood. The top rung brings him to the fulfillment of his destiny, his Oneness with the Divine.

Man's climb is always illuminated by God's eternal Light and Love. Just as the sun by the very nature of itself must radiate heat and light, so does the Divine Nature of God constantly radiate Love, Power, Wisdom, Truth and

Light. These gifts are as available to man as the rays of the sun and likewise as necessary for his growth and well-being. But he often neglects to accept these gifts or thinks they are reserved for a chosen few.

God's Light is as the noonday sun. If one stands directly in the Light, a very small shadow is cast. But if he chooses to stand where the light strikes him obliquely, the shadows are longer. The shadows of your life are determined by where you choose to stand in the Light. If you wish to experience the full Light of God in your life, you will find your ladder lighted and your climb made easier.

Keep your eyes on your goal and love in your hearts, and you will reach the top!

The School of Life

Think of your life as a school in which you are being trained to become a Divine Emissary of God. You must attend all of the classes, learn all of the lessons and pass all of the tests before you can be qualified to graduate.

Each experience has some lesson to teach you, and unpleasant situations are the tests which reveal how well you have learned your lessons. In school you were faced with your knowledge or your lack of it at examination time. This is also true of your spiritual life. If your reactions to trials and circumstances reveal that you are lacking in understanding, you must face that lack within yourself and resolve to rectify it.

All of this processing is according to God's Great Plan to refine His children. The fire of His Divine Love may seem to be destroying you at times, but it is only burning away the dross in your life and will leave you purified and ready to be used in the building of His Kingdom.

So learn your lessons well and welcome the tests that come to you. May you graduate Summa Cum Laude!

Our Purpose

So oft we question the purpose of Life,
Why must we live in struggle and strife?
Why are we here? Where do we go?
These are the answers we wish to know.

Our answers will come, when we view this span,
As a training time in God's Great Plan,
To teach us to build a Life Divine,
Complete and fulfilled in His Love sublime.

How do we make our lives complete?
By turning to victory each defeat,
And knowing each trial is meant to show
Some lesson God wishes us to know.

How do we build a Life Divine?
Each day more of God's Love entwine
About the hearts of our fellowman,
Till it binds together the Human Clan.

This is our purpose on this earth,
This was the reason for our birth,
To reveal to man God's Love, Divine,
That in Oneness with Him, All may combine.

Ships

Great advancement has been made in the construction
and propulsion of ships. Early man used a hollowed log
or dugout. Then man devised the canoe, galley, sailboat,
steam ship; now he will use atomic powered ships. Early
man was completely at the mercy of the wind and tide and
currents, but with his evolution of ships came the knowledge of how to direct their course.

Your life is much the same as the ships. In your early
understanding, your craft is crude and you cannot seem to
control it. You are at the mercy of the storms and currents
in your life. As you grow in understanding, you build a

more seaworthy craft and begin to utilize a greater power. No longer must you row arduously. You add sails to your ship and learn to set them so you can utilize the Power of God. Or you add motors and go even more easily and swiftly. As you learn to use more and more of God's Power, your tasks become easier until you have little to do except watch your compass and hold a true course. If you have a seaworthy vessel and sufficient power in the hold, you can weather any storms which might come.

During your journey, you must be alert to avoid any obstacles with which you might collide. Icebergs often float insidiously into the path of a ship and while they might seem small at the top, their bulk is mostly below the surface where it cannot be seen. So the good captain must take a wide swing around them if he would avoid crashing his ship. Some of the icebergs which assail your spiritual craft are those of ego, gossip, hatred, envy and criticism. Although they may seem small on the surface, they too are very treacherous, for their bulk also is hidden, and you are not aware of their great proportions or destructive powers in your nature. Steer carefully away from them lest your ship be wrecked.

The cargo in the hold of your ship should be Brotherly Love. As you sail the seas and reach various ports, leave this precious cargo with all whom you meet.

God Bless you and Bon Voyage!

Windows of the Soul

Your desire for spiritual understanding could be likened to the windows of a house. In building a home, much attention is given to the number, size and position of the windows. They determine how much light and air can be admitted and what the view is going to be.

Your spiritual desire opens your Soul to the Light and Love of God and determines what vistas you will view. Only when you have a great desire to KNOW God can the Light of God come to you.

Although you might have many windows, the Light could be shut out by the shades you may have drawn. You can be shutting out the spiritual light by drawing the shades of materiality, or ego, or hatred, or sensuality, or criticism, or any number of ungodly things.

The second function of a window is to let fresh air in. Just as a room can be sweetened and purified by fresh air, God's refreshing Love can sweeten and purify you.

With your shades up you can see the lovely panorama of God's bountiful creation. Your world is expanded to all that lies within your horizons.

How different is the home which is filled with sunshine from the one which is dark and gloomy and musty because it has no light or air. The sunny home seems to invite you in, while the other repels you. This is also true of you! You can keep your shades tightly drawn seeing no beauty and being repellent to others. Or you can open your heart and be a joy to everyone.

Through an unobstructed window, your spiritual light can be a beacon to all who are in darkness. Have you not come down the pathway at night and seen a light shining in the window? How wonderful to be coming "home" to that well-lighted, cheerful place for which your heart had been longing. Many tired and hungry souls are longing to come "home" to Truth and Love and Understanding. Your lighted window can be their beacon, and you can be their haven.

Light cannot shine through a dirty window, either from within or without. Keep the windows of your Soul clean and well polished so that they might be a pure channel for the Light and Love of God.

The Garden of Truth

The Garden of Truth is within the Soul of each man. It is that Inner Sanctum where he communes with God. By this communion, the garden flourishes and blooms.

Think of this garden as a refuge for your Soul. Go there in thought for harmony, peace and illumination.

This is a still quiet place in consciousness where the world is shut out by a wall of Divine Protection. There is only one pathway which leads to this lovely garden, and it is the Pathway of Spiritual Unfoldment. The gate through which you must enter is the Sincere Desire to KNOW God.

Once you have entered the garden, you behold and absorb all of its beauty and tranquility. You will see the beauty of its delicate blossoms and breathe their pungent perfume, for they are the beautiful spiritual qualities of your Soul which have come into bloom. Here you will find the Rose of Sympathy, the Violet of Tolerance, the Lily of Understanding, the Lotus of Faith, and all of the delicate godly aspects of your Divine Self. Each aspect is brought to full bloom in this lovely garden.

In the midst of the garden is an ever-flowing fountain, the Fountain of Divine Love. It overflows on all sides and sends its rivulets to water the flowers and bring them to their fulfillment. This is the life-giving Essence which must be absorbed if the plants are to flourish and bloom.

Above and shedding its brilliance over all is the bright sun which is the Christ Light within each Soul. Together the Christ Light and the Fountain of Divine Love have brought this lovely Garden into expression.

Gently cooing and gracing the garden are the Doves of Peace and Harmony. Here you will experience peace and tranquility such as you find in no other place. Here you will find love and faith and beauty. In the blessed Garden of Truth, you WILL FIND GOD!

POEMS

Part 1

Chapter 4

POEMS

A VISION

Life could be so wonderful, do you not agree,
If we could hold the vision which comes so fleetingly?
   In man's loftier moments, the portals open wide,
   And for a precious second he seems to see inside
      The very Gates of Heaven;
      And there he does behold,
God's Plan for our perfection, just waiting to unfold.

A world of Peace and Brotherhood is in that perfect Plan.
A world of Love and Fellowship, where man will honor man.
   No wars to rend the mother's heart.
   No shattered lives by hatred's dart,
      Within the Gates of Heaven.
   No lust, no greed, no prison bar,
   The beauty of God's Plan to mar.

Alas, too soon, the vision's gone,
And we again become earth's pawn.
   But, as EACH heart with LOVE is raised,
   Someday, on earth, God will be praised,
      As He is praised in Heaven,
And Brotherhood will reign supreme,
And be no more a fleeting dream.

TRUE IDENTITY

It matters not what fame we've won,
    What wealth, what race, what creed,
To know our true identity
    Is each Soul's crying need.
All else is but a will-o-wisp,
    Pursued with lust and vigor,
In a vain attempt to find
    That "Something," which is bigger.

Deep in each heart there is
    A Sacred Place, most dear,
Where Spirit speaks, if we but list,
    In a voice that's loud and clear.
Here in this Inner Sanctum,
    In reverence we kneel,
That to our searching hearts
    His secrets he'll reveal.

"Ye are My Temple, I'm your Life.
    Together we are 'ONE.'
I am your Father-Mother God,
    Ye are my blessed SON!
You need not roam to find me,
    Your 'WAY' is but 'retreat'
To this 'Holiest of Holies'
    The 'Blessed Mercy Seat.'

Here you will find your 'True Self,'
    Your futile search will end.
No longer will you feel 'alone'
    As lovingly we blend.
In Me, you'll have your Being
    And find your destiny,
In Me, you'll dwell forever,
    In bliss and harmony."

THE SEEING EYE

We look with eyes—but do not SEE,
We hear with ears—but do not HEAR,
God shows his wonders and plays his tones,
But our eyes are blind and our ears as stones.

Pain and suffering, sin and shame,
Endless striving for worthless gain,
We struggle on, through the maze of life,
Engulfed in tears and bitter strife.

We fall at last beneath this load. Then,
As Paul, upon Damascus road,
A great light dawns and a voice is heard,
And within our hearts He reveals His word.

"Behold Me—in the flower and tree,
Behold Me—in the sun,
Behold Me—in the form and mind
And heart of everyone.

"Behold Me—in the waters,
Behold Me—in the wind,
Behold Me—in the beggar
And in the one who's sinned.

"Behold Me—in the serpent,
Behold Me—in the blind,
Behold Me—in the saintly
And the dregs of Humankind.

"Behold Me—in the strife and din,
Behold Me—through your tears,
Behold Me—in the lark's sweet song
And the music of the spheres.

"Behold Me—when all love seems gone,
And when your heart is breaking,
Behold that I'm the ONLY TRUTH
For which your soul is aching.

"Behold Me—in the timeless past
    And in Eternity,
Behold Me—as my Perfect Plan
    Unfolds itself IN Thee.

"Behold Me NOW—with Open Eyes,
    I'm not from you apart,
Behold—My Works—My Love—My Plan,
Behold Me—WITH YOUR HEART!"

THE CALL

There comes a time when every Soul
    Hears ringing loud the Call
Which comes from out his own great depths,
    That one and only "ALL."

"Behold Me as your Source,
    Your Destiny, Your Life,
Behold Me as your Sustenance,
    And cease from all your strife.

"When striving for possessions,
    Great trials your Path beset,
A harried life of care and woe,
    Ending only in regret.

"No man can serve two masters,
    I'm sure you will agree,
Your only peace and happiness
    Will come through serving Me.

"My fields are ripe and ready,
    The laborers are few,
I need your help to stir the hearts
    And minds of men anew.

"No hands, no feet, no voice have I,
For this, on you I must rely.

"A world of Love and Brotherhood,
    Where peace will reign supreme,
Each man expressing as Divine,
    Is My eternal dream.

"So, this clarion Call I send to Thee,
    Be hands and feet and voice for Me."

MY ETERNAL BLESSINGS

Could I ever count the blessings
    The Father gives to me?
'Twould be like trying to count
    The many leaves upon a tree.

But, if the leaves I counted,
    How could I ever know
The bountiful supply of Life
    Within the trunk below?

As the seasons come and go,
    And the tree its leaves will shed,
When the winter of my life comes,
    They may say, "She is dead."

But this I KNOW, for it is true,
    The Father has for me, and you,
A Plan, which, tho' we cannot see,
    Is much, much, greater than the tree.

And if the tree, which looks so bare,
    Can heed the Impulse which is there
And come again to glorious bloom,
    My thoughts shall not be those of gloom.

For, from the lesson of the tree,
    I know I'm in Eternity
When from this earthly sphere I go,
    'Twill be to ever onward grow.

So how can I, my blessings count,
When, FOREVER they'll flow from the Father's Fount?

GOD'S DIAMONDS

A million diamonds sparkle, upon the dashing brook,
  As it wends its gleeful way through woodland and
  through nook.
A diamond for each time the brook, in radiant delight
  Catches and reflects again, the sun's pure, brilliant
  light.

A million diamonds sparkle, as God lights our hearts with
  love,
  And joyously we go through life inspired from above.
A diamond for each time the Soul, in radiant delight,
  Catches and reflects to man, God's Love and Truth and
  Light!

THE DAWN

Out of the depths of the misty night
  The dawn sends fingers of glowing light,
Clutching the dark shroud engulfing the world,
  They fling it aside, and the bright morning herald.

Out of the depths of our Soul's despair,
  Faith sends its rays, saying "God is here."
It tatters the mantle of fear and doubt
  And puts all our disbelief to rout.

Beautiful Dawn, of a day so bright,
  Breaks for the Soul, who SEES the Light,
All darkness dispelled, in the Father abide,
  In the glory and brightness of full noontide.

NOW

This fleeting moment we call "now,"
Furrows itself upon time's brow,
Then speeds its way, with pace so fast,
Into the dim and age-old past.

The future goes forth to Infinity,
And who is to say what it will be?
Trials and lessons it's sure to bring,
Sometimes we'll cry, sometimes we'll sing.

But, the way to face it without fear,
Is to greet each day with a smile of cheer,
And know that each trial that's overcome
Takes us up life's ladder another rung.

The past is gone, the future's not here,
So why waste time in remorse or fear?
"Each moment our best," should be our vow,
For life will always be the "NOW."

A PRAYER

Silently the snow falls
    And shrouds the earth with white.
Silently thy Spirit, Lord,
    Fills my soul with Light.
Gentle as the snowflakes,
    Wilt thou graciously impart
The mantle of thy purity
    Upon my longing heart?
Cover all my sins, Lord,
    With thy robe of white,
That I might be as pure, Lord,
    As thy earth seems tonight.

ODE TO LIFE

Oh Life, within the boundless heart of All,
How wondrous is thy majesty,
How urgent is thy call.

Each must respond in its own way,
To thy great vibrant thrill,
Propelled by thy creative power, its pattern to fulfill.

From atom small to Universe,
By thee are all things wrought,
And with thy omnipresent fire, forever they are fraught.
Content to be thy vessel, is diatom and star,
Imbued with Thee, they carry on
Just BEING what they are.

But Mortal, in eternal quest,
And blessed with power to SEE,
Would seek to wrest the secret of thy Infinity.

Could Man but know it, even this—
His search to know of Thee,
Is thy compelling Spirit, striving to set him free.

As he goes forward on his Path,
Embracing Thee in Love,
Thou too wilt give Thyself to him
And lift him to new heights above.

RAINDROPS

I watched descending raindrops,
  As they fell into the brook,
And as I watched, it seemed to me,
  God opened His great Book.

I saw my life as it once was,
  Alone, a thing apart,
And I knew again the longing
  That had been within my heart.

For I was as a drop of rain,
  Suspended in a cloud,
Which tossed me aimlessly about,
  And did my Soul enshroud.

But God in His great mercy,
  Took pity on my plight,
And opened up my eyes and heart,
  That I might see His Light.

So I know the great rejoicing,
  The raindrops must have known,
As the babbling brook received them,
  And made them all its own.

And as they join the rushing brook,
  And speed on to the sea,
I too, go forth, as ONE with Him,
  Into Infinity.

THE STREAM

As the waters of the stream flow on relentlessly,
In their rush to pour themselves into the mighty sea,
They oft are thwarted in their haste,
And their meanderings might seem like waste.

But, could they know the joy they bring,
They then would know why waters sing,
For, to countless fish they're host,
Of heavenly music they can boast.

A place to romp and shout with joy,
They make for many a barefoot boy,
A place of quiet, to sit and dream,
The oldster finds beside the stream.

The Life of God they bring the land,
To feed the hungry human band,
And they reflect, with diamonds bright,
The beauty of God's heavenly light.

So what if, in the course they take,
Some changes they are forced to make?
The joys they give will compensate,
And the sea for them will always wait.

We too rush on toward The Sea,
To reach our fulfilled Destiny,
But, thwarted we may sometimes seem,
When we cannot achieve a dream.

Our course we're often forced to alter,
To help someone whose feet may falter,
Or bring some joy to some sad heart,
Who needs our help for a fresh start.

So, as we wend our way through life,
Let us not force our way with strife,

But be content to *flow* along,
And, as the stream, let's sing a song.

Let's give of beauty, joy, and light,
And, with the Father's Love, be bright,
For, as the stream's met by the sea,
The Father waits for you and me.

GOD'S HANDIWORK

I saw the lacy pattern
    Of the shadows from the trees,
I smelled the sweet aroma
    Of the flowers on the breeze,
I heard the breaking of the surf,
    As each wave made its run,
I felt the warm and soothing rays
    That streamed down from the sun.
I drank in all this beauty
    As I rested by the shore,
And I thought of God's great Universe—
    "ALL this and SO much more!"
"No matter where I'd roam,
    In this, or any nation,
'Twould still all be a blessed part
    Of the Father's great Creation."
"And, whatever I might comprehend,
    Through senses or through thought,
Could only be a minute speck
    Of what God's Handiwork has wrought."

HOW BLESSED AM I!

MY GOD, MY GOD, How blessed am I,
Thy glories to perceive,
The majesty of mountain-top,
The beauty of the seas.

The Cosmos great, the atom small,
One pattern do portray,
Revealing Law and Harmony
Of Thy Creative Ray.

Proceeding from his Seed Divine,
As part of Thy Great Plan,
Unfolds that great potential "God,"
Within the Soul of Man.

Oh, wondrous Light! Oh, Cosmic Sun,
Shine Thou through me, and make us ONE!
For all Eternity my cry.
"MY GOD, MY GOD, HOW BLESSED AM I!"

ALL THE WAY

When you've struggled and striven with all of your might,
And it seems that nothing will ever be right,
That's the time to remember the dear, loving Lord,
And turn from your troubles and trust in His Word.

For although we forget Him, He always is there,
Ready to help with His kind loving care,
We have only to seek His dear, blessed face
To receive His rich blessings and dwell in His Grace.

So when you are weary from life's heavy load,
Walk beside Him along His well-lighted road,
Your cares will all vanish and life will be gay,
For He will go with you ALL of the way.

JESUS' BIRTHDAY

The Father, in his wisdom,
   Saw the needs of humankind,
So He placed upon this earth
   One who could lead the blind.

Our Blessed Jesus was the One
   Who gave his very life,
To show us all the Pathway,
   And guide us through our strife.

Our eyes he's helped to open,
   Our feet he's set aright,
His love and strength and counsel
   Have been our Guiding Light.

So, what could be more fitting,
   Than to celebrate His birth,
The Day the Father sent Him
   To dwell upon this earth?

Our grateful praise we give Him,
   For all the Love we share,
And pray that He will keep us
   Within His loving care.

Our Teacher, Master, Brother,
   To us he'll always be.
May we follow in His footsteps
   Throughout Eternity.

I WALK WITH THE MASTER

I walk each day with the Master,
I live each day in His Love,
I talk each day with the Master, and
His blessings pour from above.

Chorus: He takes my hand and guides my way,
He will lead me through each day,
I walk in His Light and my pathway is bright,
For I walk all the way with Him.

If I walk each day with the Master,
My Soul with His glory will shine,
If I talk each day with the Master,
His peace and His joy will be mine.

Chorus: He takes my hand and guides my way,
He will lead me through each day,
I walk in His Light and my pathway is bright,
For I walk all the way with Him.

I need not wait to know heaven,
For with Him all things are Divine,
So I walk each day with the Master,
And Heaven is Already Mine!

SPRINGTIME

Hear the voices of the robins,
Singing in the apple trees.

See the bursting buds unfolding,
Swaying in the sweet spring breeze.

Smell their fragrance, so beguiling,
Taste the heady wine of spring.

Feel again the Joy of living,
Then, God's eternal wonders sing.

LIBERTY

Deep in the heart of every man
There rings a bell most clear,
Calling for peace and liberty,
A dream he holds most dear.

Our nation, for this purpose,
From the wilderness was wrought,
To loose the tyrant's shackles
A bloody war was fought.

A young and vital nation,
Full of promise, true and clean,
A new and better way of life,
Was every patriot's dream.

Unity of purpose
Made our country strong and free,
And gave us all the heritage
Of precious liberty.

I UNDERSTAND

by
Kathleen Cain
(our daughter, 15 years old)

I understand why people fail,
And suffer pain, along life's trail.
They have no hope, or goal in mind,
So they don't succeed, you'll always find.

Draw a picture of your heart's desire,
Then never stop praying, altho' you may tire.
Sooner or later your dreams will come true,
If you always remember, God is with you.

I understand why we have war,
And men must fight to break the door
That's made of hate and bitterness,
Instead of love and friendliness.

Peace can never come to stay,
Unless all nations learn to pray.
For God's the One who holds the key,
And turns the lock, to set Love free.

LIGHT

by
Edward H. Cain

I lived in the darkness called "Knowledge,"
    Then the Light came flickering through.
The beauty—I scarce could behold it,
    And a voice said, "I'm the Real INNER You!"

How long have I lived in the darkness?
Then the answer came from within,
"The Light has been here forever,
But you failed to let it come in "

My heart cried—"God I thank Thee
For awakening in this span of life."
The voice answered, "You get what you strive for,
Light has come for you and your wife.

"So my child, spread My Light to the Universe,
Yes, in My eyes, the world is small,
Wonders of life are yours for the asking,
For *within you* lie the answers to all.

"Sin dwells in the cellar of darkness,
Man is given free choice, this you know,
It is only through sorrow and heartache
That God gives man the privilege to grow.

"So don't let this privilege pass by you.
Just say, "God, you have the answers, I know,
Take my hand and let me work for you,
I'll not stumble again, and I'LL GROW."

MY PRAYER

by
Edward H. Cain

Since my eyes are the lantern of my soul,
Teach me to see into the beyond.

Since my hands express your power,
Teach me to do Thy will.

Since my feet walk at your direction,
Teach me to walk in another's shoes.

Since my heart is completely yours,
Teach me to BE love in all that I do and see.

Since I am born for eternal growth,
Teach me to be ONE with the universe.

Teach me to drop the robe of materiality
And wear your Robe of Love.

Teach me that there are many roads,
But only one that goes directly to you,
And help me to find that road.

Teach me your short-cuts,
That I may not linger on my Pathway
In becoming ONE with Thee.

For only then will I know complete happiness,
And become Thy true Servant.

This is my purpose and my prayer!

HAPPINESS

by
Edward H. Cain

I have walked through the valley of sorrow,
I have climbed the mountain of faith,
I know what it means to go hungry
In a land of beauty, but waste.

When I questingly sought for an answer
A voice spoke to me loud and clear,
"You receive in the measure you've given,
Are you selfless, and live without fear?"

Then I stopped and thought for a moment,
And knew—happiness comes by "giving away,"
As I saw with the eyes of "knowledge"
I knew where I'd gone astray.

I had lived for my selfish ego,
Giving little of my real self,
But I've changed, and now I am happy,
I've put ego away on a shelf.

So, if you want to be happy,
Turn the other cheek and forgive,
Forget all your hurts and self-pity,
And you'll have learned how to truly LIVE.

I...THE CREATURE...MAN

by our friend
Dr. T. G. Bush

I have followed after rainbows...
I have sought the pot of gold...
I have traversed burning deserts...
I have braved the artics cold...
I have probed the restless oceans...
I have searched the endless sky...
I have climbed the highest mountains...
I have taught myself to fly...
I have builded mighty kingdoms...
I have struggled to be free...
I have split the tiny atom...
I have charted every sea...
I have fostered great achievements...
I have suffered loss and pain...
I have met and conquered tyrants...
I have fled, to fight again...
I have lived through plague and famine...

I have perished by the sword...
I have reaped abundant harvests...
I have served without reward...
I have postulated knowledge...
I have increased life and span...
I have limitless horizons...
I am...I...the creature...MAN

I am Man...the enigmatic...
I am timid...I am bold...
I am cynic...I am zealot...
I am young...and I am old...
I am white... and I am colored...
I am dull...and I am wise...
I am poor...and I am wealthy...
I am humble...and despised...
I am chaste...and I am passion...
I am honest...I am knave...
I am undisputed leader...
I am freeman...I am slave...
I am kindly...I am selfish...
I am careless of my fate...
I am quitter...I am doer...
I am arrogance and hate...
I am vanquished...I am victor...
I am tiller of the sod...
I am profane and agnostic...
I am follower of God...
I am steadfast...I am fickle...
I am virile...I am worn...
I am legions long since vanished...
I am millions yet unborn...
I am monarch...I am peasant...
I am family and clan...
I am ceaseless and prolific...
I am...I...the creature...MAN

Part 1

Chapter 5

Personal Mystical Experiences

Soon after contacting the far-eastern teachers I was told that I had been accepted by them as a novice and I was presented with the Robe of the Initiate. This was a very sacred service! I was told that the Robe carried with it a great responsibility, but also great protection. In accepting the Robe I was required to vow to dedicate my life to serving mankind in humility and love. I was also told that I would be guided and instructed by the Masters, and that their circle of protection would always enfold me, for their Light infiltrated my auric field. They said that I was now "on the Path" and that, as I fulfilled each duty and learned each lesson, I would be taken forward in my Soul's progression. Each part of the Robe of Light is significant. The *cowl* is indicative of the receiving and imparting of *knowledge* and *wisdom*. The *sleeves* mean that the arms of the pupil must be outstretched in *loving service, embracing* one's fellowmen. The *left side* indicates an *open* and *loving heart*. The *right side* means that one will give of his *strength* to others. The *back* means that the Initiate will *take up the burdens of others* and help to carry them. The *girdle* is the woven *Band of Brotherhood* which *encircles ALL*. The entire garment is the *Seamless Robe,* woven of the *Golden Threads* of Love! I was told, "Be open and receptive to the Light and Love of the Masters and call for their Divine Wisdom and Light. Knowledge,

Power, Light, and Love, come to the Initiate as he devotes himself wholeheartedly to serving the Light. Find every avenue of service and do it all in Love, and your progress is assured." Various members of our group were also later presented with the Robe, as The Masters felt they were ready to accept the responsibility it entails.

I also had many personal mystical experiences that brought great revelation and realization. I have since learned that some of them are considered "Initiations" by the Masters. To insure my remembering and the soul-response I felt to them, I kept the following account of many of them as they occurred:

Doorways to the Light

As I sat in meditation today, it seemed I was at one end of a long black tunnel. At the other end of the tunnel I could see a very bright light. As I progressed through the tunnel, the light became brighter. When I walked out of the tunnel into the light, I was lifted up to a higher level and found myself confronted with a sliding door. I pushed it aside, only to find revealed another door; this too I pushed aside. I proceeded through many doors, each of which was named. They were the doors of Impatience, Intolerance, Fear, Worry, Anger, Misunderstanding, and finally the door of EGO. What a struggle I had to open the last door! As each door was opened, the Light became brighter and I finally stood FREE, in a beautiful GOLDEN LIGHT. I realized that this was symbolic of the many things which must be pushed out of my life, if I am to enter into the Divine Light of Love and Understanding.

The Well of Understanding

During meditation today, I seemed to be standing beside an old-fashioned open well. I had this realization, and this poem came:

My Quest

I was a weary traveler
Upon a dusty road.
A great thirst was upon me,
And heavy was my load.

My soul cried out for knowledge
To quench this awful thirst,
And then I heard a voice say,
"These things you must do first."

"The Bucket of an Open Mind
You fasten to the Rope,
Which is a kind and loving Heart,
In which there is much Hope.

"Then deep into the open Well
You let the Bucket fall,
Until you know that it has reached
The one and only ALL.

"Then with the steady pull of Faith,
You pull the Bucket up,
And fill, to overflowing,
Your large awaiting cup.

"Sincere desire is the Cup,
Which then will be well filled.
Truth is the nectar you will drink,
Your thirst forever quelled.

"No more the dusty road you'll tread,
Your load you'll cast aside.
When all these lessons you have learned,
In Peace you will abide."

As I stood by the well I had the promise of the cup
being filled to overflowing, and was told to give the filled
cup to every thirsty wayfarer whom I met. Then I heard

these words. "This is the FULL CUP of the Living Christ in each man. It is the Holy Grail, or the Golden Chalice, which has been sought throughout the ages but never found except by the few who search and find it WITHIN themselves. SEEK WITHIN."

The Christ is Born

It is just before Christmas, and I am deeply aware of a new significance of Christmas. This poem has just come. This is a tremendous *Inner Realization,* not just casual thoughts.

The sky is clear, chill is the night,
The stars are near, the moon is bright,
The earth stands bathed in Light Divine,
This sacred Night, forever mine.

I gaze upon a shining star,
Which sheds its radiance from afar,
And feel within that wondrous glow
The shepherds knew so long ago.

I hear an angel Choir proclaim,
"Your life will never be the same,
For unto you this night is born
The Christ of your Eternal Morn!"

And in the manger of my heart,
I feel the Christ Child wake and start.

Babe, tho' the Christ in me may be,
'Twill grow to full maturity,
As up the Path I ever climb,
Secure in this great Truth sublime.

So Christmas Bells, ring out with glee.
This night "The CHRIST" is born in Me!

This is the first Real Awareness I have had of my own CHRIST BEING. What a beautiful revelation this is for me and how wonderful it will be to observe this "Christ Child" grow in stature and understanding!

The Temple

A few months ago I had an experience in which I seemed to climb up a winding pathway, at the top of which was a BEAUTIFUL TEMPLE. It was surrounded by a high wall, in which was a beautiful, ornate gate. I was taken to the gate, but I was not allowed to go through into the temple. I was then told that I was not ready to enter the temple, but to return to the physical or earthly realm and give out the lessons I have received. I had been greatly disappointed that I was not allowed inside the temple, for it seemed to be my greatest desire.

As I sat in meditation this morning I directed my attention to the teachers. I sent out my call to them in the form of the prolonged AUM on the outlet of the full breath. I ran the entire scale of notes in this way until the pitch was so high I continued it in mind only. As I finished this, my consciousness was filled with innumerable entities of the Brotherhood, who all stood about me in an immense circle. I could not identify any of the faces, but I had a wonderful sense of peace and joy. As they were all gathered around a voice spoke, saying, "No one enters with you into the Inner Sanctum; there you must go alone." Immediately they all withdrew and I was left alone. I could not understand what they meant, and I was sad that they had left, but I sat quietly for a few moments and then had this wonderful experience:

I was first aware of a *pure white Light.* Then I was inside a beautiful temple which seemed to be of white marble, but with an iridescent quality. It was suffused with the same white Light, which seemed to have no specific source, but seemed to be alive and scintillating. Then I was no longer "seeing" the temple, but I actually BECAME the Temple, and a thundering voice said, "YE ARE THE TEMPLE OF THE LIVING GOD." It is impossible to put this experience into words. I had often heard these words, but this was REALIZATION beyond which words can convey. Then I saw the Soul of myself, within the Temple of myself, kneel at the altar and receive a benediction. The voice said, "This is my beloved Son, in whom I am well pleased. Well done, good and faithful servant. You have been faithful in lesser things; you will become master of greater things." I knew the word "son" had no gender connotation, but meant child. As I stood up I saw a great storm approaching. There were dark ugly clouds, lightning flashes, and a black tornado funnel which came twisting toward me. As they reached the light with which I was surrounded, they parted and passed on either side of me. Again the voice spoke, saying, "Walk in the Light and no harm can come nigh Thee."

When the storm had passed, I saw my spirit as "The Christ" driving the money changers from the Temple. I knew the money changers to be the defiling thoughts and deeds which had inhabited my Divine Temple, and that there could be no room for them in this Holy Place.

As I looked, I saw seven niches or recessed places between the marble pillars surrounding the circular walls of the temple. On the floor of each niche I saw a broken idol lying in many pieces. I knew these idols to be all of the things which had kept me from experiencing the Oneness of the Divine. They were Pride, Selfishness, Fear, Intolerance, Misunderstanding, Love of Material Possessions, and Egotism. Now as they lay upon the floor, the Light filled each niche. I knew that when they had been standing, the niches had been darkened by their shadow, but when the Temple is purified and the idols are destroyed the WHITE LIGHT FILLS THE TEMPLE and there are no idols or shadows left within it.

Soon each niche became a column of shimmering, living color until the entire outer wall of the Temple was a living rainbow, each color blending and merging into the next in a complete circle. I was given the significance of each color. Red is indicative of Power, Orange is for Service, Yellow means Wisdom, Green means Life, Blue is Love, Indigo is Spiritual fulfillment, and Violet is Illumination.

All of these qualities are necessary for the Soul's evolution and are all a part of the Great White Light which is Divine Love. In this "Divine Temple of Self," all of these qualities must be achieved. As they merge together in Oneness, we then become the Pure Light of Divine Love.

How long I had searched for the Temple "outside," only to find that it had been this close all of the time, but in my blindness I could not SEE. What a WONDERFUL realization this has been! Thank God for such a wonderful experience. I am indeed Blessed! If Spirit can reveal these things to me, I am sure it can also accomplish them within me!

The Light of the World

Today during meditation I saw a vast sea filled with ships. I knew the ships to be symbolic of human souls. They were being tossed about in a violent storm. Into the sea protruded dangerous points with rugged shore lines, but upon each point stood a tall lighthouse from which a bright beacon light was shining. I recognized each light as a Divine Being who had been a Beacon Light for Humanity—Jesus, Buddha, Mohammed, Krishna, and all the others. As I watched, I heard a voice say, "The same light is within you that is within them. You, too, must become a beacon light unto others, for YE ARE THE LIGHT OF THE WORLD." I know that I have a great and wonderful work to do, and I am sure I am divinely guided and inspired!

Let the Light Shine Through You

As I sat in meditation this morning I heard these words, "Be as the hole through which the light shines into a darkened cellar." In the third eye, I saw a picture of a black cellar, in which there were no windows, but only a small hole in the ceiling through which a shaft of light was shining. A green vine, which had grown toward the light, lay across the floor. Above the cellar was brilliant sunlight, but so little was shining into the cellar. I had this realization: "Most of humanity lives in the dark cellar of Consciousness, but all is Light in the higher levels of Consciousness. Your work is to be as a hole between the two. Above is the Light, below is the darkness. Allow the Light to shine through you, that others might have the Light, for All things require Light for growth. But always remember the NOTHINGNESS OF A HOLE. Be Nothing except a means by which the light is passed into darkness." No place for ego in this assignment!

AT-ONE-MENT

Here in this lovely spot, I am filled with the realization of the Divine Presence in ALL things. These words have just come and partially express what I feel.

God's Symphony

God played for me a symphony,
    As I lay dreaming 'neath a tree,
And sweeter music I'll ne'er hear,
    Until angel choirs reach my ear.

The babbling brook, splashing o'er the stones,
    Created the rhythm with its sweet tones,
And all of nature then joined in,
    'Til my heart was thrilled with its heavenly din.

I heard the woodwinds in the tall pine trees,
    As they swayed so gently in the breeze.
The meadow lark upon the hill,
    Was praising God with his flute-like trill.

The buzzing bees, in their droning din,
    Portrayed the part of the violin,
And the big bass viol was a croaking frog,
    Who was sunning himself upon a log.

The chirping cricket, the singing bird,
The rustling grass, all wished to be heard,
And they all joined in God's symphony,
As He was playing it for me.

The music was soft and sweet and low,
Then it swelled to a mighty crescendo,
And swept me on its lofty wing,
'Til my ONENESS I felt with Everything.

Then I seemed to be everywhere, and within everything, all at the same time. I was the LIFE within each blade of grass, I was in the flowers, the birds, the stones, the rivers and oceans, and even within all humans EVERY-WHERE! I was the UNIVERSE!

This was an AWARENESS OF *ONE LIFE* such as I have never experienced before. Truly, Spirit is working wondrously in me. I am indeed blessed!

The Chain of Brotherhood

As I entered meditation today I repeated several times these words, "Take my life and let it be dedicated, Lord, to Thee."

Suddenly I was aware of a heavy golden chain being placed around my neck. From the chain was suspended a golden medallion which seemed to be a sort of filigree of open work design.

Almost immediately there was a brilliant light and I saw my LIFE in a great crucible, with white flames surrounding it. I saw it melted down, and melted down, by this Divine Fire until there was nothing but PURE GOLD left. I knew that every experience which I have ever had has been the Divine Fire which has been purifying me.

The gold seemed to be in individual large drops, like quicksilver. Then a hand reached into the crucible and re-moved each drop, fashioning it into a large heavy link. Each Link was fastened to another until the gold was all used and the chain was complete. Then a voice said, "Out of the Pure Gold of Truth and Love and Understanding you must help forge the Chain of Brotherhood. The medallion will be yours to wear when the work is finished." Then the chain and medallion disappeared. This appears to be my assignment! With the help of the Blessed Masters and the Power of God at work in me, I know I can fulfill it. Thank God for this revelation!

....

A few weeks later I again saw the medallion. In the center was a large, pure white CHRIST JEWEL, and all around it were places for other jewels to be set. Apparently the medallion is to be filled with the jewels of Illumined Souls, and it is my task to do this. What a blessed opportunity and challenge this is. I pray I will some day deserve to wear the Medallion!

The Christ Star

Prior to this, two things have happened which now have great significance.

Sometime ago one of the ladies in our class thought it would be nice if we each had a pin with which to designate our group. She sent to New York for them and asked to have them shipped C.O.D. When they arrived there was no charge for them, so she wrote and asked how much she should send to pay for them. She received the reply that there was no record of any account against her and according to their records the bill was paid. We were all astonished but took this as a sign that we were truly accepted by the Masters, and this was their way of proving it to us.

A few weeks ago I was told, "Nellie, I am happy to tell you that you now have your Master Teacher Jesus Incarnate within you. Love your Master and follow in His footsteps. Watch for your star." This seemed pretty far-fetched to me and I was reluctant to accept it and I put it out of my mind, but after today's experience I KNOW it is True! I am in such a high state of vibration that it is hard for the physical body to stand. Every cell is vibrant and there is a terrific agitation of the solar plexus and a constriction around my head, but I am so GLOWING

and so thrilled that I hate to return to the physical frequency.

As I sat in meditation I was taken through a review
of my work with my beloved teachers. I was told, "You
first worked as a struggling Soul, searching for the 'Way
of Life.' With the help of Harmon, whom you attracted,
you were guided to some degree of understanding. When
you proved sincere in your efforts you were initiated into
the White Brotherhood. As a novice, or apprentice, your
work was watched. You were given the Robe and told of
its significance. You were also given a pin, the symbology
of which was not revealed to you at that time. You were
given many lessons to guide you in your unfoldment, and
you were told to pass them on, that others might also be
helped. The lessons serve a two-fold purpose; they help you
to receive intuitively and, as you absorb and apply their
essence, you are raised to a new level of consciousness.
As you share them with others, they too are helped, and you
become more firmly established in your new understanding.

"You were faithful in your assignments and in the pursuit of greater understanding. You were therefore allowed
to enter the Temple, at which time you received the Seal
of the Inner Circle. Then came your illumination pertaining to the Divine Beings who have been the Light Keepers
for humanity, and your assignment as a Light Keeper.
Next came a great expansion of Consciousness in which
you experienced your Oneness and your presence throughout All of creation. Then came your experience of the
melting of your life by the Divine Fire in God's great
crucible. Here you saw All experience as good and necessary, and you were told to forge the chain of Brotherhood
out of the Pure Gold of Truth and Love and Understanding. These are all steps leading to your fulfillment. I now
reveal to you the symbology of the pin which you received.

"The pin is in the shape of a five petaled rose with a
cross in the center. The cross is the symbol of the crossing
out in your life of that which is material and carnal. The
rose is the flowering of Spiritual Understanding. The Rose

now is in full bloom, and you are ready for the next step. The Rose now becomes the CHRIST STAR.''

Then it seemed that the Light which had been before me, which I was beholding with the third eye, moved into my Whole Being and I was FLOODED with it. The center, or core, was PURE LOVE. It was as if I had become the Rose. Then the rounded edges of the five petals of the rose became elongated until I BECAME a RADIANT STAR, shining and shimmering and shedding a tremendous brilliance. Each point of the Star then was named; they were Purity, Peace, Power, Wisdom, and Service, and all were emanating from the pure center of Divine Love. As I came back to my human-self awareness, I asked if this could possibly be true; then Jesus stood before me with a beautiful white light all about Him. He said, "You are the CHRIST STAR. Shed your radiance abroad that humanity might become illumined." Then He moved into my very Being and I felt His wondrous presence IN ME. I KNOW He is my Divine Teacher and works through me. Thank God for such a wondrous thing! May I be a faithful, true, humble, channel for His Divine Work.

I understand the beautiful significance of the Christ Star. In perfect balance, by the shining light of The Christ through me, I must radiate all of the star's qualities and carry the Light to All who will see.

....

I was later told by the Master John that the five pointed Star becomes a six-pointed star when one becomes fully illumined and Christed. This is complete integration with the Divine and comes when one is ready to leave the human expression of life and work in the Christ Octave of expression.

The Mystical Marriage

How can I ever put into words the magnificant thing which has happened to me? It is so incredible and so beautiful that it almost seems to defile the sacredness of it to put it into words. However I want to remember every precious detail, so I must try as best I can to record a Divine Experience in mere words.

Yesterday I was in an extremely high state of awareness all day. Last night after the family had gone to bed I sat in the window looking out at all of the beauty in the yard. It was a beautiful clear night and the moon was full and bright. The stars seemed to twinkle more than I had ever noticed since the wonderful night when I experienced the birth of the "Christ Within." I realized that the prophecy of that time was being fulfilled. "Babe tho' the Christ in me may be, 'Twill grow to full maturity," and I was happy beyond expression to be aware of the CHRIST WITHIN.

As I was in this Consciousness, I was shown a plain golden wedding band, and I was told, "Prepare for your Mystical Marriage." Then it seemed there was a dress rehearsal of a marriage. I was walking down a long aisle upon the arm of Jesus. I was in a white bridal gown with a *very heavy* veil. As we reached the end of the aisle, Jesus said, "Search your Soul to know if you are ready to take this vow. When the vow is made, the bridegroom lifts the veil and you no longer see through a veil 'darkly' but you KNOW and are KNOWN by Him." I was told to weigh every aspect of this marriage to KNOW if I was ready and willing to accept its responsibilities.

That was all. Suddenly I was alone and in my normal state of awareness. I was very puzzled and I could not understand the meaning of the experience. After much pondering, I went to bed. I hardly slept because my mind was too filled with the importance of so beautiful an experience. After the family left this morning I sat again in meditation, and Blessing of all Blessings, this wondrous thing happened:

I was extremely conscious of my heart center. It seemed that it swelled and swelled within my body until my chest would burst. Then I seemed to break through the bonds of my body and I expanded and expanded until I was swallowed up within the Heart and Love of the whole Universe. Soon I was again clad in bridal raiment and on the arm of Jesus. As we proceeded down the aisle, He spoke. "As your elder brother I now commend you into the Divine Keeper's hands. This was my task, to bring you to your fulfillment." Then it seemed there was an immense congregation lining both sides of the aisle. I saw everyone who had ever been of any help to me on my spiritual pathway. My parents, grandparents, ancestors, children, husband, friends, teachers (both human and invisible) and the Masters, but as I saw them, I also heard these words, "All these you must leave and CLEAVE ONLY UNTO ME, even as a wife must forsake her father and mother and cleave only to her husband, thereby establishing a NEW household and a NEW family." I had a great realization of what this meant. From this time forward, only the things of the Spirit could have any significance, if I took this vow. The NEW family and household meant I could have only pure and holy thoughts and deeds, be concerned only about things of the Spirit, and embrace ALL Life in ONENESS.

I was then asked, "Are you prepared to make this vow?" I replied, "I am ready and I do so VOW." Immediately the veil was lifted. I saw nothing but a PURE WHITE LIGHT which engulfed me. Then I was FUSED with and BECAME ONE with the Creative Power of the UNIVERSE. I KNEW myself as the Feminine half of the Creative Power with which the Holy Spirit unites to bring about ALL manifestation. I was realizing this not as the individual Me, but as the whole human family. In this consciousness, through the impregnation of the Holy Spirit as we unite in ONENESS, comes forth only Divine offspring, conceived in Love and Purity. This means that we are co-creators with the Holy Spirit upon all levels of our Being. When we unite, in our conscious minds, with the Divine we will conceive only pure and perfect offspring in the form of thought and word and deed upon the physical, mental, and spiritual levels of our Being.

This, then, is the PERFECT CONSUMMATION, PERFECT UNION, PERFECT BLISS! This is complete submission, for I have no will but to be Divinely used by the SPIRIT of God! SO BE IT!

Consummation

"Here we have fused in Oneness,
In that Mystic Union rare,
Co-habitation with Me,
Is Bliss beyond compare.
Co-Creators we shall be
Of loving thought and deed,
In this sacred nuptial bower
Are all pure things conceived.
The Perfect Consummation,
In precious Unity,
Is ours, in sweet fulfillment,
For all Eternity."

Note: At a later date, after having allowed myself to become involved in, and upset by, some trivial material matter, I was chastized thusly: "When you allow your mind to become impregnated with inharmonious thoughts, you are committing fornication against the Holy Spirit. Be true to The Divine!"

PART 2

Teachings of John, the Beloved

Preface

After several years of guidance and lessons from the Far-Eastern teachers, we were surprised to receive a message from John, the Beloved Disciple. This was hard for us to accept, as it seemed sacrilegious, and we could not believe that one of his stature would come to us. We felt unworthy and of so little importance in the great scheme of things that we were sure we were contacting an imposter. We had learned from past experience that one must be very careful in communicating with the "unseen" intelligences, for there are many pranksters and imposters who are earthbound, or in the lower astral levels. They will make claims just to be able to express in the earth vibration and have led many people into very distressing situations. However, we were assured of his identity by the things we received from him.

We were told that communication with his level of consciousness is possible in this way. The Masters function upon, and within, certain "frequency bands" just as radio and television are transmitted over certain wave-lengths. Those who can attune to their wave length can receive what is within their consciousness. He said that since we were sincere seekers and never entered into meditation without invoking the Light and Love of God, and since we were dedicated to our work, we were able to touch his frequency. We were told that it was not a matter of our being expecially "chosen," but a matter of our own "attunement." We could accept this explanation since we truly had been sincere and dedicated.

John told us that each of the Disciples work within the Hierarchy to develop certain qualities within humanity. He is the Director of what is known as the "School of Divine Love." It is his, and his co-workers', assignment to develop the Love Nature of the human family.

We continued to receive lessons from John for about three years. Many of these were pertaining to the Laws of Soul Progression and to the correlation of the various Octaves of Life within the Cosmic Spectrum. I was shown many diagrams revealing this. He also gave us lessons explaining the metaphysical meaning of a portion of the Book of Revelations and other Biblical stories. We also received a series of lessons on the Nature of God and many other topics. As I review the vast fund of information he gave us, I realize that it would take several volumes to contain all of it. So I shall have to edit it in as concise a manner as possible. The next six chapters will therefore be my condensation of his beautiful, revealing gift to us.

PART 2

CHAPTER 1

THE JOURNEY OF THE SOUL: CONSCIOUSNESS

Each Soul is on an exciting and rewarding spiral of unfoldment. Each upward step brings greater awareness and expanded realization of the beauty and precision of the Universe, and of the progressive states within it. As man works upon the various levels and absorbs the lessons he experiences, he grows in consciousness, raises his vibratory frequency, and qualifies to move forward and upward on his Soul's Journey.

It would seem that in this training there are specific lessons to be learned and certain gradations to be attained, just as a child must pass through each grade in school. It is therefore most important that we make the most of our opportunities and learn our lessons well, lest we be required to repeat many grades while working upon our problems until we have them understood and solved.

During our journey, we experience earthly expression through a wide range of unfoldment, from the completely unawakened Soul, who is operating in an animalistic, or materialistic, consciousness, to the Illumined Soul, who finishes his earthly lessons. Each step must be experienced and absorbed. There can be no side-stepping and no cheating, for this is a process of BECOMING. This cannot be merely an intellectual understanding, nor an award which is bestowed, but it is the GOAL which each Soul MUST Achieve! Only then is the Soul liberated and free to function in the higher dimensions. Only then do we become a Master!

Mastership being the goal which the Soul must attain, let us attempt to find what steps are necessary and how this is brought about.

We must first recognize the fact that the Pathway to Mastership will never be exactly alike for any two individuals. It could not possibly be, for we have embodied at different levels of consciousness, as well as having had various experiences which have caused us to be different from each other. However, there is a general pattern through which all Souls evolve.

In essence, man is a Spiritual Being, inhabiting a body through which to express for a brief span on this earthly sphere. Man's misconception of this fact through the ages has resulted in a feeling of separation from his Divine Source and of his thinking that his body is HE. He spends most of his time and effort providing for the body, but gives little consideration to *who* he really is or to his purpose for being here. He vaguely considers a hereafter, but makes little effort to prepare himself for it and is almost totally unaware of the Divine Law of his own Being.

The first step in the long "Process of Becoming" is for man to be awakened to the fact that he is a Spiritual Being NOW! Not that he will become one in some mysterious way after experiencing so-called death, but that he already *IS*. Withdraw the Spirit from the body and nothing is left but physical material which in time reverts to the elements. What is it that causes us to breathe, our blood to circulate, our digestive and eliminative processes to function, all with no awareness or effort on our part? It can only be the Indwelling Spirit, the REAL Inner SELF, which is Divine. Man's progress is dependent upon his willingness and ability to identify himself with this Indwelling Spirit; when he is able to completely make this identification, he becomes a Master, even as the Master Jesus who said, "The Father and I are ONE!"

Once having become aware of his own spiritual nature, man can then apply Conscious Effort to accelerate his long journey. Prior to that time he has been operating in a mechanical, material consciousness, where he has been the slave of his possessions and emotions. With this new understanding he begins to *want* to free himself from the shackles of fear and misunderstanding and the endless striving for material gain, which, when gained, had not brought the happiness he had expected. He catches a glimpse of a better Self and a peace and happiness which he had not known existed. He then sets out to find HIMSELF. He attempts to understand and apply the laws which will bring him into a greater realization. His feet are ON THE PATH!

As he then works to erase his old negative thought patterns and habits and replace them with positive and constructive ideas and deeds, he advances, step by step, until he achieves his goal. No wonder this is spoken of as a journey! For this is a long and ofttimes discouraging trek. How many times one thinks they have conquered some fault, perhaps jealousy or selfishness, only to have it again rear its ugly head? However, as we persist and earnestly strive to identify ourselves with our Divine Center, we gradually establish ourselves on a new level of consciousness and another step has been taken on the Path.

It is perhaps well that we think for a little on the nature of Consciousness. Consciousness is the innate "That which KNOWS." It is operating upon an infinite number of levels according to the evolution of that through which it is expressing.

It is what causes the electrons to combine in the proper combinations to form the atom and in turn form the molecules and cells, all according to the pattern of the element which is being brought into manifestation.

It is what causes the tree or flower to proceed from the seed and bloom, also according to its own pattern.

It is that which causes the bird to grow within the egg, then hatch and instinctively migrate as it needs to change its environment. It causes the bee to gather nectar and convert it into honey, and the butterfly to emerge from its chrysalis. It causes the animal to care for its young, and each species to propagate itself.

It is what causes our blood to circulate, our lungs to

breathe, our bodily processes to function and our minds to comprehend. In fact, it is that which *KNOWS* and CAUSES ALL things to BE!

Over eons of time this Consciousness has evolved ALL things through which it now expresses. We see it at work in everything, but we are prone to think of it as operating only through what we can comprehend through our five senses. Is it not reasonable to assume that it is also operating upon much higher levels than we can now perceive? If it operates throughout all physical and mental manifestations, can it not operate in frequencies beyond those of which we are presently aware? It seems we can safely assume that it does, and it is into these realms that we progress as we travel The PATH.

As we take each step on the path and attain a new level of Consciousness, we BECOME that of which we are aware. We enter into a new state of "BEING."

Let us know that it is only in Consciousness that we can experience anything. If we are not aware of a certain event, so far as we are concerned, it has not happened; but when we learn of the incident it becomes a reality to us. The mineral is not aware of the higher form of vegetable life, for it has never experienced that degree of Consciousness. The vegetable is not aware of the higher form of animal life and the animal is not aware of the powers of man. As long as man is functioning in the limited Consciousness of a material and emotional slave, he is unaware of the higher levels of Spiritual existence.

Man has one great advantage over the lower species. He has been endowed with Self-Consciousness and the power of Reason. He can recognize the fact that he is not only physical, but Spiritual as well, and he can then take the necessary steps to develop his AWARENESS of the higher aspect of his nature—his SPIRIT! As he becomes more acutely aware of, and more finely attuned to his Divine Center, he will experience moments of great revelation and illumination.

Just as the animal is a higher form of life than the vegetable, and man is higher than the animal, so is the realm of Spirit higher than the physical of man. How limited we would think ourselves if we were suddenly forced to function in the Consciousness of an animal. How wonderful then our life can be when we learn to operate in the Consciousness of Spirit, or Divine ONENESS! With our barriers down our identity becomes complete and we, too, can say "The Father and I are ONE!"

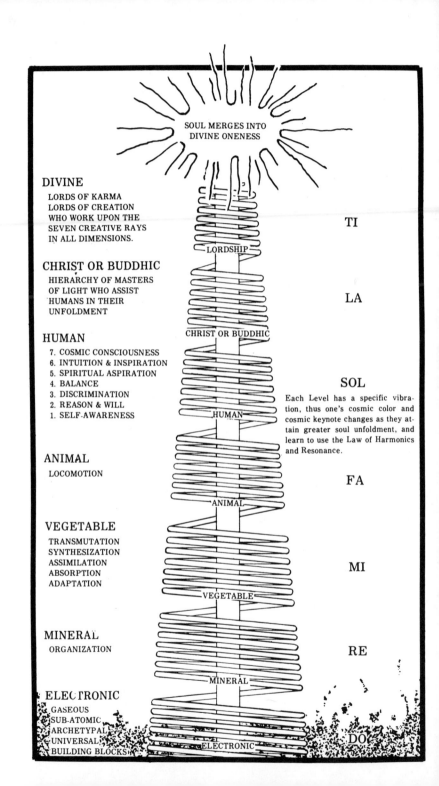

SOUL MERGES INTO
DIVINE ONENESS

DIVINE

LORDS OF KARMA
LORDS OF CREATION
WHO WORK UPON THE
SEVEN CREATIVE RAYS
IN ALL DIMENSIONS.

TI

LORDSHIP

CHRIST OR BUDDHIC

HIERARCHY OF MASTERS
OF LIGHT WHO ASSIST
HUMANS IN THEIR
UNFOLDMENT

LA

CHRIST OR BUDDHIC

HUMAN

7. COSMIC CONSCIOUSNESS
6. INTUITION & INSPIRATION
5. SPIRITUAL ASPIRATION
4. BALANCE
3. DISCRIMINATION
2. REASON & WILL
1. SELF-AWARENESS

SOL

Each Level has a specific vibration, thus one's cosmic color and
cosmic keynote changes as they attain greater soul unfoldment, and
learn to use the Law of Harmonics
and Resonance.

HUMAN

ANIMAL

LOCOMOTION

FA

ANIMAL

VEGETABLE

TRANSMUTATION
SYNTHESIZATION
ASSIMILATION
ABSORPTION
ADAPTATION

MI

VEGETABLE

MINERAL

ORGANIZATION

RE

MINERAL

ELECTRONIC

GASEOUS
SUB-ATOMIC
ARCHETYPAL
UNIVERSAL
BUILDING BLOCKS

ELECTRONIC

DO

PART 2

CHAPTER 2

SPIRAL OF ATTAINMENT

Just as each species has its pattern to fulfill and does so by progressing from its embryonic state to its fulfillment, so does the Soul have its pattern and its various stages of growth and development. The seed could not become a full blown flower instantly, and we must take each step of our Soul's progression.

The seed first BECOMES the seedling, then it BECOMES the plant and finally it BECOMES the flower and fruit, emerging from that which it appeared to be, into a greater and lovelier creation. As the potential flower is within the seed, so is the potential MASTER within our own Being, and it will come into expression when we have been nurtured and watered by the Spirit sufficiently to fulfill our Divine Pattern.

The Process of BECOMING could be likened to an ascending spiral, each turn bringing us closer to our objective and marking an Octave of Being in our Cosmic Spectrum. Each octave has its own notes or scale, and these notes are the steps we must take in BECOMING. As we progress and *become* a new note, our Consciousness is established in a higher frequency. The completion of each Octave is double the frequency at which the octave was started just as the notes of a piano are doubled in frequency with each octave. Low C has a frequency of 32 vibrations per second, the next C is 64, the next 128, middle C is 256, and so on to high C with 4,096 vibrations per second. This same principle applies to the frequencies of the Soul, each octave bringing us into a higher frequency of Consciousness, where we are more sensitive to, and in resonance with, the Infinite.

The Divine Law of Octaves is a very complex study as each note also has its inner octave of notes, which explains some of the ancient symbology of seven within seven, etc.

The over-all Divine Cosmic Spectrum, or Octave of Life, is composed of seven notes or degrees of Being known as Kingdoms. These could also be thought of as seven different ranges of frequency, through which the thread of Consciousness is ever expanding and creating higher forms of life.

The first is the electronic stage. This is the energy, or life-force, of the universe. These units of energy are the building blocks of which all things are made and each has sufficient Consciousness to determine whether it will be of a positive, negative or neutral nature.

In the second, or mineral stage, organization has come into manifestation. Here the electrons, protons and neutrons combine to form atoms of the various elements, each according to the pattern of its innate degree of Consciousness. For instance, carbon has six negative electrons revolving around a nucleus of one positive proton and neutron. The ratio of oxygen is eight to one. Gold is seventy-nine to one, and uranium is ninty-two to one. Thus, each element has its own unique pattern and its own frequency of Being, but all are composed of the same electrical energy or life-force.

The third, or vegetable stage of life, has the added faculties of absorption and adaptation to raise it above the consciousness of the mineral. The vegetable can reach out its roots for sustenance and absorb through its roots and leaves. It synthesizes what it absorbs and is transmuted in the process. It can also adapt to its environment.

Locomotion is the added factor in the animal, or fourth kingdom. Unlike the plant, the animal has the ability to move about from one location to another to obtain its sustenance.

The Human is the fifth kingdom, or note. Man has acquired the faculties of Self-Awareness, Reason and Will. Thus, he has the ability to be aware of his own nature and his environment and to reason about both. As he evaluates and perceives a better way of life, he is then able to exercise his will in an endeavor to improve both himself and his environment.

The sixth note is that of the Christed Beings and the angels, and archangels. From their realm they inspire, guide, and teach those in the human domain.

The seventh and final note is that of the Lords who have great creative powers. They direct the various Creative Rays, controlling creation, birth, karma, etc. These Beings are of such character and quality that it is impossible for our human minds to conceive of their frequency or power. They are finally merged into the ALL where they are ALL Power, Wisdom and Being.

Each kingdom or note has its own inner octaves through which Consciousness has evolved, always creating more perfect vehicles through which it can express. This is a very gradual process, so we find the higher species of one kingdom very much like the lower species of the next kingdom. As we consider the Human Octave of expression we find those who are little above the animal in Consciousness, but we also find those who have attained such a degree of perfection that they are about to finish this octave and proceed into the Christ Octave of Being.

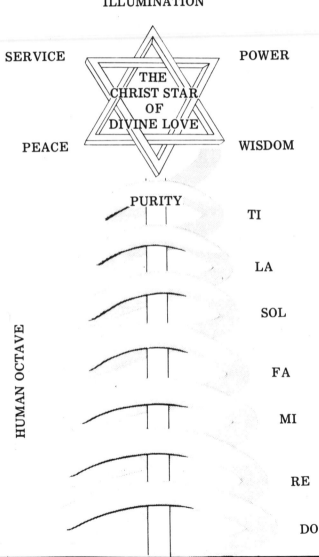

ILLUMINATION

SERVICE

POWER

THE
CHRIST STAR
OF
DIVINE LOVE

PEACE

WISDOM

PURITY

TI

LA

SOL

FA

MI

RE

DO

HUMAN OCTAVE

PART 2

CHAPTER 3

THE HUMAN OCTAVE

Our primary concern, as human beings, is to study the Human Octave of Expression, to know that we are evolving through it, and what it is bringing us. Let us also think of this as a spiral with its seven notes and their inner octaves. This means that we have much work to do and many gradations to acquire in our progression. By considering the human embryo we see the mark of its evolution through all of the lower forms of life, but we also are all potential Gods. As we apply Reason and Conscious Effort we are ascending the Human Spiral, which culminates in Christhood. From there we will proceed through the Christ Octave and enter into the Octave of Lordship and finally into the Divine ONENESS of the ALL.

Jesus "grew in wisdom and favor with God" and became "THE CHRIST." We, too, can BECOME Christed Beings when we attain his level of Consciousness and can operate upon his frequency. It was the high frequency of His Being which made it possible for him to perform what seemed like miracles to those in a lower Consciousness, but were really done in strict accordance with Divine Law at his Frequency, or level of Being. "These things which I do, ye can do also," is the promise that this measure of attainment is for us. But each note MUST be played, the entire scale must be run before we will attain that degree of perfection. Again, IT IS A MATTER OF BECOMING!

As we evolve through the various notes of the Human Octave we *become* new creatures in Consciousness.

The awakened man does not live in the same Consciousness that he did when he was merely trying to satisfy his physical appetites. But, his awakening only comes through the pain, suffering, and frustrations, which he creates while going through that phase of his unfoldment. In accordance with Divine Law, man must evolve through the Human Octave to attain the Christ stature. If we do not fulfill our pattern in one human expression, we must repeat in human form until we do.

When we re-embody, we return upon the frequency level of Consciousness which we have thus far attained, usually at the same note from which we left, with the possible exception of the little we may have learned in other dimensions between embodiments. We then proceed to complete the note or octave, as the case may be. This explains why there are so many different levels of Consciousness among human beings. Should we embody with no understanding of spiritual values upon an extremely low note of Being, we would be as one of the cannibalistic, or very primitive people. But if we have attained a high level of Consciousness, we will embody into the environment which will give us the experience necessary to help us attain our Christ Light, or frequency. When we have become the Christ Light, we stay upon that note until we are completely established in it, and it in us; in fact, until we BECOME A CHRISTED Being. Each note requires a time for the fixation of its frequency in the Consciousness.

When we have become a true Christ, it will no longer be necessary to embody in Human form unless we should choose to return, as the Master Jesus and other Christed Ones have done, to become a world avatar. Should we choose, we can become one of the vast multitude of Divine Beings who are constantly assisting the human race through the activities of the White Brotherhood from the higher frequencies beyond human sight. By means of inspiration, intuition and illumination, these devoted souls are guiding and aiding humanity as it struggles up the Pathway of Attainment.

As we take our various steps, we become a new note, color, tone and frequency through expanding Consciousness. We then come under the influence of the Masters who are working upon that specific frequency. This is very much as the gradations of our school systems, with some teachers working at the primary level, some at the elementary, others at the high school and college levels. They work patiently and diligently with much repetition until we finally comprehend and become established at each new level of Consciousness. Then we are ready for the next grade. But until we have learned our lessons well, it is as impossible for us to understand the activities of the higher frequencies as it would be for a child in the lower grades to comprehend a college course.

As each Soul proceeds on its journey, it will have many experiences which aid in its progression. It if often difficult to appreciate or understand the purpose of some of the more painful ones, but in retrospect, one can perceive that ALL experience, whether it seemed good or bad, is necessary if one is to become a Master.

When one is consciously ON the Path, he will have moments of awareness and realization far beyond the average human comprehension. When the intuitive faculty is activated, the Soul is able to tune in to the higher frequencies and obtain inspiration and instruction from the Christ Octave.

Many things then become clear to him and much is revealed. He becomes aware of his Divine purpose. He becomes filled with Divine Love and his only desire is to serve the Divine. He sees ALL things as Divine and all circumstances and situations as part of the Divine Plan. He knows his body and his Consciousness to be the Temple of the Living God!

At a certain point in his unfoldment, the Soul is made aware of the fact that he has been accepted as an apprentice in the Universal White Brotherhood. Here he must work diligently and unselfishly in the service of his fellowmen. When he has proven his sincerity, greater Truths are revealed to him. He learns of his Divine Power and that he is surrounded by an armor of Divine Light which is impregnable to lower frequencies. He recognizes his Oneness with ALL life, everywhere, and demonstrates health, abundance, and harmony.

Finally, the Soul becomes so aware of its Oneness with the Divine that it experiences a Mystical Marriage in which it is completely FUSED with the Divine. Regardless of sex, the Soul now realizes that it is the feminine aspect of the Creative Power of the Universe. As it gives itself in complete submission and is impregnated by the Holy Spirit, it conceives and bears Divine Offspring in word, thought and deed. Thus, the Soul becomes co-creator with the Holy Spirit. This is the Perfect Union! Perfect Consummation! Perfect Bliss!

Tragically, it is sometimes hard for the Soul to sustain this exalted level of Consciousness. It allows itself to slip back into its old thought habits and patterns, and it is then committing fornication against the Holy Spirit. When this happens, it bears the ugly offspring of inharmony, unhappiness and ill health.

By bitter experience, the Soul realizes its mistakes and seeks a reunion with the Holy Spirit. Ultimately, it remains faithful and is permanently established in Divine Oneness. It becomes the CHRIST STAR! It is now a MASTÉR and proceeds into the Christ Octave. This is our DESTINY and our PURPOSE.

CHAPTER 4

COSMIC COLOR AND COSMIC TONE

Each note of Being has its own Cosmic color and Cosmic tone. If we were to spin a top fast enough, not only would its tone rise to a pitch beyond which our ears could discern, but it would also change color as it became hot. It would run the full light spectrum from red to violet and finally to white where it would be revolving so fast there would be no separation into the various colors. During its acceleration, each color and each tone would be denoting a different frequency. In the same manner, as we increase our frequency, we change our Cosmic color and our Cosmic tone.

Each degree of Consciousness which we attain is only a partial expression of the complete Octave of Being, just as each color is only a portion of the One Light. As we complete the spectrum, or octave, we finally become THE LIGHT, all parts becoming integrated into the ONE Divine Light.

A single note is only a portion of an octave of tone, but each acquired note gives us a new KEY with all of its Cosmic chords and harmonies in which to operate. Each KEY NOTE in music has its own harmonic chords in every octave of the keyboard. As we come into a new KEY of Being, we are in harmony and resonance with everything in the Universal keyboard which is within the harmonics and resonance of our key. It is this Divine Law which enables us to receive inspiration and illumination from those enlightened Beings in the higher octaves of life.

Within us at all times is the Divine Light, or our Divine Center. It is as a Golden Pole about which we are constantly building our Spiral of Life. As we make each turn up the spiral, we draw closer in Consciousness to this inner Light, until we finally merge into it. When we are completely harmonized with the Divine, we become the pure CHRIST Light or CHRIST Star. Previous to this complete identification with the Divine, we have been expressing only a portion of THE LIGHT. Just as a prism will deflect light into its various colors, wrong thoughts and deeds will deflect our Divine Light and cause us to express only a portion of it.

With the Christ Light comes great power because it is of an exceedingly high frequency. It transcends all human power and gives Mastership over the material world. It brings what the ancient teachers termed LIBERATION, and makes one a FREE SOUL. It also brings with it the desire for Lighting the way for others who are treading the Pathway of Spiritual Attainment, for when one becomes "Christed," they are "Love Personified," and their ONE Desire is to serve others.

The Christ Star is the complete integration of the Human with the Divine, and marks the completion of the Human Octave of expression. We could think of its six points as emanating from a center of DIVINE LOVE. The one who becomes the Christ Star will have attained these six qualities of Being: ILLUMINATION, POWER, PURITY, WISDOM, PEACE and SERVICE, and will be a MASTER!

PART 2

CHAPTER 5

INVOLUTION and EVOLUTION

All of Creation is brought about by the involution and evolution of Consciousness in dual spiral action. As we become a new Spiritual Creation, we evolve in Consciousness in an ascending spiral. At the same time, Spirit is involving into us in a descending spiral. In this process, we are greatly influenced at specific points in our unfoldment. It is at these times that our Consciousness takes a new direction and unfolds along different lines. Thus, we create a triangular pyramid within the spiral. This is the Triune nature of Man—physical, mental and spiritual.

Let us first understand the construction of an octave. Each octave is composed of seven full notes, five of which are aided by half notes and two which have no half note. Between Mi and Fa there is no half note, also between Ti and Do. It is at these intervals where there are no half notes in each scale that great changes take place in our unfoldment.

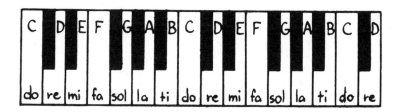

In the ascending and descending scales of frequency, each note has a definite ratio to the preceeding and suc-

GREEN—EVOLVING SOUL
RED—INVOLVING SPIRIT

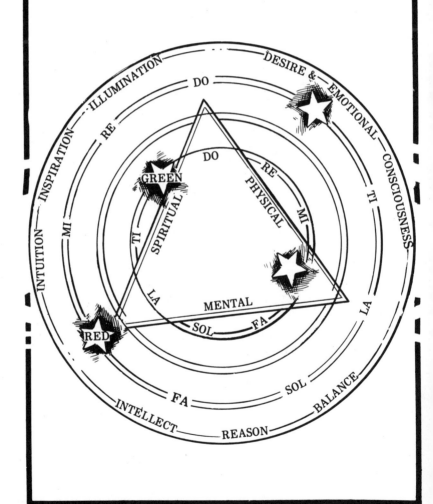

ceeding notes, but between the notes of Mi and Fa, and again between the notes of Ti and Do, the ratio is not uniform with the others of the scale. This is where the half note is not included. At these points of interruption in the ratio of our increase in frequency, or Spirit's decrease in frequency, there is a slight retardation of the frequency ratio. At these times, our frequency of Being takes a change in its direction, either because of our change in ratio, or the change in ratio of the involving Spirit. These points of hesitation, or retardation, are called intervals. They are designated on the chart by an asterisk (*).

As we embody on the human level, we come in on the note of Do. As we proceed to the note of Re, we are influenced by the interval of the involving Ti. This gives us reason, self-awareness and will, and makes of us a human rather than a lower species.

At our interval between the notes of Mi and Fa, we are touched by the involving La. This causes us to realize that we are not merely a physical machine, but that we have some power over our emotions and our environment. Our direction is then turned toward the fulfillment of our mental nature, and the mind achieves mastery over the physical. Upon the notes of Fa and Sol, we are strengthened and balanced by the involving Sol and Fa. There is an intermingling of the Spiritual and physical, and we have many experiences to refine and purify us and prepare us for the higher spiritual frequencies to come. This is also the level where Karma is being worked out.

As we reach the note of La, the interval between the involving Mi and Fa touches us. This brings us into Spiritual Consciousness where we again change our direction to complete the Triangle of Being. Here we attain a frequency which reveals our color and light to the Masters. They will then work with us through inspiration and intuition to help us in our unfoldment.

Our interval between the notes of Ti and Do, plus the full power of the involving Re, brings us into the Christ Light and helps us complete the Human Octave. This brings us into the new frequency of Do in the next octave. We will then proceed through the Christ Octave of Being, again to repeat the process and be brought to Lordship.

This principle is working throughout all octaves, constantly bringing more highly evolved forms and expressions of Consciousness into manifestation.

PART 2

CHAPTER 6

NOTES OF LECTURE SERIES & SUMMARY OF HERMETIC, UNIVERSAL LAWS

The following is the outline of the interrelationship of all Life, which we have used in our lecture series.

Also, a summary of the Hermetic, Universal Laws of Vibration, Correspondence, Cause and Effect, Rhythm, Polarity, and Gender, from the book "The Kybalion," by the Three Initiates.

I am including this to help the reader better understand the process of Soul Unfoldment.

....

OCTAVAL STRUCTURE OF THE COSMIC SPECTRUM OF LIFE

The Universe is comprised of ONE Essence—positive and negative units of electricity, or Energy. Form is determined by the adherence of these electrical units to each other in different relationships.

Each unit of energy is endowed with a degree of *Consciousness* which causes it to respond to and maintain specific relationships with the opposite polarity according to the Divine Design for every form.

As these energy units relate to each other, they VIBRATE according to their ratio—one to the other. Every atom has a specific vibratory frequency, determined by the number of negative electrons rotating about a positive proton. For example, Hydrogen= +1 to -1; Helium= +1 to -2; Oxygen= +1 to -8; Iron= +1 to -26; Gold= +1 to -79; Uranium= +1 to -92.

All of Life is a highly intricate and precise organization of Divine Energy as it precipitates by going into spiral motion and forms the different Octaves, or Kingdoms, of Life to comprise the overall Cosmic Octave of Consciousness which Divine Mind has designed and indwells.

Just as a musical octave is comprised of seven notes, there are also seven kingdoms. They, in turn, are each divided into seven inner octaves which, again, are comprised of another seven notes, etc.—ad infinitum. So, the framework of the Universe is built upon multiples of seven. Thus, we have the mystical number of seven and the ancient theory of seven within seven within seven within seven, etc.

The Seven Kingdoms, or Octaves, as they apply to Life within man's present comprehension are:

1. Electronic
2. Mineral
3. Vegetable

4. Animal
5. Human
6. Masters, Adepts, and Christed Beings

7. Lords of Karma, Creation, etc.

Man, with his mind and developing intuitive powers, is the bridge between the higher and lower kingdoms, and he has been "given dominion over all." (Genesis 1:28). But, he must learn to use his power in loving appreciation or he becomes a destroyer, as our ecological situation now proves.

Electronic Kingdom

(before manifested form)

1. Divine Mind
2. Unassociated positive and negative aspects of Divine Energy

3. Archetypal Patterns
4. Sub-atomic
5. Atomic
6. Molecular
7. Gaseous

Mineral Kingdom

(Has the quality of "Organization" of Divine Energy
into Elements)

The Graduated Table of Elements is comprised of seven periods and seven different groupings. Each of a grouping has a relative position within each period, separated by seven. For example: Alkaline Metals—Lithium, Sodium, and Potassium are third, eleventh, and nineteenth on the table. The grouping of Alkaline Earths—Beryllium, Magnesium, Calcium, etc, are fourth, twelfth, and twentieth in position, etc.

Previously unknown elements have been found because scientists were aware of this precise progression and knew what to look for.

Vegetable Kingdom

(Has the qualities of adaptation, absorption,
synthesization and transmutation)

1. Primeval Open Sea
        Microscopic organisms, Algae, Diatoms
2. Seaweed
        Life moved to earth
3. Fungi
        Molds, toadstools, mushrooms, etc.
4. Lichens
        Mosses, ferns, etc.
5. Flowering plants
6. Vegetables
7. Shrubs and trees

Animal Kingdom

(Has the qualities of locomotion, and response
on an instinctive level)

1. Amoeba   Invertebrates
   Single celled
2. Mollusks   ”
   Snails, oysters, lobsters, etc.
3. Fish   Vertebrates
4. Amphibians   ”
5. Reptiles—Birds   ”
6. Mammals   ”
7. Higher mammals and early man   ”

Each Kingdom has all of the qualities of the preceeding
kingdoms inherent within it.

Human Kingdom

1. Self-Awareness
2. Reason and Will
3. Discrimination
4. Balance
5. Spiritual Aspiration
6. Intuition and Inspiration
7. Cosmic Consciousness

Christed or Buddhic Kingdom

1. Ascended Masters   4. Maha-Chohans
2. Adepts   5. Angels
3. Chohans   6. Archangels
               7. Elohim

Divine Kingdom

Pure LIGHT Beings

Lords of Karma and Creation who work upon the
Seven Creative Rays in all dimensions, forming and
fulfilling all of the archetypal patterns.

....

The NUMBER SEVEN

(as it manifests throughout creation)

The Musical Scale—Seven notes
Do—Re—Mi—Fa—Sol—La—Ti—Do with half notes
to assist the progressive pattern. The half-note principle is also involved in all of Creation and its interplay in the Involving and Evolving process causes genetic changes to produce new forms.

The Solar System—Seven Major Planets—Sun, Mercury, Venus, Earth, Mars, Jupiter, Saturn.
Five Lesser—Uranus, Neptune, Pluto, Vulcan, Asteroids. Each planet has a different metallic core emanating different vibrations into the universe.

Earth Seven Layers—iron core, aleveen, basalt, crustgranite (all solid). Atmosphere, stratosphere, ionosphere (all etheric).

Basic Metals—Lead, Mercury, Gold, Silver, Iron, Tin, Copper.

Electro-Magnetic Spectrum—Radio, Infra-red, Heat, Light, Ultra-Violet, X-Ray, Gamma or Cosmic Rays (thoughts, or mental activity).

White Light—Seven Colors—red, orange, yellow, green, blue, indigo, violet (one, three, five are the primary colors just as the musical harmonic chord of each key).

Organic Life—Seven steps—electrons, atoms, molecules, cells, organs, systems, Man, Society.

Man's Seven Bodies—solid, liquid, gaseous, etheric (invisible framework on which the bodies are supported), emotional, mental, Soul (which is our individual share of Universal Spirit).

Man's Seven Systems—Circulatory, Nervous, Respiratory, Digestive, Eliminative, Lymphatic, Endocrine (the Secretive glands).

Man's Seven Chakras—relating to the Endocrine System
1. Gonads   Sex, Creative or Reproductive Center
2. Adrenals   Navel—Kidneys
3. Spleen   Solar Plexus

4. Heart   Heart-Life Center
5. Thyroid   Throat
6. Pituitary   Third Eye (key gland)
7. Pineal   Crown Chakra—top of head

Man is moving into higher levels of Consciousness according to his individual aspiration and work in adapting his life to the Laws of the Universe. By sincerely seeking, he attracts the Master Teachers to him. They then infuse his aura with their Light and Love and help him develop his intuitive and spiritual faculties and raise his vibration and state of Being.

By the Law of Resonance and Harmonics, Man can attune himself, through meditative practices, to all of that throughout the whole Cosmic Spectrum which is in harmony and resonance with his particular vibration, or Cosmic Keynote. For instance, the harmonic chord of C-Major is C-E-G, and every C-E-G upon the piano keyboard is in harmony with all the others, as are the harmonics of every key. Also, each Octave doubles the frequency of the Keynote. Low C vibrates at the rate of thirty-two times per second. C of the next higher octave has a vibration of sixty-four times per second. The next is one hundred twenty-eight, then two hundred fifty-six, then five hundred twelve, then one thousand twenty-four, then two thousand forty-eight, and finally High C is vibrating at four thousand ninety-six times per second. This same principle is in action as the Human Soul progresses through the Octaves of Human and Christed Consciousness in ever higher states of vibration and Being. Man is moving toward Godhood and his eternal work is to become ever more aware of his Divine potential and devote himself to the perfecting of himself, and to the expressing of his total Divine capacities at whatever level he may be. Life then becomes an exciting and glorious adventure and progress along the Eternal Pathway is assured.

THE LAWS OF CORRESPONDENCE AND VIBRATION

Kybalion—"As above, so below—as below, so above."

There is Correspondence between the laws and phenomena of the various Planes of Being. The form, or manifestation, is different in each plane because of the increased vibratory frequency on the ascending Scale of Life, but that which is on each Cosmic Keynote has its counterpart in the preceeding and succeeding Octaves.

Man can understand the Microcosm and the Macrocosm by observing the laws ruling the things that he is familiar with, and then using the same laws as a basis for his study. For example, by studying the atom he can understand the solar system, and vice versa, or he can understand his various interpenetrating bodies in this way.

For purposes of study, the Universe may be divided into three great classes of phenomena known as the Three Great Planes: 1. The Physical Plane, 2. The Mental Plane, 3. The Spiritual Plane. These are the ascending degrees of the Great Scale of Life, the lowest of which is undifferentiated matter of the lowest form, the highest, that of Spirit—with no great line of demarcation between, but a gradual shading through matter, and mental, and spiritual substance.

A Plane is not a place determined by length, breadth, and height, but by the Fourth Dimension which is VIBRATION. That which has its being within a certain frequency range is said to be on a certain Plane.

The whole Universe is an "ocean of motion," and everything is in vibration. Matter is vibratory. Thoughts are vibratory. Life is vibratory, and each plane encompasses a wide range of frequencies and is subdivided into Seven Minor Planes. *The Physical Plane* is comprised of Matter and Energy:

1. solids, liquids, gases
2. X-ray, radium, etc.
3. Higher Matter
4. Ethereal Substance (the connecting link between mat-

ter and energy, and the medium of transmission of
heat, light, etc.)
5. Heat, Light
6. Mental Phenomena
7. Divine Power

The Mental Plane comprises that which animates the forms
of the various Kingdoms. These "entities" are not the atoms
or molecules of the form "itself," anymore than a man's
body is "himself." They are the "Soul Entities" of the
form.

1. Mineral Mind	4. Plant Elemental Mind
2. Mineral Elemental Mind	5. Animal Mind
3. Plant Mind	6. Animal Elemental Mind

7. Human Mind

The Elementals are as the black keys on the piano (the
half notes). The white keys can produce music, but the
black ones are necessary for certain harmonies and melo-
dies. They also act as connecting links in the Process of
Evolution, bringing Higher Forms into being, and New
Kingdoms, or "leaps of Life."

It has taken the Human Race millions of years to reach
its present Fifth Plane of the Human Mind. (This is the
Fifth Root Race, with some stragglers from the Fourth, and
a few more-advanced of the Sixth who come as teachers of
humanity, or who have attained Self-Mastery and reached
Cosmic Consciousness.) Man is now moving toward the
Sixth Plane of Human Mind and will develop greater mental and intuitive powers (the Sixth Sense is Intuition).
The Race Consciousness is raised only as each individual
becomes motivated to seek and express his Higher Self.

The Spiritual Plane

It is impossible for the finite mind to comprehend the
nature of the Beings on the Great Spiritual Plane, but undoubtedly they, too, function on various vibratory levels
according to their level of Consciousness—from simple Self-
Mastery to Lordship.

As each man moves upward on his Pathway of Spiritual Unfoldment and his pursuit of spiritual verities takes precedence in his life, he is guided and inspired by these great Beings who act as the Guardians of the Human Race. As man is *receptive* and *responsive* to this guidance, and to the inner promptings of his God-Self, he will also attain Self-Mastery and move into the higher Spiritual Planes.

Response is the Key Word. Man must first become Respons*ive* to his God-Self, then he becomes Respons*ible* in fulfilling his Divine Pattern and Mission. Just as one must first become *ABLE* to Love before they become LOVEABLE. For, as one gives to Life, one receives in like measure—by the Divine Law of Cause and Effect.

....

THE LAW OF CAUSE AND EFFECT

Everything in the Universe is in motion by the Law of Vibration. Every vibration, in its activity, sets up new vibrations, or *re*-actions. This is called the Law of Cause and Effect and it manifests on all levels, or planes. Nothing happens by chance, everything that happens is the result of some chain of action which has preceeded it, and it in turn is the Cause of succeeding results.

The Hermetic Philosophy says, "Every Cause has its Effect; Every Effect has its Cause, everything happens according to Law. 'Chance' is but a name for Law that is unrecognized. There are many planes of Causation (physical, mental, emotional, and spiritual), but nothing escapes the Law."

If all things were not functioning according to Law— what a chaotic world this would be! The word "Chance" is derived from a word meaning "to fall" (as the falling of the dice). But there is really no "chance" to the falling of the dice, the results depend upon the position of the hand— or box, the energy expended, the condition of the table, etc. Under *exactly* the same conditions, the results would always be the same.

Cause and Effect deal with "events"! No event "creates" another event, but is merely a preceding link in a chain of events. There is a continuity between all events—precedent (before), consequent (present), and subsequent (after).

We are not here by chance. There are so many factors to our being here that it staggers the mind. Our very physical presence is phenomenal. We each have two parents, four grandparents, eight great-grandparents, etc. It is calculated that in forty generations the number of ancestors would run into the millions. Suppose one of them had not met their mate—would you be here?? Or what chain of events has caused you to pursue this study? Suppose you were to get a piece of soot in your eye. It is not just the result of your eye being open and the soot flying in, but all that has preceeded in your life and before. Also, why you were there at that exact spot at that particular time, how and why the soot was there (perhaps as the result of coal being burned for industry). Then going further back—to the coal being the result of the decay of forests, the growth of the forests from the seeds and absorbing from the earth—the sun, the rain, etc., etc.

Most people are blind slaves to the Law of Cause and Effect, being influenced by their heredity, environment, customs, the opinions of others, and their own emotions, desires, moods, etc. They manifest no mastery over themselves, or their lives. They are involved in the world of Effects and complain about their "bad luck." Or they sometimes think they are doing "as they please," but they fail to realize why they "please" to do certain things in a certain way. They allow themselves to be as pawns on the chessboard of Life.

When one begins to understand the Law of Cause and Effect, they realize that by their thoughts and actions they can set new Causes into motion which will produce new Effects in their lives. The Masters, knowing the Law, rise above the material plane of Life by placing their thoughts and desires in touch with the higher aspects of their Mental and Spiritual Nature. They can then dominate their moods and characters, and their environment. They then become the Players in the chess game of Life, rather than the Pawns. They then live as Causes, rather than as Effects. However, they are always subject to the Law of Causation on the Higher Planes, but they *rule* on the Material Plane, for the Higher Laws will always prevail against the lower.

The Law of Cause and Effect is equally in action on all three levels of Man's Being, and ignorance does not excuse one from the outworking of the Law. If one puts his finger on a hot stove (the Cause), he gets burned (the Effect). If one drives over an embankment (Cause) he has an accident (Effect). If he is angry (Cause) and has driven too fast—that is Effect, but also Cause of the accident. To go back a step further—why was he angry? And so on.

On the Mental level, we could use the same illustration. The anger was the emotional and mental Effect of some Cause, and in turn became the Cause of undesirable results. To carry this back we could explore what chain of thought caused the anger, etc. Happy and loving thoughts are Causes for happy and loving Effects, for oneself and for others. A cheery "Good Morning!" and a happy smile will set the tone for a happy day, but a grumpy frown can do the exact opposite.

On the Spiritual level, each act of loving service, each true soul aspiration, each contact with the God of one's own Being in the Inner Sanctum of one's SELF, becomes the Cause for a wonderful Effect, which is Soul unfoldment, greater understanding and awareness, and a more loving and happier life. Lack of spiritual objectives keeps one in the prison of materiality, emotionalism, fear, lack, and unhappiness, for they are the Effects which one Causes, either through ignorance of the Law, or willfully. Every man can achieve Mastery as he learns and *Uses* the Law. He then BECOMES the LAW unto himself.

Every thought, deed, and feeling of Love and Joy brings forth fruit of its own kind in one's life, as do thoughts of hate, intolerance, ill-will, etc., for that IS THE LAW!! It was well phrased two thousand years ago when Jesus said, "Can a fig tree bear olives?" and "As a man soweth, so shall he reap."

THE LAW OF POLARITY

Kybalion—"Everything is dual; everything has its pair of opposites. Opposites are identical in nature, but different in degree."

The Fourth Hermetic Law is called the Law of Polarity. It propounds the Truth that all manifested things have two sides, two aspects, two poles, with many degrees between the two extremes. It states that the difference between things which seem diametrically opposed to each other is merely a matter of degree and that the pair of opposites may be reconciled through the process of neutralization.

We see this law in operation in all of the manifested Universe, from the Highest Point of Life and Intelligence, which we think of as Universal Spirit and Mind, to the grossest matter. They are the opposite poles of the same Divine Essence.

This principle is easier to understand as we consider the opposites on the physical plane. For example, heat and cold, high and low, up and down, slow and fast, big and little, East and West, short and long, darkness and light, etc.

There are no "absolutes," everything is relative to its opposite. These opposites are the positive and negative aspects throughout all of Creation, and together they maintain the Balance of the Universe. One cannot exist without the other and they are both dependent upon the third factor, the neutral pole. If there were no neutral separator between the two forces they would rush together without balance and destroy each other. A battery must have a neutral pole as well as positive and negative poles. An electric circuit must also have all three aspects. There is a point of neutrality, or motionlessness, or perfect balance between the polarities in all things. The Infinite is in perfect balance and all of nature strives to maintain that balance. It is only Man, in his ignorance, who destroys it.

Heat and cold are identical in nature, the difference being merely a matter of degree. Hot water, tap water and ice water are of the same essence, but differ in their degree of heat. However, their position in relationship to each other along the Scale of Polarity determines whether we would consider any of them as hot or cold. Tap water would be warm if compared to ice water, but cold compared to heated water. But, hot water would be cold compared to steam, and ice water would be warm compared to ice or frozen' water. So all is relative and yet functioning somewhere along the Scale of Polarity of its own nature. There is no place on a thermometer where heat ceases and cold begins. It is all a matter of higher and lower vibrations. So we see not only the Law of Polarity involved but also the Laws of Relativity or Correspondence, and Vibration. This is also demonstrated in the musical scale and in the color spectrum of light, for all tones and colors are degrees upon the Scale of Polarity of their nature, but in different vibratory levels.

Man is related to all that is in the Universe and in his environment. Everyone's living conditions are determined by their mental activity and by how they react to these relationships. Man labels things "good" or "bad." His mental processes constantly involve themselves in hate or love, fear or courage, faith or worry, anger or patience, etc. Here again there is no point which can be called "absolute." Beginning at any point on the scale we can find more love and less hate, or more hate and less love, etc. An understanding of the Law of Polarity helps us to realize that we have polarized ourselves at specific points in our thinking and actions. Then we can begin the process of Transmutation. For instance, by thinking lovingly and giving more love we raise ourselves upon the Scale of Love, or by calling forth more courage we can overcome our fears, etc. So Man's Mind, or Consciousness, is the Neutralizing Factor in his life, and through conscious effort we can transmute and balance the conditions of our lives.

Things belonging to different classes cannot be transmuted into each other, but things of the same class may have their polarity changed. Thus Love never becomes East or West, or short or long, but it can become Hate or greater love. By negative thinking and actions one descends the Polarity Scale but ascends by positive thinking and deeds. The Positive Pole throughout all of creation seems to be of a higher degree than the negative and has the greater power of attraction. It is the proton, or positive particle of the atom, in conjunction with the neutron, that attracts the negative electrons in sufficient numbers to balance itself so it can fulfill its Divine character. The Positive is constantly attracting what it needs to itself, the negative repulses. This is well demonstrated in our reaction toward people we meet who give off either negative or positive vibrations. If we react to them either positively or negatively, this is called Mental Induction. Others are also constantly reacting to our vibrations, so it behooves us to raise ourselves upon the polarity Scale to where we are emanating, and attracting more Love and Light.

On the Spiritual level the "Law of Relationship" also exists. We exist only in relationship to the great Cosmos, and we could have no existence apart from it. Here the Positive Polarity is also dominant. As we raise our vibrations and establish ourselves at new levels of Consciousness, we are responding to that Divine Magnetism which is the Source of our Being and has implanted within us the desire for greater understanding and Love, and the desire for a fuller expression of our TRUE-SELF, which is the Divine SPIRIT of LIFE *within* each and every man. For we ARE LIFE! Birth and Death are seeming polarities but if we establish our consciousness in the Soul, or in the Eternal of ourselves, we transcend the polarities of time and space, and of the finite and infinite worlds, and we become stabilized in the ETERNAL NOW!

THE LAW OF RHYTHM

Kybalion—"Everything flows out and in; everything has its tides; all things rise and fall; the pendulum-swing manifests in everything; the measure of the swing to the right, is the measure to the left; rhythm compensates."

The Fifth Hermetic Principle is the Principle of Rhythm. It states the truth that in everything there is a measured motion; a to and fro movement; a flow and inflow; a pendulum-like motion forward and backward; high tide and low tide. This motion takes place between the two poles, or opposites, which was discussed in the last lesson, but the "swing" is not necessarily to the extreme poles of the opposites, but "toward" first one pole and then the other. There is always an action and a reaction, an advance and a retreat, a rising and a sinking, in all of the phenomena of the universe. The Brahmans call this the Out-Breathing and the In-Breathing of Brahm. This manifests in solar systems, planets, men, animals, energy, matter, mind, and even in Spirit. All planes are subject to this law, the physical, the mental, and the spiritual. Solar systems are born and die, civilizations rise and fall, all forms come into manifestation and later disintegrate. Everything has a period of birth, growth, maturity, decadence, and death, and then new birth—as the Eternal Divine Substance, of which it is composed, is re-cycled.

Night follows day and day follows night; tides ebb and flow; summer follows winter and the reverse. All atoms, molecules, etc., follow the cycles of their nature. This rhythmic motion, or vibration, is in and through all things. There is no such thing as absolute "rest" for the swing is constant.

Man's body is also functioning in Rhythm. He breathes rhythmically; the heart beats in rhythm; he wakes and sleeps; his respiratory, circulatory and digestive systems, etc., are all subject to this law.

The Law of Rhythm is equally invariable in the area of mental activity and accounts for the bewildering succession of moods and feelings and the perplexing changes that we find happening in ourselves. The Hermetists have understood this law and have learned to work with it to attain Self-Mastery. They call this the process of Neutralization. By understanding the Principle and the Process, we can learn to control our "Mood-Swings." Much of our fear, anxiety, frustration, etc., comes because we allow ourselves to be "caught" in this rhythmic swing at the "unaware" level of our minds and we get trapped in the emotional consequences of our undisciplined mental activities. The one who attains Mastery learns to "polarize" himself at a higher level and refuses to allow his mind to become enmeshed in the negative swing. He uses his "WILL" as the "neutralizing factor" and controls his thought processes. He catches himself before he allows his thoughts to take the full negative swing. He deliberately replaces his negative thoughts with positive ones before he becomes emotionally involved. So it is possible to escape many of the "effects" of the Law, but the Law itself is not destroyed, only transcended at a particular point; and we must keep constant vigilance, for the pendulum does swing, although we may escape being carried along with it if we establish our "consciousness" at a higher level.

Another aspect of the Principle of Rhythm is known as the Law of Compensation, or Counterbalance. This states that the swing in one direction determines the swing in the opposite direction. On the physical plane this is very evident in the swing of the pendulum of a clock or in the seasons, tides, etc. Man's mental states are subject to the same law. The man who enjoys keenly can also suffer keenly. A pig suffers little mentally, and he enjoys little, but he is compensated. But, there are other animals who enjoy keenly and who also suffer keenly. There are temperaments of men which allow only low degrees of either enjoyment or suffering, while others are capable of intense joy or pain. The rule is that the capacity for pain and pleasure in each individual is balanced.

Again, the Hermetists go further and teach that the Negative preceeds the positive in this matter. So, in experiencing a degree of pleasure it does not necessarily mean that one will have to "pay for it" with a later corresponding degree of pain. On the contrary—the pleasure IS the compensation for a degree of pain previously experienced, either in the present life, or in a previous incarnation. This throws a new light on the problem of pain. The Hermetists regard the chain of lives as continuous; all as a part of the ONE Eternal Life of the Soul. The Law of Neutralization is also applicable in this area as we endeavor to expiate any Karmic debts that we may have incurred, and we resolve to establish our consciousness in the Eternal part of our Being. Recognition of our present problems and concerns as being the negative swing of the pendulum which, by the Law of Compensation and by our acceptance of them as being the means of our soul unfoldment, will surely help us swing to the opposite extreme. Hopefully, by understanding the higher Law of Polarization, we can establish ourselves at a new level through each experience. It is thus that we find our True Identity, and travel the Eternal Pathway of the Soul's Progression and grow in Wisdom, Love, Truth, and Divine Stature.

THE LAW OF GENDER

Kybalion—"Gender is in everything; everything has its Masculine and Feminine Principles; Gender manifests on all planes."

The last Hermetic Principle is the Principle of Gender. It proclaims the truth that Gender is manifested in everything, that the Masculine and Feminine Principles are ever present and active in all phases of phenomena, on each and every plane of life.

In considering the Law of Gender we are not merely thinking of Sex as it is most commonly thought of, but in its broadest, universal connotation. Sex is a manifestation of Gender on the physical, or organic, plane.

The word "Gender" is derived from the Latin word meaning "to beget; to procreate; to generate; to create; to produce." The Creative Process requires a Masculine and a Feminine interaction, or union, to bring anything into manifestation on any, and all, levels.

In the Biblical story of Creation there is reference to Elohim, meaning God, or Gods. Eloh—is a singular Hebrew noun, meaning Creative Energy. The Feminine plural is Elohoth; the Masculine plural is Elohim. Just as God is referred to in the Bible as "He," so is the Masculine form used here, but the phrase, "Let *US* make Man in *OUR* image," surely implies both Masculine and Feminine factors at work. Eloh—means either male or female, either as separate qualities, or Beings, or androgynous (dual-sexed)

Beings, such as the Lords of Creation who function in either capacity to shape the universal archetypal patterns and lend their Creative Love Energy to the fulfillment of those patterns.

The function of Gender is solely one of creating, or producing, and its manifestations are visible on every plane, from the simple adherence of one negative electron to one positive proton and a neutron to form an atom of hydrogen in the world of matter, to the highest of Mental Creation as well. It is the constant interplay, and attraction for each other, of these two forces, which causes Vibration—which in turn is the basis of ALL life and manifestation on all levels.

The role of the Masculine Principle is to direct its inherent energy toward the Feminine Principle which receives it and adds its own qualities, thus setting the Creative Process in motion. The Feminine Principle always does the active Creative work, yet each is incapable of creating without the other.

Energy, or electricity, must have both the positive and negative principles to function; all organic life requires both to be generated; the Omniverse became manifest as Divine Mind (the Masculine Principle) impressed its ideation upon Divine Essence (the Feminine Principle, or Womb of Creation). Our thoughts (masculine) also act upon Divine Essence (feminine) to bring into manifestation that which we image, or give our thought power to.

Much could be said concerning the well-known phenomena of the attraction and repulsion of atoms; chemical affinity; cohesion of Molecules; magnetism; and the Law of Gravitation—that strange attraction by which all particles and bodies of matter in the universe relate to each other; but suffice to say, it all occurs because of the Law of Gender which is the eternal Law of Attraction between the Masculine and Feminine energies of the universe.

MENTAL GENDER

Modern day psychology propounds the theory of the dual aspects of the mind, conscious and sub-conscious, voluntary and involuntary, active and passive, etc. This is considered a comparatively "new" field of research and endeavor, but in reality, it was known and propounded in the most ancient of teachings as a part of the Hermetic Philosophy, under the Law of Mental Gender.

In relating the new and ancient concepts we can say that the Masculine Principle of Mind corresponds to the so-called Objective, or Conscious Mind; the Voluntary, or Active Mind, with originative powers. The Feminine Principle of Mind corresponds to the so-called Subjective, or sub-conscious Mind; the Involuntary, or Passive Mind with executive powers.

In the interaction of the two aspects of Mind, the Masculine, or Conscious Mind, is constantly accepting or formulating ideas from outer sources and experiences, and through the thought energy devoted to these ideas, they are impinged upon the Subconscious, or Subjective level of Mind, which, true to its Feminine nature, accepts this impregnation and proceeds to do all in its power to bring forth the outer manifestation of the idea. This is why T.V. and radio advertising is interjected so frequently during programs, for each time it is repeated, the thought is fixed more firmly in the Sub-conscious of the viewer, or listener, even though it may not have been seriously considered at the Conscious, or Objective level. Children are particularly vulnerable because they do not reason or reject the idea, so it goes directly into the Sub-conscious.

This is also why "denials" of that which one does not wish to experience is unwise, for the Sub-conscious does not register the denial, only the image of that which the denial is about. Affirmations of a positive nature are much more effective. For instance, if one wishes to stop a habit such as smoking, they should not say, "I must *stop* smoking." Thought energy about smoking only fixes the idea of smoking more firmly in the Sub-conscious. One might better say, "I command and expect my body to require only pure, clean, air to oxidize my blood stream and energize each cell, organ and system." This is impregnating the Sub-conscious Mind with the image of health and perfection and, if done often enough and positively enough, in a short time the desire for smoking will be gone.

In like manner, one should not say, "I will not indulge in fault-finding," for "fault-finding" is the order the Subconscious receives. Rather, one should say, "I will be tolerant of my fellow-men, or the individual, as the case may be." This same method can be used with any habit, or characteristic that one wishes to change. We must learn to "Accentuate the Positive," as the song-writer has said.

Both the Masculine and Feminine Aspects are within everyone, regardless of their body sex. We all play each role at different times. Whenever we accept an idea from any source, we are playing a Feminine role. When we give out an idea that is accepted by another, we are playing a Masculine role. A mother plays a Masculine role when implanting an idea in a child's mind, who at that moment of acceptance is functioning in a Feminine capacity regardless of its sex. Then if the child passes the idea on to a friend who accepts it, he has functioned in a Masculine capacity. This same principle is at work in all sorts of relationships; for example, the teacher and pupil, the doctor and patient, the salesman and buyer, the actor and his audience. Preachers, orators, statesmen, all magnetic persons are those who are able to use the Masculine Principle as a way of impressing their ideas upon others, although most of them are not aware of the law they employ. This is also true in the area of hypnosis, mental telepathy, psychic influence, and various psychic and mental phenomena.

Hermetic teachers ask their students to turn their attention inward upon the Inner-SELF, as many young people do now in searching for "Reality." Many conclude that they are a unit of Consciousness; therefore, they declare "I AM" and feel they have found the "Ultimate," but it takes a deeper analysis to reach the Inner Depths of Oneself. There must come a recognition of the "ME" Self as being different from the "I" Self, for it is usually with the "ME" Self that the average person identifies himself.

Man thinks of himself as being composed of certain feelings, likes and dislikes, characteristics, education, background, physical attributes and appetites, etc., all of which go to make up his Personality. But the very word "personality" comes from the Greek word "Persona"—meaning Mask. So his personality is not his True SELF. Many cannot conceive of a "Self" independent of their body, or at the most, consider themselves as bodies possessing a Soul, rather than as Eternal Souls having a body as a means of expression and experience for a short earthly sojourn.

As man rises in the Scale of Consciousness, he gradually can disentangle himself from the body and the material aspects of his life, but he is still apt to identify the "Self" with his mental states and feelings, and it takes much effort and experience before he learns that these, too, are the results of his own misdirected mental energy. In time, he discovers that he has great mental powers latent within him and that there exists a mental "Something" which is able to WILL that the "ME" act along certain creative lines, and which is able to stand aside and witness the Mental Creation. This "Something" he can call the "I." He learns to project this "I" Consciousness to the "ME" by a process of WILL, which is Vibratory Energy.

This "I" represents the Masculine Principle of Mind, the "ME" represents the Feminine Principle. The "I" represents the Aspect of Eternal BEING, the "ME" represents the Aspect of BECOMING.

The majority of persons employ the Masculine Principle but little, and are content to live according to the thoughts and ideas instilled into their "ME" from the "I" of other minds. They are polarized in their Feminine Principle of Mind and are too lazy to exert their Will and exercise their Masculine Principle of Mind. They are as sheep following the leadership of those whose Masculine Principle is dominant. Proper balance of the two Principles within one is the desired objective. Then one can be receptive to new ideas, thus assuring his growth, but one must also be able to summon the Will and the thought power to execute that which they hope to bring to pass. Only by employing the two Principles can one be assured of a happy, vital life.

While the dual characteristics of the Creative Power is ONE at its root, they are uniquely different from each other. The Feminine Aspect is Receptive, Magnetic, and Attractive. The Masculine Aspect is Radiative, Electric, and Impulsive. In Astrology they are represented by the Moon as the Feminine, Intuitive, Imaginative faculty, and the Sun as the Masculine, Inspirational, Will faculty. When these faculties unite in a Truth Seeker he is said to be well on his way to Illumination and Self-Mastery, for he has become open, receptive, and responsive to the "I AM" of himself, and to the great Cosmic Intelligences who guide and direct humanity. He recognizes that, as he responds to the Divine Magnetism that draws him ever upward and onward in his Soul Progression, he can be inspired and guided. He allows Divine Mind to be the engendering power in his life. He is willing to assume a Feminine Role and allow his mind to be impregnated by the Divine Spirit of all Life which runs the Universe. He no longer puts his petty "ME" on the throne of his mind. He attunes his mind to Divine Mind and he acts upon the inspiration he receives. He harmonizes his life with all of the Universal Laws. His mind becomes the womb where the conception of Love, Harmony, Joy, Peace, Service, and Illumination takes place, and he brings forth this progeny into his life.

This is truly the MYSTICAL MARRIAGE of which the great Mystics speak, and it is to be sought, and ultimately found, by all travellers on THE PATH.

Recommended reading: THE KYBALION, or HERMETIC PHILOSOPHY, by The Three Initiates.

PART 2

CHAPTER 7

THE SEVEN ASPECTS OF WHAT MAN CALLS GOD
(as given by John, the Beloved)

The Intelligence and Power that brings all things into
manifestation has been given many names throughout the
ages, some being Divine Mind, The Creator, The All-
Knowing One, The All-Powerful, Infinite Intelligence, Atma,
God, etc.

As far as the human mind can comprehend, this Creative and sustaining UNKNOWABLE REALITY which
has caused and is within ALL things, has Seven Aspects.
They are:

1. Power	4. Life
2. Law	5. Love
3. Wisdom	6. Soul

7. Spirit

All aspects are integrated into all of Creation and no
one aspect can function independently of the others. Each
manifested thing has all aspects within it, so in reality, the
various aspects are ALL ONE. It is here broken down into
its various components that it may be better understood.
By the Law of Octaves, the seven aspects are each comprised of seven distinct qualities.

1. *POWER* or Energy, or activity, expresses in these
ways according to the vibrational frequency of its mode of
expression.

1. Radio, audio or sound
2. Heat and infra-red

153

   3. Light
   4. Ultra-Violet
   5. X-Ray
   6. Gamma-Ray
   7. Cosmic, Mental

2. *LAW*
   1. Mentalism (Everything first has its Being in Divine Mind)
   2. Correspondence, Relativity (As above, so below)
   3. Vibration
   4. Rythm
   5. Polarity
   6. Cause and Effect
   7. Gender

3. *WISDOM,* or Divine Mind
   1. Consciousness, or innate awareness
   2. Memory
   3. Reason
   4. Discrimination
   5. Balance, or Law
   6. Adaptation, Acquisition, Assimilation, Synthesization, Transmutation
   7. Quest, or Evolution

4. *LIFE*, or Consciousness
   1. Electronic
   2. Mineral
   3. Vegetable
   4. Animal
   5. Human
   6. Christ, or Buddhic, Masters, etc.
   7. Lord Octave (Directors of Creative Rays, Lords of Karma, Creation, etc.)

5. *LOVE*
   1. Attraction (The cohesive and creative power of the Universe)

2. Devotion (Consecrates all things to their Divine Expression and Purpose)
3. Generosity
4. Humility
5. Kindness
6. Patience
7. Service

6. *SOUL*, Individualization (Each individualized unit of Consciousness)
   1. Life
   2. Power
   3. Wisdom
   4. Love
   5. Service
   6. Ability to expand and evolve
   7. Intuition (Ability to be receptive and responsive to higher frequencies)

The word Spirit comes from the Latin word "Spiritus" meaning Breath in action or motion, or ENERGY. Spirit encompasses all of the foregoing aspects.

7. *SPIRIT*—All the Attributes of the Divine
   1. Power—Creative Mind in motion
   2. Law—Creation, Evolution of Consciousness expressing through all form, species, and Souls.
   3. Wisdom—Divine Mind, Imagery or imagination, inspiration, illumination.
   4. Life—Consciousness expressing through all form, species, and Souls
   5. Love—Creativity
   6. Soul—Individualization, the ability to function on ALL frequencies, at ALL levels, as an individualized unit of Consciousness
   7. SPIRIT—Total Awareness and BEING.

By analyzing these various aspects of the Divine and their inner qualities, we can come to a better understanding of ourselves as evolving Souls moving to our Divine Destiny within the DIVINE PLAN.

PART 2

CHAPTER 8

THE BOOK OF REVELATIONS

(The following metaphysical interpretation of a portion of the Book of Revelations was also given by John. These lessons were interrupted when classes were recessed for the summer and were not continued when classes were resumed. This is unedited, just as it was received in three class sessions.)

"It is my privilege to help take you to the doorway of the next Octave of Being. There are requirements which are necessary to bring this about. IT IS ONLY AS YOU BECOME THE PERSONIFICATION OF LOVE, and as you give yourself in complete SERVICE to the Divine and to your fellowmen, that the final attributes which complete the Human Octave become yours. I repeat, COMPLETE LOVE and SERVICE, and complete identification with your Divine Center, or GOD-SELF. Then you receive direct Divine Inspiration and Illumination.

"This was also true of me. As I walked with the Master, I gave myself completely in Love and Service, and I was privileged to have Divine Revelation. This is very necessary, for it opens the door into the next octave for you. For this reason I have urged you to give much time to meditation—to seek to identify yourself with the Divine, to be completely receptive, and to give yourself wholeheartedly in Love and Service. As you do this, you will be illumined, you will be instructed and guided, you will know the Truth

157

of your own Being, and you will be made aware of the
power WITHIN and its rightful use for yourself and to
help others.

"As I received revelation, even in such magnificent
experiences, I did not conceive of their full nature, but I
have been taught by various experiences since that time,
and have been allowed to grow and understand. I realize
that there were many things which were revealed to me that
had a deeper significance than I attributed to them at the
time. Some of these lessons have already been given to you,
but there are others of which I would speak. The Spirit
revealed to me that which I was to relate to the world.
Much of this has seemed like riddles to those who do not
understand, but has great significance for the awakened
Soul. As I stated, "I was in the Spirit and I *SAW!* This
is likewise true of you, when you are "in the Spirit"—with
your mind fixed on Godly things, when you are filled with
pure desires and wish with your whole heart for spiritual
progress, you will be illumined and great revelations will
come to you. You will KNOW the LIVING PRE-
SENCE of GOD, guiding and inspiring you. This is
being "in the Spirit."

"I would now speak of the seven churches, the seven
candles, and the seven stars. The seven churches, as they
pertain to the progression of the Soul, are the seven major
steps which the Soul takes in its unfoldment. They are the
seven notes of the Human Octave of Expression. Thus,
you will understand what is meant by "instruction to the
seven churches." They are the seven notes through which
the Soul must proceed, learning each of life's lessons along
the way, becoming ever more aware of his Divine origin,
purpose, and Oneness in the Divine Plan.

"The seven candles denote the lighting of the Human
Consciousness upon the various notes of Being. Each aspect of Man's Being must be recognized, illuminated, and
brought into activity, in a Divine way. The LIGHT must
be brought forth upon each note. As this is done, and as
he becomes established in Divine Consciousness, the
LIGHT of each note is accomplished and ESTABLISHED,

and it becomes a STAR. The Seven Stars are the lights of the completed notes. As all the notes are completed, and the octave is finished, they merge together to become the CHRIST STAR, or the 'MORNING STAR' which brings the dawn of a new day, or cycle, for the evolving Soul. This is the striking of the note of "Do" in the next octave, or the first note of the Octave of Christhood. As one becomes the Christ Star, the Light is INCARNATE WITHIN, and they become the "Light of the World," as the great Masters and Jesus, the Christed One, have done. He lights the planet today, and he Lights your Pathway. You, too, are Christs in the making, and you will become the Christ Star when all of your seven "Stars" merge into the ONE GREAT LIGHT.

" 'To him that overcometh, I will give to eat of the Hidden Manna, and will give him a White Stone, and in the stone a NEW NAME written, which no man knoweth, save he that receiveth it.' The 'Hidden Manna' is Understanding, Truth and Revelation. This precious gift comes to the one who opens the door with Love and a burning desire to grow in spiritual understanding. This is the food of the Christ Consciousness which comes to the one who masters the carnal self. The 'White Stone' is the refined Soul which has gone through all of the refining process of life's experiences. The ancient alchemists called this the 'Philosopher's Stone.' This is what is happening *in* you. You are becoming the Pure Essence of Divine Love and Being, or the pure 'White Stone' of Being, which is the fulfillment of the Human expression, or Octave. When this is achieved, you will no longer function in the human level of Consciousness. You will have become a CHRISTED ONE, and your 'NEW NAME' will then be 'CHRIST.' While the Christ Principle is within each man, it does not come into expression until such time as he is sufficiently evolved in Consciousness to bring it into manifestation. It is as the seed which must be nurtured, unfolded, and brought to its fulfillment. You are now working in this refining and unfolding process. The WHITE STONE and the NEW NAME become yours when you become fully aware of your

Divine Nature and *identify* yourself *as* that. This is what is meant by the words, 'No man knoweth save he that receiveth it,' for this is something which happens in the Consciousness of the individual. When he has become completely identified with the Divine Center of his own Being, he then recognizes his Divine Nature and that his true name is 'Christ.' Others may see this as it outpictures in his life, but it is only the Inner Man who truly *knows* whether or not his identification is complete.

"May your hearts embrace the true meaning of these words and may you walk in the Light. Yours is the Path of Light which will bring much experience and illumination. Unto you will be given the WHITE STONE, the MANNA, and the NEW NAME, for you are becoming in all of its brilliance, THE CHRIST STAR.

"Many other things were promised to the seven churches, some of which you have already attained. 'He that over-cometh shall be clothed in white raiment.' This you know, for the Robe of Initiation has been given to some of you as you have attained the note of Being where you were accepted and were brought under the tutelage of the Masters of the White Brotherhood.

" 'You will eat of the Tree of Life,' signifying the ac-quisition of Wisdom and Understanding.

" 'You will not be hurt of the Second Death,' meaning that you will painlessly die to the things of the carnal world as you come under the dominion of your Divine Self, which will 'Sit upon a throne and wear a Crown,' and rule over all.

" 'He that overcometh I will make a pillar in the temple of my God, and he shall go out no more,' which means that you will be established in Christ Consciousness, that you will have completed the Human Octave, and will have stepped into a more highly spiritualized dimension which is the 'New City of Jerusalem' from which you will 'Go out no more,' except by choice to serve in lower dimen-sions, as many great avatars have done.

"All of these things, which were promised to the churches are likewise promised to you as evolving souls. I give you these few examples of that which is yours to achieve, and what you can expect, as you grow in Understanding, Love and Service. Remember, this is the Divine School of Love and these things are accomplished in no other way. As the New Age comes, there is great need for these things to be revealed. Many have been trained throughout the ages, so when mankind reached the stage in his evolution where he could understand these Truths, there would be teachers sufficiently prepared to present them to him. Keep the door open that we might touch each of you, for this is not something that is designed to be given through only a few channels. It is our purpose that ALL become Illumined, through Direct Revelation to each one. It is to this end that you are being instructed, that you might *not* be dependent upon *anyone*, but might each receive Direct Communication and Revelation to fulfill your Divine Pattern.

"In the Revelation which I recorded, I told that 'I saw One who was as the son of man, clothed in long raiment and girded about with gold; Whose feet were established as in shining brass and fire; Who had hair as white as the snow; Whose eyes were as fire; Who spoke with the voice of many waters, and who had coming from his mouth as a sharp two-edged sword. I fell at his feet and he put his right hand upon me and said, "Fear not, I am the first and last. I am He that liveth, and was dead, and behold, I am alive forevermore." '

"I beheld this as 'The Christ.' It is likewise 'The Christ' of one's *own* Being. When this is made manifest to you, you, too, will be overwhelmed by Its beauty, and it will symbolically have the same characteristics.

"It will be as the Cloak of Divinity about you, which is girded with gold, bringing to you that which is pure and true.

"It will have feet of fiery brass, meaning that the basic unfoldment of 'The Christ' in each individual is the Fire of Refinement. This is known in some philosophies as the 'Kundalini Fire,' which spirals up through the body and activates the seven chakras to bring awakening and fulfillment. The Fire of 'The Christ' burns up through the

Human Consciousness until the person is completely transmuted and brought to fulfillment.

" 'The hairs of his head were as white as wool, or snow.' This, too, is significant, for at the culmination of the Human Octave, with Christ Consciousness, will come the White Light. During the fulfillment of the various notes, one has run the full Light Spectrum, to become the combination of all its comprising colors, or, the White Light.

" 'The Voice, which was as many waters' means that out of the Pure Essence of Being comes many streams of understanding, at all of the various levels of soul awareness. By this you are taken through your many phases of unfoldment. It is from the 'waters' that all life forms originated, and it is by the many 'waters' of the Voice of 'The Christ' that you are brought into new expressions of Being.

" 'There was a sharp two-edged sword, which came out of his mouth.' This means that as you attain Christ Consciousness, the two-edged sword of Truth will be declared by you. Truth is a two-edged sword which cuts down all that is not pure and true. You will speak, from your Christ Center, the words of Truth which will destroy all that is not true in your life and will help to destroy what is not true in the minds of others.

" 'His eyes were as fire' means that 'The Christ' within you beholds and knows all that transpires within your hearts and minds. Its burning, piercing sight reveals all your faults and virtues. It allows nothing to escape its scrutiny. As the lower nature comes under the scrutiny of the Indwelling Christ, you must perfect yourself until those eyes behold only Divine Perfection within you.

"As I was stricken by this wondrousness, you, too, will be awed by 'The Christ' within you. As you behold Its beauty, you will prostrate your human self before It. You will know that you are, and ever have been, under Its guidance and tutelage, that all things will be made right for you, and that you can *never* be separated from The Christ within you.

" 'Fear not, I am the first and the last, and behold, I am alive forevermore.' The Christ has eternally motivated you, but was not consciously activated by you. Now that you are aware of this Indwelling Presence, It will forever be a Conscious Reality to you. May you work diligently to bring It to Its fullest expression.

"God Bless you!"

PART 2

CHAPTER 9

JOHN GIVES A TECHNIQUE FOR ENTERING
UNIVERSAL REALIZATION

"Beloved:

"Tonight we open new doors for each of you. Let us develop a technique whereby you can enter into the vast, unexplored, infinite realm of Spirit. Each of you have said the words, 'The Father and I are One,' and you have experienced this realization to some degree. Let us attempt to make this an ordinary experience of your daily lives, that you might engage in it at will. This should be a personal experience, so use words of the first person, and let each word burn itself upon your hearts and consciousness.

"Think of the area just between the eyebrows, known as the Third Eye. Turn your inner eyes to that point and see ONLY that point. Think of it as a star, or a great light, then just lose yourself in that light. BECOME it, and say to yourself:

" 'I AM NOT JUST FLESH AND BLOOD. I AM NOT JUST MY BODY, NOR MY BRAIN. I AM NOT JUST (your name). I AM THAT WHICH DIRECTS, MOTIVATES, AND INHABITS THIS BODY. I AM THAT WHICH USES THIS BRAIN AND THIS NAME. I HAVE A TRUE NAME. MY NAME IS 'THE SON OF GOD,' 'THE ALMIGHTY,' 'THE WONDERFUL,' 'I AM SPIRIT'!! I AM SPIRIT AND I AM NOT LIMITED TO THE PHYSICAL BODY. I AM ABOVE AND BEYOND THE PHYSICAL. I

AM SPIRIT AND I AM FREE!! FREE TO GO WHERE-
EVER I CHOOSE, FREE TO DO WHAT I CHOOSE,
FREE TO EXPRESS AS I CHOOSE, IN GOD'S IN-
FINITE UNIVERSE. FREE!! FREE FROM ALL
SHACKLES OF FEAR, DOUBT AND MISUNDER-
STANDING. FREE IN THE TRUTH THAT *I AM
SPIRIT*!! THAT WHICH I KNOW AS THE PHYSICAL
OF ME IS MERELY FOR THE PURPOSE OF *MY*
EXPRESSION AND TRAVEL IN THIS LIMITED
EARTHLY EXPRESSION.

" 'If I were to be in a town in China, and the only
means of travel was by rickshaw, I would use it, but if I
were in another country and the best means of travel was
by airplane, I would use the airplane.

" 'I have been placed upon this earth plane to fulfill
a mission, to learn lessons; and to express, as best I can,
this Divinity which I AM. That which others know as 'me'
is only my mode of travel and expression. The physical
body is related to the Real ME in the same way the plane
or rickshaw would be—a means of travel, a vehicle for the
Spirit. I am the same ME whether in a rickshaw or plane,
and the Real ME is the same whether in this body or another. I AM above and beyond any particular mode of
expression, for I AM ETERNAL SPIRIT, unrestricted
and FREE. A UNIVERSAL BEING, ONE WITH
GOD!!

" 'I AM LIGHT! This light which I have become has
all the attributes of Light, the power of Light and the speed
of Light. I can be anywhere in the flash of a second. I can
bring Light into all circumstances and situations, for I AM
LIGHT, and Light is understanding and Truth. I am not
only Light for myself, but I am Light for others. I behold
all situations in which mankind becomes entangled in the
Light of Spirit, and I see them only as the tangled web of
man's imagination, not as the Truth of his Being. In
spheres of misunderstanding he is caught in his own web,
but in the Light of Truth I behold that he is also a pilgrim
upon the Pathway, and he is also LIGHT. When he steps
from misunderstanding into the Light, he will leave his
tangled web behind.

" 'I AM LIFE! I AM ONE with ALL Life! As I see Life expressing in its myriad forms, I am a part of it, and I feel my kinship with it. I do everything possible to promote life and growth, and to bring forth the perfect expression in all life forms.

" 'I AM LOVE! I now embrace ALL that God IS, and God IS everything! I embrace ALL and am ONE with ALL, IN LOVE!

" 'I AM TRUTH! In Spirit there is only TRUTH! All that is false has been left behind. I am of the Universe and I AM UNIVERSAL! This is the REAL ME, and I KNOW that the FATHER AND I ARE ONE! From now on, although my seeming abode is my physical body, I KNOW that I am free to step into the Star of Light at any time and extend my Consciousness out into Universal Awareness.

" 'Now I turn, in introspection, to the very core of this which I know as the physical of me. I can be in it and yet see it. I behold the perfect functioning of my body temple, for it is Light and through the SPIRIT, which I AM, giving it life and expression, it has the perfection of Spirit. Each cell is doing its perfect work, alive and vital, responsive to the power and Love of God. So, I do not depend upon outside measures for my comfort, health, or wellbeing, for I KNOW that the Spirit of GOD, which I AM, revitalizes, purifies, and sustains my body temple. I behold this perfection of body and affairs not only for myself but for everyone, all ordained and accomplished in Love. I project this Love and perfection into all individuals who are in need of it, as well as into all dimensions of Life. I project the quickening of the Spirit into the hearts, minds, and bodies of all people that they might experience the peace of the Spirit.

" 'I KNOW that when God revealed Himself to Moses, saying "I AM THAT I AM!" this was meant for all men. I AM! I simply AM because God "IS," and I am made in God's image. God is Spirit and I AM SPIRIT. This is my True Nature. Who then can place limitations upon me? It is impossible as long as I remain aware of my TRUE IDENTITY.'

"This, Beloved Ones, is the Consciousness which will bring you to the fullness of your Divine Nature. Live in this Consciousness and be not bound to the world. Walk in the world, but be not OF it, for you are Spirit. Walk in the Light and the shadows will all fall behind you. God Bless You!!"

PART 2

CHAPTER 10

MONAS EL EKA

On several occasions my husband had heard the words "MONAS EL EKA," but did not understand their meaning. We had asked for an explanation and had been told that it meant "God is ALL." A few years later we transformed our basement into a meeting room for our class work. My husband commented that he would like to use the words as a slogan over the fireplace. I had been reluctant to use then without further verification of their meaning. We then received the following message from JOHN, the Beloved.

"My Beloved, I come to you with Love and Blessings and with a great thankfulness for the opportunity to speak to you. As you have previously been told, my work is the conducting of the Divine School of Love through which each soul is taken to become the Personification of Love before being ready to 'graduate' from the Human Octave of expression. Love is the uppermost theme of the teachings of this school, but you must also become acquainted with Universal Law that you might understand and apply it in your soul's progression. The time has now come for a more specific definition to be given of the slogan Ed received many years ago, 'MONAS EL EKA.' I am most happy that you wish to adopt it for your classroom.

"You were told, very simply, that it meant 'God is ALL.' This gave you some realization of the all-encompassing power and presence of the Divine, but nothing specific, since, at that time, it would have been hard for you to com-

prehend. As you have grown in realization and understanding of the ONENESS and the all-pervading Presence,
you can now come to a better understanding of this in its
many areas and activities. You can now align yourselves
with it and begin to utilize this power more constructively
in your unfoldment. The Hierarchy rejoices that you have
sufficiently accepted this idea that you want it to be present
in this classroom, for this denotes growth on your part.
It is with great rejoicing that we see this manifesting in
your consciousness, for it is no longer only words, but
CONSCIOUS AWARENESS, which is a greater and
more wonderful thing. So, I would speak to you of the com-
ponent parts of the slogan MONAS EL EKA.

"Let us first consider the word MO-NAS or MON-AS
(later found to be Greek). This means the great Tidal
Wave of Life and Creation of the ONE Divine, Infinite,
ALL-Encompassing Power. It not only means the activity
of Divine Wisdom and Power in the heart of all of the manifested universe, but it is also all of that which is beyond
the manifest. It is ALL of Divine Wisdom and Being flood-
ing forth in a never-ending Cycle of Being. There is always
this Flow of Life from Divine Mind, or from the unmanifest
into the manifest. It moves down into ever and ever lower
frequencies, or rates of vibration, from the undifferentiated
into the differentiated, forming, cohering, and vivifying the
various aggregate of atoms composing form and substance according the pattern held in Divine Mind. Then,
as substance disintegrates, the power is released to return to
the undifferentiated state and again engage itself in another
cycle, or range of frequencies. Thus, it is the TIDE of Creative Life, ever and ever flowing forward into manifestation and returning again to its source. In other words, it
is ONE and yet it is MANY. The word MONAS, meaning
many, comes from the root word MONAD, WHICH MEANS
ONE. So, out of the ONE comes the many, in that it ce-
comes individualized as it steps down into form, but it
returns again to the ONE, and is innately of the same
quality while engaged in form. So 'MONAS' is LIFE in
all of its tide of manifestation. The MANY within the ONE,
both potential and in manifestation.

"The word El is a word which denotes power—the Creative Power of the Universe (later found to be Hebrew). This is the unleashing of the Creative Energy into motion. But again, it is not only the unleashing of it but also the potential. It is that which is potentially able to come into expression by this power, and also that which causes the flow to take place.

"Perhaps an analogy which would help you understand is your word for power and energy—ELectricity. The Divine Power which brings all things into manifestation and which manifests in all things. Electricity is the Divine Creative, cohesive and sustaining power of the universe. It is the power at the heart of each atom, it creates, rejuvenates and fulfills ALL things and is within the electromagnetic field of all things. It indwells all of creation and it is also the potential Life of all things. Just as potentially there is greater power in the water behind a dam, the EL power is ever present and waiting to be released into activity through Its many expressions. It is the power within the differentiated forms, but also the Intelligence which brings about the differentiation.

"There is much reference to the EL in scriptures. ELO, meaning the ONE. ELohim, meaning the plural or many. ELI, the high priest. ELisha, ELijah, these names with EL prefacing them signified the potential of that which was to come. Elijah and Elisha and Eli were prophets and priests. We have often spoken of the High Priest of your own Being; this is the EL, the high priest within you waiting to reveal and fulfill your own Divinity.

"Many names in the scriptures end with EL. This designates those who recognized and used the power. MichaEL, all powerful. GabriEL announced the birth of the Christ. DaniEL who was victorious by the use of the power. This same EL is WITHIN you and can be used by you, it forecasts the fulfilled Divinity of you which it also brings into manifestation. It is Creative Mind bringing its creations into manifestation and fulfillment.

"EKA means the serpent of Divine Wisdom (Sanskrit). In ancient Egyptian times the serpent was the symbol of regeneration and the immortality of Being. It means there is never an end to Divine Life but it is an ever-cyclic process bringing the Soul into the fullness of its Divine expression by experience in all dimensions. This has great significance concerning the many dimensions in which the Soul functions during its unfoldment. It is also significant as the great unfolding power which works in and through the body as the Kundalini, while the soul is functioning in the earth dimension.

"As a human being, you inhabit a physical body which is your means of expression and the vehicle for the unfoldment of your consciousness. As you come out of the ONE into the world of form, you must take the many turns of the spiral which bring you back into the ONE-NESS as an enlightened, perfected Being, who has EXPERIENCED LIFE in its many dimensions. You are then ready to take your place as a Divine Creative Power in the Universe. Each must WORK his way through the full scale of Being, experiencing all aspects of human life, then moving into and through the Christed Octave of Being, and finally in and through the Octave of the Lords of Creation. An ever-upward progression, becoming more aware of, and utilizing more of the inherent Divine Power and Wisdom. Your body is your tool to use while in this classroom of Life. As you learn more of its function, and its connection with the other subtler bodies, you will see the correlation between it and your eternal unfoldment. Understanding and utilization of the Divine powers within you will help you fulfill that for which you came into embodiment at this time.

"We have spoken before of the spinal column and the nerves surrounding it as being likened to the Rod of Aaron within the ARK of the Covenant, within the Holy of Holies, which is YOU. The two main nerves, the Ida and Pingala are balancing polarities, one being positive, and the other negative. They spiral up the spine in clockwise and counter-clockwise fashion, crossing each other at various points; thus they coil about the spine in a serpent-like manner—hence, the EKA or Divine serpent. These nerves carry the Divine Energy, or EL; at their points of junction they polarize and balance the Chakras which can then become activated as great vortices of power for the various bodies which interpenetrate the physical form.

"This Serpent of Fire, or Divine Creative Power, the EKA, manifests itself in the first Chakra at the base of the spine as sex, or creativity. For those who operate in the lower levels of consciousness this energy is utilized almost entirely in the sex act. As one grows in consciousness, he learns to use this power in other creative ways, both mentally and spiritually, until the regeneration is complete and one has learned to use it with wisdom to create only those things which are good and right for all. This is the full and rightful use of the great EL power and it sustains and fulfills its user. As the EKA, or polarities of the EL power, activate the chakras, more and more power is released, more knowledge is acquired and more soul progress is made. Mental powers are activated, emotional power is stabilized, and one begins to seek for the answers to the eternal questions, 'Who am I and where am I going?' One wants to know more about oneself and the world in which they live. They find that they are a Divine, Eternal Being, inhabiting a body which then becomes a tool rather than the servant of their emotions, desires, and drives.

"As you work diligently in converting this wonderful EL power to its proper use, the time will come when the two components will make their final junction at the Crown Chakra. As they arc together, the pineal and pituitary glands are activated, this releases the intuitive powers and you are then able to receive Light and Instruction from the higher octaves. This brings ILLUMINATION and is the Divine Alchemy of which the Masters speak. Man then transmutes himself in all areas of his being, the lower physical into the higher and more refined physical, the lower mental into undreamed-of mental capacities, and he finds and expresses his true Divine SELF.

"But do not think that this alchemy ceases when you leave the physical body, for you merely go into a new dimension of Being, but this same power is with you carrying you forth. It will take you through the full Octave of Christ Expression and release more of itself to bring you into the fulfillment and completeness of your Divine Being and Power, where you will function in a world that is so wonderful you could not now conceive of its beauty, magnitude, power and Light. This then, is what is in store for you as you are swept along the Divine 'Tide of Life,' the 'MONAS-EL-EKA.'

"I leave you with this to ponder and practice. Hold onto the picture of the great Stream of Life carrying you forward into greater awareness and expression. Utilize this power and be open and receptive to it. Do not block it for IT IS YOU and YOU ARE IT! In the DIVINE ONENESS there is NO separation. The separation can only be in your own lack of awareness and understanding— even then you are still being carried forward, although you may not be aware of it. However, when you become consciously AWARE of and work WITH the Divine Power, your progress is much more rapid and your life becomes more beautiful and harmonious. For with the knowledge of the INDWELLING PRESENCE there is no more resistance and you are carried on the Stream of Divine Love and Light to your fulfillment in the ONE. God Bless you!!"

PART 2

CHAPTER 11

THE SYMBOLOGY of the LIFE OF the MASTER JESUS

The record of the life and experiences of the Master Jesus has been the best seller of all times, and his life and teachings have probably influenced more lives than any one person in history. This is all very well for he has always been an influence for good as people attempt to live by their various concepts of his philosophy and purpose. However, there is a deeper significance of his life which is seldom realized or understood, for each experience which he had, and his entire life on earth, depicts the journey which each Soul makes in its spiritual unfoldment.

The CHRIST PRINCIPLE is within each individual, just waiting to be brought into manifestation, but man must go through a long process of growth and unfoldment before he becomes aware of this and finally becomes established in CHRIST CONSCIOUSNESS. It is this growth which is taking place as man evolves through the Human Octave of Expression. When he begins to understand his purpose in life and knows that he is an evolving Soul, the life of the Master Jesus has a much greater beauty and significance for him, for he knows that he, too, will ultimately achieve Mastery over the Human Expression of Life.

In reviewing the life of the Master Jesus, let us see its correspondence as man evolves into Christ Consciousness.

The angels herald the coming of the Christ. These are

the spiritual perceptive faculties, innate within man, which make him aware of his greater spiritual potentialities.

The Star in the East which led the way for the shepherds and wise men is the Inner Divine Light within man which is ever pointing the way and urging him onward in his Soul's progression. The East is symbolic of a new and enlightened state of Consciousness.

The sheep are indicative of the thought processes of man, being watched over by the Shepherds of Reason and Will. Think for a moment of the blind way in which sheep will follow their leader. Thoughts will do the same, one thought will follow another until a veritable chain has taken the mind over. Reason and Will are the Shepherds which keep the thought processes under control.

The Wise Men are the three aspects of man's Being, his physical, mental and spiritual nature. When the Star appears to the Shepherds and Wise Men, they leave their present state of Consciousness and seek THE CHRIST. Then all the human faculties are turned in one direction, toward the East. The physical, mental and spiritual faculties, and the Reason and the Will then follow the Inner Light in quest of the Christ State of Consciousness.

Mary represents the Soul which is impregnated by the Holy Spirit to bring forth the Christ Child. This is the Immaculate Conception and the Virgin Birth. Joseph, the intellect, does not understand this and is resentful. In his ignorance he would put Mary away, or deny this beautiful thing which is happening. But the angel, the perceptive or intuitive faculty, causes him to understand and accept the situation.

Mary, the soul, and Joseph, the intellect, go to Bethlehem, which is the Place of Substance or Supply, to pay their tax. This means that the Soul and the Intellect give up whatever is required of them of their material Consciousness and enter into the realization of God's Supply and Divine Plan. It is now time for the CHRIST CHILD to be brought forth. They go to the Inn, but there is no room there. The INN is a place of many or varied degrees of Consciousness. Think of the many who enter an inn, bringing with them their various states of misunderstanding and confusion. The CHRIST cannot be BORN in this kind of Consciousness. They must go to the stable, or away from all materialistic desires and emotions, into a state of humility. Here the Infant Christ is born. This is the birth of the Spiritual Consciousness, the first realization of the INDWELLING CHRIST.

CHRISTMAS

The sky is clear, chill is the night,
The stars are near, the moon is bright,
The earth stands bathed in Light Divine,
This sacred night, forever mine.
I gaze upon a shining star,
Which sheds its radiance from afar,
And feel within that wondrous glow
The shepherds knew so long ago.
I hear an angel choir proclaim,
"Your life will never be the same,
For unto you, this night, is born
The Christ of your Eternal Morn!"
And in the manger of my heart,
I feel the Christ Child wake and start.
Babe, tho' the Christ in me may be,
'Twill grow to full maturity,
As up the Path I ever climb,
Secure in this great Truth sublime.
So Christmas Bells, ring out with glee,
This night THE CHRIST is born
IN ME!

Now the Shepherds and Wise Men come to kneel before this new king. The Wise Men bring their gifts of frankincense, myrrh and gold. Frankincense is the gift of the physical or emotional nature, this is the symbol of feeling and devotion. The mental aspect brings the gift of myrrh, which is the fragrance of holy thoughts. Gold is brought by the spiritual nature, which is symbolic of that which is most precious, Man's Eternal Being. All of man's Consciousness and activities will now be directed toward the growth of the Indwelling CHRIST CHILD.

Herod, the materialistic Ego, seeks to destroy the Infant Christ. The Soul and the Intellect, Mary and Joseph, flee with the child to Egypt, which is the subconscious state of awareness. They remain there until the death of Herod, or until the Ego has capitulated and is submissive to the Higher Self.

At the age of twelve the Christ begins to teach in the temple. The Temple is the Consciousness as well as the body of man. The number twelve indicates that the five senses and the seven psychic centers are now activated by the Christ principle. The Christ is now attaining stature and wisdom, it is "About my Father's business," and it is influencing every aspect of man's Being.

Before he began his ministry Jesus spent forty days in the Wilderness. The Wilderness is symbolic of the undisciplined human, materialistic Consciousness. Here man is tempted and tried. The number forty is based upon the number four which represents the square or perfect balance. With the circle added this means the completed cycle or the completion of the work. (Moses was in the wilderness for forty years [symbolically] before reaching the perfected [Canaan] state of Consciousness.) By fasting, which means refraining from worldly thoughts and deeds, the Christ resists temptation and comes forth from the wilderness purified and strengthened and prepared to take up its ministry.

Jesus then called his Disciples and went about teaching and preaching for the next three years. The Disciples represent all of the faculties of man's Being. They are Love, Faith, Power, Order or Law, Imagination, Generation or Creativity, Understanding, Reason, Judgment or Discrimination, Zeal or Enthusiasm, Will and Intuition. All of men's faculties are now called into the discipleship of the Christ of his Being and he goes through a period of time learning, teaching and demonstrating his Divine powers.

Now The Christ makes its triumphal entry into Jerusalem to fulfill its destiny. Jerusalem is the Divine Love Center of Consciousness, here all souls must come for the completion of their Human Expression. Although it comes triumphantly, The Christ is still denied by its disciples and it is scorned and crucified by its enemies. This is the final effort of the materialistic Consciousness to overcome the Christ Self. As the emerging Christ hangs upon the Cross and suffers great agony and humiliation, the human, carnal aspects are completely crossed out or erased. As The Christ becomes completely submissive and commends itself into the Father's hands, it is released from further Human suffering and experience. The Veil of the Temple is then rent and the Holy of Holies is revealed.

The Christ is now entombed for three days, and the door of the tomb is sealed with a stone. This is the time of going WITHIN in Consciousness, to evaluate past experiences and to become established in a NEW awareness. It is a time for the fixation of the new state of Consciousness. When the stone is rolled away, The Christ walks forth, into the LIGHT of a new dimension. Man is now free from ignorance, materiality, and the Karma of past experiences. The angel, or perceptive faculty, proclaims the RISEN CHRIST.

For another symbolic forty days The Christ walks upon the material plane. Now, in its resurrected body and Consciousness, it demonstrates its Divine Power, Love and Wisdom. It completes and fulfills its final note of Human Expression.

Finally, in a glorious ascension, it is lifted into the wondrous Light of the Christ Octave, where it will proceed to function as a Christed Being. It has become the CHRIST STAR!!

PART 2

CHAPTER 12

CHANGING WATER INTO WINE

(From John, The Beloved)
"Each individual has a great work to do within himself.
If he is to achieve Mastery, he must experience the union
between the Spiritual SELF and the material self. This
might be understood by thinking of an instance in the life
of the Master Jesus. You will remember that the first
miracle he performed was changing the water into wine.
You have been told that all of the Master's life revealed
that which each person must accomplish within himself.
Symbolically, the first miracle is what each individual
must do if he is to transform himself from the material
man into the GOD MAN.

"You recall that a wedding was taking place to which
Jesus and his disciples had been invited. In applying this
symbolically, there must be a marriage between the lower
self and the spiritual Self. When Man comes to realize that
there is really no separation, except in his own Consciousness, he knows that he must merge these two aspects of his
nature into one program of Divine expression. Then a
marriage comes about.

"The mother of the Master was at the wedding. The
'mother' is symbolic of the Soul-quality of man. The disciples are symbolic of the twelve aspects of man's nature,
his strength, wisdom, faith, love, etc. The 'Christ' represents
the God-Self. All of these faculties must be present at the
wedding.

"To celebrate the marriage, wine was being served at the wedding feast, but there was insufficient wine for the group. So the mother asked Jesus to provide more. Symbolically, this happens at the time of each 'inner' marriage. The Soul recognizes the transmuting power of 'The Christ,' and calls its activity into expression. At first the Master was reluctant, for he did not feel the time had yet come for him to make his demonstration. Is this not also true of the highest in man, even though being aware of its presence, he is reluctant to let it manifest for the first time? But, Jesus responded to the request, just as 'THE CHRIST' will always respond to the request of the Soul.

"He asked to have six earthen jars filled with water. The 'water' is symbolic of an undecided, or fluid state of consciousness, in which there is no substance or power. There is a double symbolism in the number six, for there were six jars which were filled with water that was transmuted into wine. The 'jars' are man's five senses, plus his sixth intuitive sense, which are the means by which he learns and progresses. The number six also represents the first six notes of the Human Octave through which man proceeds. When he reaches the seventh note, 'THE CHRIST' has become active in his life, transmutation has come. He is no longer filled with misunderstanding and indecision, and his six senses are now utilized in a spiritual way. When 'THE CHRIST' performs its miracle in the Human Nature, the 'jars' are filled with the rich 'wine of the spirit'.

"In the ordinary process of making wine, fermentation takes place which transmutes the organic substance of the fruit into the potent elixir which it becomes. This is accomplished over a long period of time. As the Master performed this miracle, the transmutation was instantaneous. This symbolizes the magical working of the 'Christ Spirit' in the human consciousness, as one finally awakens to 'THE CHRIST' *in* himself with its transmuting power, which transforms him into a 'Christed Being'.

"The term 'fire-water' has been rightly used. Think of the power, or fire, within the water after it has been changed to 'wine'. This is the 'fire element' of Life, known by the Masters as the 'RUBY ELIXIR' or the great spiritual power which comes with 'Christhood and Mastery'.

"This, which is taking place 'in you,' is likewise taking place in all men. Your work is to help others find this experience for themselves. Whenever you touch another with Love and Light, you help to arouse 'THE CHRIST' within them to perform Its miracle. Then they, too, will be able to partake of the 'Ruby Elixir' which brings Wisdom, Truth, and Love into their lives. 'The Christ' of you fills the earthen jars with the 'Ruby Elixir' and also places it in the GOLDEN CHALICE of your heart to be passed to others that all who drink from it might be lifted and brought to a new awareness of their own Being.

"We walk together in Love, sharing the Golden Chalice, which you must in turn share with others. God Bless You!"

PART 2

CHAPTER 13

Perception and Use of Higher Frequency Levels

This message came from the Master John after we had been discussing how it could be possible for those in other dimensions to see us and each other.

"We say that we 'see' you and the question arises in your minds, 'How can they see without physical eyes?'

"In the first place, you do not necessarily 'perceive' through your eyes or ears. They are merely the means of relaying certain impressions to the 'perceptive faculty' which sorts, and then records those impressions upon the brain cells. This implement of perception is within the area of the Pineal and Pituitary glands. This is the true 'seat of perception' in the physical body. It also receives, translates, and records upon the conscious and subconscious minds that which it perceives in the finer, or higher frequencies. This is the INNER EYE, or the Intuitive Faculty.

"This 'inner perceptor' is a part of the soul aspect and continues after one leaves the physical body. We, too, have perceptive faculties which are in keeping with our rate of vibration. This enables us to know what goes on about us in our dimension, and we can also 'project our consciousness' to your dimension. So we 'see' you, for we know you by your vibration.

"We, as you, can have glimpses of that which is in the frequencies above us. When your perceptive and intuitive

185

faculties are sufficiently developed, you can perceive what is in other dimensions. By the Law of Harmonics and Resonance you can attune to what is on your specific 'Keynote' in the higher octaves of the Cosmic Keyboard of Life, and receive great revelation.

"Each of you is a vortex of Cosmic Energy, spinning, or functioning at your own particular velocity. As we perceive your force-field, we are aware of its frequency. Just as *everything* within the Cosmic Spectrum has its own vibratory rate, so do you each have your own specific rate of vibration, and therefore your own Cosmic Color and Cosmic Tone, or keynote, which is evident to us.

"As you progress in Spiritual awareness, your frequency is stepped up and your color and tone change, for you assimilate the infusion which comes from the same note upon a higher octave. This is done by aspiration, meditation, and attunement. As you are lifted in consciousness to the point where you are in tune, or in harmony, with your keynote on a higher octave, your electromagnetic force field is infused with the color and tone of all the notes within the harmonics of your Key. Then your tone becomes purer and your color is no longer the red, or yellow, or blue that you know. It is the same color but, being suffused with the higher frequency, it has a beautiful glow. LIVING LIGHT is perhaps the best term for it—a scintillating, shimmering, vibrant Light, not the dead, set color it is without the infusion from the higher frequencies.

"This outpouring of energy *can* come to you from the higher octave of Being. This is the great ability that awaits you as you grow in understanding. You can consciously step up your vibrations and absorb more Cosmic Light and Power. Being a vortex of cosmic energy, you always attract that which is necessary to sustain your state of consciousness. You pull cosmic energy into your magnetic force-field and assimilate it. You also expel it at the rate of your particular vibration. Picture yourself as a magnet of Cosmic Light spinning at a tremendous speed, drawing to yourself all that you need of cosmic power, utilizing it but also returning it to the Cosmos. Think of yourself as a dynamo, receiving energy and transmuting it into a concentrated, more potent form. By coming into you it can be accelerated. Having passed through you, its character has been changed according to your use of it. It can be made more potent by your right use, or, if misused, it becomes besmirched for having passed through you.

"You are a unit of Divine Energy! By being aware of its operation in and through you, you can absorb more of it, you can utilize, direct, and amplify it. You can raise your frequency to very high levels, far beyond that which is necessary to maintain the physical body, for the power of mental and spiritual energy far surpasses what is necessary to merely maintain the form. So, STRETCH out with your mind! Reach into this vast reservoir; grasp and bring into yourself the Divine energies of Mind and Spirit, and utilize them for the uplifting of your state of Being, your Cosmic awareness, and your consciousness. As you appropriate and assimilate these frequencies, you are transformed, for they are Divine Mind and Love in action within you.

"Mind is Cosmic energy in action, and it is not limited to specific areas. Cosmic Mind is present in whatever area of the Cosmos you might touch. Therefore, the higher the level into which you can project your consciousness, to that degree will Divine Mind become yours! There are no limitations in Mind. Anything you can touch is yours to appropriate. This is also true of Spiritual energy, for they are one and the same.

"You can enlarge your spiritual, mental, and physical energies through appropriation, but mere appropriation is not enough. What you do with the power is the important thing. He who reaches into this wondrous reservoir for these great energies and uses them in a destructive manner destroys himself and all he touches. But, if he uses them for Divine purposes, he not only elevates himself, but all else as well.

"You can assimilate these great energies which will activate all the chakras (the force fields that link your various bodies together) within you. As you absorb these powers into your various Centers and bodies, you become increasingly aware of the Cosmic power WITHIN yourself. As the Centers become activated, they draw each of your seven bodies into perfect alignment. With all of your Being united, activated, and brought into harmony, you become a literal dynamo, rightly using Divine Creative Energy and releasing it back into the Cosmos, intensified through its creative use.

"This is truly the great Creative Power of the Universe. It is the sex, or Gender Principle, as it manifests in the physical world. It is the Divine Creative Mental Principle on the mental level, and it is the Father-Mother Principle on the spiritual level. You have the choice of whether you will use it constructively or destructively. Those who indulge in promiscuous sexual activity dissipate their Divine power. Great artists, or musicians, or those who engage in creating beauty and lovely things, are using the power in the right way.

"The same thing is true of the use of Divine energy upon a mental level. It can be used for the betterment of your life, or it can be dissipated in anger, hatred, fear, jealousy, and many other inharmonious thoughts and deeds.

"On the spiritual level, your Divine powers are dissipated unless they are directed toward the highest unfoldment that is possible for you. Earnest Desire for spiritual understanding unleashes Divine energy, but being content with living in a material state of consciousness is a dissipation of the power.

"The great work that lies before Man is for him to become aware of the vast Sea of Cosmic Power in which he lives. Then he must learn to appropriate it and make the right use of it. When he does this he becomes Master of Himself and a LIGHT for others, for he becomes unified with the Father-Mother Creative Power and he comes into the CONSCIOUS awareness of his own Divine SONSHIP. He KNOWS that he is the offspring of Divine Creative power, that it is inherent within him, and is fulfilling Itself in and through him. He claims his SONSHIP and all that it encompasses.

"So, Beloved Ones, this is a lesson we hope you understand and use. This realization MUST BECOME YOURS if you are to make spiritual progress! The Power is *ever present*, but you determine how much of it you will claim, and how you will use it. You are building a Temple not made with hands. You are uniting the forces of heaven and earth IN you, and from this union can come the Divine offspring, the SON, or Christ Consciousness. This is using the Divine Principle of Gender at its highest level, to bring forth an ever more perfect expression of the wonderful power of Love and Life.

"*YOU ARE LIFE!* Never forget, You are Divine Life, the Son of God, with God's qualities *within you!* You tread the Divine Pathway of fulfillment until you become so closely aligned, unified, and identified, with Divine Life, that you become Its perfect expression upon whatever level of unfoldment you might be. As you go forth in this realization, life holds no insurmountable obstacles, for you walk in Light and Love. God bless you, My Beloved!"

At another time we received this message from a deceased friend, who had been an electrical engineer, and was very interested in the process of perception in other dimensions.

"We always wondered about Light and how Souls function here. Light is just another word for vibration. The higher the vibration, the greater the light, or power. It is our means of travel and expression. We recognize each other by vibration, for each *is* his own vibration and is known by it. I cannot fully explain it in words, for you have no words for it. But, each soul *is Consciousness*, individualized and unique.

"We have a built-in perceptive faculty, which causes us to know each other, and what is around us. It is as capable of discernment as your eyes and ears in your dimension. I can only call it Consciousness, or Knowingness. We KNOW, just as you know, and it is still by the ONE MIND and the ONE SPIRIT which has always been our means of knowing and expressing. Life is just as real here as it is in your dimension, and I am fully as *aware* now as I ever was, but I can now function on a much broader basis.

"I know now that I need have no limitations. If I can imagine strongly enough, I can experience that image, for our thoughts, or images, form the design of what we experience. I am learning the Law of Imagery, and what a wonderful thing it is. My experience is only limited to my ability to IMAGE. I can have, or be, whatever I can image. This is Creative Law. Earth man will grow in this understanding and, when he does, he will change his world."

PART 3

CHAPTER 1

ANCIENT ORDER OF OSIRIS and KEEPER
OF THE FLAME

On January 23, 1966, another phase of our unfoldment started to develop when we were first contacted by an intelligence that identified Itself as "Keeper of the Eternal Flame." This came about in a very unusual way during class, when we were in meditation.

About ten years prior to this, on June 3, 1956, we had received this message: "I am Khufu, Mighty ruler of Egypt. I was King in the valley of the Pharaohs. I saw the building of the temples of Thebes and Karnak. A member of your group was my slave girl in that day. Her name now is Nellie. I am of the 4th Dynasty. Perhaps, in your modern civilization, you might think of us as barvarians, but we were not, for we contributed much to civilization. Many things which can be seen in Egypt today are testimony to our knowledge. We were great builders and erected many temples with beautiful art and statuary. We served our Gods, as you serve yours, and we had our sorrows as you have yours. Life was cheap and many children died young, or were sold into slavery, as was Nellie. But she learned many things. I leave you now with the blessings of the great God of Light, Ra."

(This was followed by the first visit from one named Amala, who said: "Tama-Ho-Tep, my beloved sister, Tama-Ho-Tep," meaning Nellie.) "The span of years cannot keep our love apart. My name is Amala. I left you long ago when I was sold and you remained in Karnak. I left, never to see you again until we now meet in the loving care of Moco. I am to stay with you and be of service in any way I can, for I am to help you in your work. Call upon me, I will come again. God Bless you!" (She has come often in the intervening years and has been very helpful, especially in helping new students who have come to us for guidance.)

On June 12, 1965, Amala had also given us the following message: "Ageless lines of Divine Love bring us together again. We gave a life of service in the land of the world's birthplace, Egypt. I am now here to help you. You belong to the Ancient Order of Osiris. Now we are to bring LIGHT for this Age. You were once an Initiate in the Order of Light Bearers. Mastery of 'self' and Divine Wisdom are our objectives. Knowledge of the True SELF must precede mastery of the carnal self. You have advanced from Initiate to Apostle, and you must now carry the Light to mankind. We light your pathway in Love. You are all brought together now to carry on the work of the Masters, and I now open a new path of service to you. John's school of Love has prepared you for your work. Now Go and TEACH your wisdom by Life, by Deed and Word. This is the most ancient of Orders of Brotherly Love and unites ALL life in Divine ONENESS. Never question—All is ONE and Life is *eternal* and it repeats itself in ever-ascending expressions. *Know* that as you serve Life, it brings you to new and fuller manifestations of Itself. You are to be Life's ambassadors for this Age. Carry the torch of Light, the insignia of Osiris, the God of Light. You are my beloved Sister of Light. ALL IS NOW REVEALED!"

To the group:

"You go to new Divine cordons in great temples of Light. Osiris lights your Flame and YOU ARE LIGHT. Before the altar of Light, kneel to receive your Scepter of the Sacred Flame. With this scepter, you will carry the Flame of Truth. This sacred rite is an Initiation in the Lodge of the Masters. You become KEEPERS OF THE SACRED FLAME! You have always been in this lodge, but you come now as Light Bearers for this Age. You will be Light to the weary and unlearned. Light and Love dispel the darkness.

"It can now be revealed that Karmic ties have been resolved between Nellie and Ed. When we were slaves together, Ed was our slave-master and literally wielded the whip. This caused great resentment on her part, which was necessary for her to overcome to complete her Human experiences. Ed too, had to be given the opportunity of being loving to her. This has been accomplished and they will now serve together as Bearers of Light. Blessings to all!"

(On January 23, 1966, the new phase started in this manner, while in class meditation:)

I saw a processional of robed figures. They were marching by twos away from me down a gradual incline. Each figure was carrying a lighted torch in his right hand. This was all taking place in a great columned temple. All wore high Egyptian headdresses, and each torch had a three tiered square-type base of burnished gold. The following words were heard:

"My Dear, you are seeing the processional approaching realms of after-life. Osiris followers have a ceremonial procession depicting the approach to death. (This perturbed us, for it seemed morbid.) All is well, be not alarmed. Osiris followers honor death as the gateway to Light. Death of the body releases the soul to new dimensions.

"I am Keeper of the Eternal Flame. As the procession enters the lower chambers, this signifies the body entering the grave. It also signifies the end of materiality in the consciousness. The Flame depicts the Eternal Spirit in every man, which lives on through every outer expression that the Soul experiences. Taken through the portals of death, it arises in a new dimension and greater awareness. Osiris followers regard death as a liberation to be celebrated with rejoicing, both the death of the body and the death of limiting concepts. The Flame burns all materiality to ashes and from the ashes arises the Phoenix of Liberation, to soar to new and wondrous heights. Osiris followers carry the Flame through the portals of many lives, always to arise to a new and higher existence, with the old consumed by the Sacred Flame to make way for the new. The Flame is the universal symbol of Eternal Life perpetuating Itself into It's *every* expression.

"You ARE Light and Light Bearers. Fear not death, my children. Your Flame is Eternal. Light the way for others with your understanding. You will hear that Osiris followers were cultists worshiping the after-life, but many untruths have arisen through misunderstanding. We hold sacred the FIRE of LIFE in its journey through all of the burning away of the lower consciousness, and the refining of the Soul until it becomes the PURE expression of the Divine.

"Keep the Flame lighted in your hearts, step into the Flame, BECOME the Flame and allow it to purify and refine you. Welcome all experiences as opportunities to burn away materiality and bring about your fulfillment, and you will finally find yourselves LIBERATED into the BOUNDLESS UNIVERSE!"

(On January 26, 1966, the Keeper of the Flame came with these words:)

"Light brings Wisdom. Wisdom brings growth. Growth brings fulfillment, and fulfillment brings peace.

"Light comes only with heartfelt desire. When your desire for wisdom exceeds all other desires, then your mental powers, your physical powers, and your Soul all unite to lift you into your Master's Light. Then his Light infuses you, and you walk together on your upward journey. Be lighted from within by Divine Life and Love; then you become *your own light* and a light for others. Bright is the Flame within My Bearers of Light. Nothing of earth can daunt the Light of the Eternal Flame.

"Osiris Light Bearers are being assembled for the New Age, but each must have proven himself by overcoming negation in body, mind, emotions, and conditions before qualifying as Light Bearers. I have come to you now because you have proceeded through the lesser schools of life and now enter the School of Light. Here you will receive instructions in the Inner Mysteries, and you are to carry the Scepter of Light for the Cosmic Vibrations of Light. This is Universal Truth revealed to the heart and ear of the diligent student, who has prepared himself to assume his Divine responsibility in serving the Source of ALL Life. A new work now becomes yours.

"Lost Truths, long hidden, are now to be given to the world. Wonderment is in the minds of thinking people, and confused and frustrated people make little progress. Many Masters are being called to action to light their minds, and you are to help them." (We asked the identity of the one speaking and remarked that we were blessed to have the guidance of the Masters.)

"You must consider *no* Master more godly than your own God-SELF. I am Keeper of the Eternal Flame, with each attribute of its creativity. You must make your Mastery of life evident. Correlate your Divine SELF with your human self. All become Masters when this is accomplished.

"Come with me to the Ghizeh Temple of Wisdom. Come to the Chamber of the Eternal Flame. In the Light of the Masters we will pass the Scepter into your hands. You are of the Ancient Order of Osiris. You were initiates long ago. Now you will bear the Light in the New Age. Now the Light is passed into your hands. The probationary time has passed. In each incarnation, each initiate must prove himself in that age. The New Age is now being ushered in, and you are ready to proceed with your work. Carry the Torch of Light into the world. Become Bearers of the Scepter of the Eternal Flame."

(Nellie relates what she sees:)

I am in a *large* chamber in the middle of which is a huge altar. The altar is square and each side is composed of twelve steps. The steps are in series of three, each third step being wider than the previous two. The third steps are rather like plateaus, or places of demarcation. The steps are indicative of the many steps Man, as a three-fold

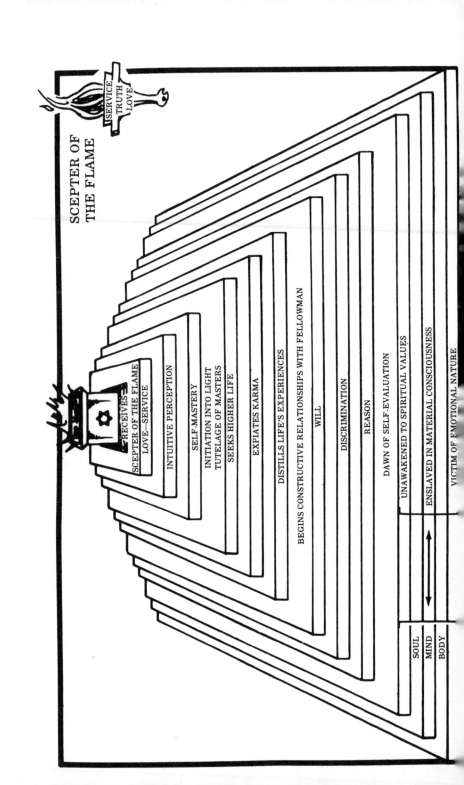

SCEPTER OF
THE FLAME

SERVICE
TRUTH
LOVE

RECEIVES
SCEPTER OF THE FLAME
LOVE—SERVICE

INTUITIVE PERCEPTION

SELF-MASTERY

INITIATION INTO LIGHT
TUTELAGE OF MASTERS

SEEKS HIGHER LIFE

EXPIATES KARMA

DISTILLS LIFE'S EXPERIENCES

BEGINS CONSTRUCTIVE RELATIONSHIPS WITH FELLOWMAN

WILL

DISCRIMINATION

REASON

DAWN OF SELF-EVALUATION

UNAWAKENED TO SPIRITUAL VALUES

ENSLAVED IN MATERIAL CONSCIOUSNESS

VICTIM OF EMOTIONAL NATURE

SOUL
MIND
BODY

Being, must take in his spiritual unfoldment to come into the full realization and utilization of his Divine powers.

On the lower level, Man is unawakened to spiritual values; his body, mind and Soul are enslaved in material consciousness, and he is the victim of his destructive emotional nature. At the first plateau he has become aware of the possibility of a different life and begins the process of self-evaluation.

During the next three steps, he develops the faculties of Reason, Discrimination, and Will. He learns to direct his powers positively, but mostly still for selfish reasons. At the second plateau, he begins to relate to others in a positive, constructive way. He begins to extend his consciousness beyond his own selfish interests, and he realizes that he is a part of something bigger than himself.

He then proceeds through the next series of steps. Here he learns to distil the spiritual values out of life's many experiences. He does all he can to expiate his Karma, and he seeks the higher life. At the third plateau, he comes under the tutelage of the Masters, and he is INITIATED into the Light.

In the final three steps he *consciously* works in the Light. Here he attains self-mastery. His intuitive and perceptive faculties are opened. He becomes the Personification of Love, and he dedicates himself to the service of his fellow-men and the Divine. He is now ready to receive and carry the Scepter of the Flame. This is the torch of Truth, Light and Love, and he carries it forth to light and bless the world.

However, this will not be the completion of the work, for above the final plateau, rises still another series of steps, which will take him into the work and Light of the Cosmic vibrations. Ever upward and onward into new areas of activity and expression, to finally unite in conscious At-One-Ment with the ABSOLUTE.

On the top plateau, there stands a smaller altar, with a lighted brazier upon it. A white robed figure, the Keeper of the Flame stands beside this altar. The brazier is not flaming, but the fire seems to be LIVE coals, with an intense radiation arising from them. We are all kneeling before the altar and the Keeper of the Flame. He reaches his right hand out and when he brings it before him, he is holding an unlighted scepter with the words Love, Truth, and Service engraved upon it. He dips it into the live coals and it is ignited. He raises the scepter in three salutes saying, "Your material way is lighted, your mental way is lighted, your spiritual way is lighted. This sacred rite is performed that you might become Bearers of Light. Lighted from the Receptacle of the Divine Fire within the Inner Chamber of your own Being, you now go forth with the Scepter of the Flame, that the world might be LIGHTED by its LIGHT, WARMED by its LOVE, and PURIFIED by its POWER. YAHANA! YAHANA! YAHANA!" A lighted scepter is then passed to each of us, and I am aware that we must now prepare ourselves to proceed up the next set of steps, but also work simultaneously in the earthly realm as Light Bearers.

(Keeper of the Flame continues:)

"A New Age dawns and into the hands of my Light Bearers is placed the Scepter of the Flame. The Flame is the symbol of the Eternal Spirit in each man, and it lives on through every outer expression through which he passes. As you are given the Scepter, it signifies your awareness of your *Eternal* Being and your knowledge that YOU ARE SPIRIT, eternal and indestructible. I am gathering my Light Bearers together, that the world might learn of My Light and open their hearts and minds to My IN-DWELLING PRESENCE, which is in every man. SELF-awareness and INNER Knowledge is to be the hallmark of the new Aquarian Age. YAHANA! YAHANA! YAHANA!"

We were to find that each communication from the Keeper of the Flame was signed off by repeating the word "YAHANA" three times. We asked what this meant and were told that it meant that all Light Centers and Light Bearers throughout the world were being activated and brought together in ONE mighty purpose for the New Age. I had spelled the word as it had sounded to me and was surprised to receive the following message during class a few weeks later:

"That you might verify and understand My Blessing— My scribe has spelled the word as it sounded to her, 'YA-HANA.' However, in your language, it would be spelled 'YOJANA.' It means that I am drawing ALL together in one great circle. The encirclement of ALL My people in the loving bonds of peace and brotherhood. This I am doing as I bring My Light Bearers together to fulfill MY PLAN! YOJANA! YOJANA! YOJANA!"

It had been stated that this might be verified, so I did some extensive searching in various books. I finally went to the Theosophical library and in the glossary of The Secret Doctrine, by Madame Blavatsky, I found the word, spelled as we had been told. It is a Yoga term meaning "The act of joining, or yoking." Needless to say we were delighted at this confirmation of our most recent assignment.

Accustomed as we were to receiving all of our messages from "entities," we constantly asked for more specific identification of the Keeper of the Flame, with the following results:

"I AM THAT I AM! I AM the ALL in ALL, the ONE in ALL and the ALL in ONE! I am above and beyond personality. Consider me not as ever having been earth-man, except as I AM in all men. I AM the everlasting Flame in each of My Children. I have come throughout the ages in many forms and guises. My Christian children have known me as Jesus, the Christed One. My Buddhist children have known me as The Buddha. Others of My Children have known me as Krishna, and Lao Tze, and all great avatars. I have come always to the highest of Man's conception, and that which he could embrace according to his background and understanding. But I HAVE COME ALWAYS IN THE *ONE SPIRIT!*"

We have concluded that this can only be the "I AM"

Consciousness, and we feel awed, humble, and very blessed to have touched such a "SOURCE."

Part Five of this book is a partial account of the many and varied lessons we have received from Keeper of the Flame in the intervening years.

PART 3

CHAPTER 2

THE UNIVERSAL LINK

The idea of our being involved in a PLAN of Universal magnitude was hard to accept, and we were very skeptical. However, it proved to be true and events occurred rapidly to bring it about.

I had been told repeatedly by the Masters to get "the book" published, but I had procrastinated for almost ten years. Now I was *commanded* to do it immediately. I protested that we had neither the time, nor the money, but I was told that it MUST be done.

So we published what became "Gems of Truth from the Masters" and surprisingly the money was available when the books were printed. Then the question of sales and distribution arose. An authoress friend, Ann Herbstreith, told me that Merta Mary Parkinson of Kansas City had purchased several of her books, and Ann suggested that I send a sample copy to her. Merta Mary replied immediately, ordering 20 books to be sent to various friends, one of whom was Liebe Pugh of England. Both Merta Mary and Liebe were authoresses and journalists and especially interested in various aspects of metaphysics. They were co-operating in what has come to be known as the Universal Link Operation.

Both of these newfound friends and co-workers asked for additional material that we were receiving from the Masters, which they included in their publications. The response was overwhelming. Within a few months after "the book" was published we found ourselves an integral part of the Universal Link, exchanging ideas and channeled material with Light groups in many parts of the world.

Widespread knowledge of the Universal Link came about when Liebe documented and circulated the story of the "Weeping Angel Picture Phenomenon of Worthington," in England. This has been called a modern day miracle and has proven the existence of "higher powers and Beings." It is the story of a Christlike figure appearing to an English real estate agent, Richard Grave, with the assertion that He had instituted "The Plan" and "Operation" whereby the consciousness and frequencies of mankind and the earth would be raised to new dimensions. He identified Himself as "TRUTH" and said, "By Christmas of 1967 I will have revealed Myself through Nuclear Evolution." One of the immediate, and also intermittent, demonstrations of His presence and power has been the emanation of "tears" which have come from the eyes of an angel in the picture which Richard was carrying when the "Master" first appeared to him.

A few years prior to the Master's appearance, Liebe had sculpted a plasticine bust of a Christlike figure which she had entitled "Limitless Love." When Richard saw the piece he immediately recognized it as the exact image of the one who was coming to him. Richard and Liebe joined forces and, acting upon explicit instructions from the Master, set up a center, documented and distributed information, and received interested visitors from many parts of the world. Many witnessed the phenomenon of the "Weeping Angel" as well as the filling with water of a "Chalice" which Liebe had also sculpted.

The fruitful years of Liebe's dedication, in the earth frequency, came to an end in December 1966. A sealed letter, which she had left with instructions for its opening at the time of her death, revealed that several months prior to her passing she had a visitaticn from the Master and was given the exact date on which her earth mission would be completed, which proved to be right.

Kathleen Fleming, a co-worker with Richard and Liebe and an artist with the unique ability to paint "Beings" as she saw them in finer dimensions, also contributed much to the Universal Link Operation. In her final days, with great physical effort, she made a tour of the United States showing her pictures, lecturing, and acting as a "linking agent" of Love, Light, and energies wherever she went. She was accompanied on her tour by Father Francis Cuzon, a priest and teacher, who had been a missionary to China for twelve years. He introduced the World Harmony Program as they moved across the U.S.A.

Among Liebe's protegees was a lovely girl by the name of Mollie Thompson, who also toured the United States. She has written many New Age songs, and sings charmingly. It has been interesting to see the similarity of the "messages" received through different channels in different parts of the world, proving the "ONENESS" and the overall scope of "The Plan." During Mollie's visit we received a statement from the Keeper of the Flame concerning "breath," which had never been mentioned to us before. We were all amazed when Mollie received a letter four days later from England in which was a message that had been received there, containing almost the exact phrases.

Our message read: "Bless Mollie, she merges My Centers into one unified, vital, active Light. Her presence enables the focusing of the Power and Light as she carries My 'breath' in her heart and breathes it, as Life, into my Light Centers." The English message read: "The Master wishes that the English Segment how return to the Universal First Cause, through their OWN BREATH, THE ENERGY OF THEIR BEINGS IN SONG, which will now become THE SACRED FIRE BREATH OF GOD HIMSELF, RETURNING TO HIMSELF, HAVING MADE THE COMPLETE CIRCUIT VIA THE PRECIOUS BODIES AND BEINGS AND UNITS OF THE UNIVERSAL LINK."

One of the focal points of the Universal Link is a dedicated group, under the direction of Peter and Eileen Caddy, in Findhorn, Scotland. The activities there, which are all divinely directed, have grown into a world renowned example of "The Operation." Cooperation with the Devic Kingdom has helped them to produce fantastic floral and vegetable gardens, and experience many other dramatic events. Documents are available concerning this phenomenon.

One of the international key figures, and ambassador-at-large for the Universal Link, is Anthony Brooke. He is a descendant of a famous English family and served for a time as the 4th White Rajah of the country of Sarawak, on the island of Borneo. He is completely dedicated to the promoting of understanding, goodwill and brotherhood among all peoples and travels extensively to that end.

Almost immediately after we became involved in the Universal Link, Anthony wrote that he would like to meet with us after his forthcoming appearance as one of the speakers at a Spiritual Frontiers Conference in Chicago. We knew nothing about him except that he had once been the ruler of Sarawak. The following experience served to further substantiate the fact that we had a definite role to play, as the Keeper of the Flame had said.

Two days before Anthony's arrival, our daughter, Kathleen, asked if I could suggest some material she could use for a school assignment. I referred her to a stack of National Geographic magazines that were stored in the attic. Being rushed for time, she asked me to find it for her. Without searching through the magazines, I reached into the middle of the stack and pulled one out. It opened to a map of Indonesia, with Sarawak in red, which immediately caught my eye. Upon reading the article I found that it contained a complete account of the Brooke family who had ruled the country for four generations, Anthony having been the last ruler and having ceded the country to England during World War II, after having had a profound spiritual experience in which he realized that he had, in his words, "A larger Kingdom to serve."

A figure well-known to many in the Universal Link is Merta Mary Parkinson, mentioned earlier. She has not only served a journalistic function through the years but has brought many Light workers and centers into a greater awareness of their essential Oneness through the Sister-of-the-Amber. This is a loose-knit organization of women of all races and nationalities, as well as all social and cultural backgrounds, who are linked by loving service to others. They feel a special kinship, having been made aware of each other through Merta Mary, and all proudly wear the Amber beads which she has presented to them.

The amber beads, many of which were a part of the King Tut tomb treasure, apparently have a greater purpose than merely linking the "Sisters" together. They must also be used by those who own them as a focal point for the receiving and disseminating of the Cosmic or "nuclear" energies of which the Master spoke.

During a visit to Merta Mary we received the following message about the Amber. It came from the "Keeper of the Eternal Flame," which is undoubtedly simply another name for that which also identifies as "TRUTH," "LIMITLESS LOVE," the "ALL-KNOWING ONE," and countless other "SOURCES" from which other Light Centers receive their inspiration and guidance. The message read:

"Beloved, the Osirian Light is now in full focus in the Earth vibration and your distribution of the Amber has provided focal points for its emanation. It is the wish of the Guardians of the Amber beads to light the earth by using the beads as a point of concentration for the distribution of the inner Light and Power. Sisters-of-the-Amber have been aware of the Light within the beads, but they have not understood that the beads are the crystalline substance *of* Light which, as amplifiers, are to be used for the distribution of the Light and Love which is the essence of the Consciousness of the Awakened Ones. Beloved, the power is not in the beads, but in the hearts and minds of those who are inwardly attuned to Me. However, the beads do have amplifying power, much as the Ruby crystal acts as a focusing point and an amplifying center for the Laser beam. The crystal of the Ruby is the heart of the Laser emanation; the Amber is endowed with the same capacities—both being crystalline forms *which is Light solidified.* It is not the form that is important. I merely cite the function of the Laser beam as being the same in relationship to the Ruby, as the Amber is to the 'Inner Light and Power' which My Light Bearers give to the world. Through concentration and amplification, with the Amber energy, a mighty release of Light, Love, Wisdom and Power is conveyed into Earth frequencies. Also, the Light can be sent to specific regions and individuals, as the Sister images and directs it to the recipient. These are not just gifts to have and allow to lie in a jewel case. They are potent foci for energy release, and it is important that they be used to the fullest extent. To most of the Sisters they have been objects for the focusing of Light for themselves, but now they must realize that the Light is the Inner God Self, with all of Its powers of creation, moving into ever-ascending spirals of eternal beauty and wisdom, and carrying humanity in Its breast to new and wondrous heights of purity and perfection."

In a later conversation with Dr. Robert Lustig, who has a fine scientific background, he pointed out that the Ruby is crystalline substance of the *mineral* kingdom and is therefore the concentration of Light, as was told. But, the Amber is of the *organic* kingdom, since it is the sap of ancient pine trees that has crystallized. The sap, having been the Life Essence of the tree is therefore also Light, but a full octave higher in the Cosmic Scale and therefore higher in frequency. In considering the tremendous power manifested through the Ruby of the Laser beam, it staggers the imagination to think of the possibilities of using the Amber with mental and spiritual energy focused through it.

The entire story, entitled "Drama of the Amber," as well as a full report of the Universal Link Operation and other equally enthralling stories, are available from Merta Mary Parkinson, 4117 NW Willow Drive, Kansas City, Mo. 64116. The Story of the "Findhorn Gardens," and current "Revelations" they receive, can be ordered from the Findhorn Trust, 27 Findhorn Bay Caravan Park, Forres-Moray-Scotland. Information is also available from the Universal Link headquarters at #1 St. George's Square, St. Anne's-on-Sea, Lancashire, England.

The Universal Link Operation has truly been the means of linking together Light Centers and individuals throughout the world, with an enormous exchange of channeled information, ideas and energies. The energy exchange is undoubtedly now the more important aspect, and what the Master was referring to when He said He would reveal Himself "through Nuclear evolution." Many people had anticipated an outer revelation or "happening" by Christmas of 1967 and were disappointed when it did not occur. However, it is now very evident that since that time a great sifting, sorting, cleansing process is taking place in every area of Man's experience and thinking; and we can expect ever greater changes as the planet continues to be bombarded with increasingly stronger Cosmic, or "Nuclear" energies.

It has been made apparent to us, in a current message just as we go to press, that the "Linking" is complete on the outer levels, and it is now the work of every "Light Bearer" to BE and Radiate the Light in an individual and collective "Nuclear Evolution" Operation. Thus creating an amalgamation of "the Energies" of ALL levels that will transmute and transcend all of Man's old concepts and limitations, and raise his consciousness to the point where he can function harmoniously and simultaneously in many dimensions.

As the message came, I, as the channel, was first aware of a great "sunburst" before me, much like the Egyptian Solar Disk symbol. However, it seemed to predate our former Egyptian relationship, and also the sun of our solar system. I sensed it as being the "Inner Light" which every individual serves, and is served by, throughout their many steps of soul unfoldment. It is the ONE LIGHT which opens the doorway of Man's consciousness and floods him with "SOUL-AR" LIGHT. It is the first edict of Divine Mind—"Let there be Light"—which then became manifest within all of creation. It is the "Source of all Being" with which each must ultimately identify himself. This seemed to be of Nuclear Essence, yet not active nor explosive. Then these words came:

"All that takes place on the 'outer planes' is but a small fragment of that which is 'real and total' *within* each individual. The outer activity of the 'Linking Operation' has been necessary but it is not the real crux of the matter, only a means to an end. The crux of the matter is that EACH INDIVIDUAL FIND, BE, AND LIVE THE INNER LIGHT. The emphasis is no longer to be put upon the outer activity of the Linking, you must now go directly to the heart of the matter by recognizing 'The LIGHT' as the 'Source of ALL Being' and inherent within yourself and others.

"As this consciousness develops throughout the entire populace and Man becomes aware of his At-One-Ment with 'The Light,' with all life forms, and with that which is even beyond 'form,' it will no longer be necessary for him to function solely in his 'form aspect.' He will learn to *consciously* function in his mental and spiritual aspects as easily, in fact more easily, than in the physical aspect. Communication with all levels, without outer means, will be possible for it will be mind to mind, heart to heart, regardless of time, space or density.

"This *is* a New Age in which Man will understand and live so totally in his LIGHT BEING that he will have immediate communication with all 'Beingness' in all dimensions. He can go into past or future, distance or 'within,' with instant 'knowingness' for he transcends body and brain and moves into UNIVERSAL MIND where ALL is known and ALL is ONE; and from which can be absorbed as much as the individual is capable of comprehending and absorbing.

"As you become All Light, All Love, All Wisdom, then is My world perfected. Then is My PLAN complete.

"Yojana!   Yojana!   Yojana!"

PART 3

CHAPTER 3

THE WHITE ROSE

Liebe Pugh's favorite flower was the White Rose, for she regarded it as the symbol of the purity and perfection of the Soul as it unfolds to its Divine fulfillment. Shortly after her transition, we had a series of incidents and messages pertaining to it that were very interesting and inspiring. As our group sat in meditation one evening we received the following from her:

"Dear Ones, My Light lives in all the Links. Come with Me, Beloved, and we will travel the Highways of Light. As Cosmic Bearers of Light, we bring Light and Love to the Master's feet, where it is blessed and magnified and wafted to the world on the perfumed zephyrs of Light as it descends into the hearts of ALL who will receive. It is a soft, caressing breeze of Love as it carries petals of *white roses* to My Beloved Children. A garden of white roses I leave with you. As the breath of LIMITLESS LOVE lifts and carries each petal, it finds its way into the hearts of My Light Bearers and My Awakened Ones. This is MY BEING *IN YOU,* MY LOVE *IN* YOU, MY LIGHT *IN* YOU. We are ONE LIGHT, ONE LOVE, ONE LIFE. Fused in ONENESS we move into realms of Light and SERVE our Creator. My Peace attends you. LINKING IS ACHIEVED!"

Ray and Dorothy Davis (also a channel for messages from the Masters and author of Robin's Return) had been at our home that evening. Four days later they had shopped for a picture for their living room. None had seemed "just right," until Dorothy found one that was half hidden behind some furniture in about the fourth store they visited. It is a muted, impressionistic type of picture—in brown tones— a city scene with the suggestion of skyscrapers, but all suffused with a golden glow, as if light were shining on the rain. They had taken the picture home and hung it, and placed some new furniture they had also purchased, then called us to come over and see what they had done to their home. The picture was hung opposite the front door, so one sees it when entering the house. As I stepped in, I was immediately struck by the arrangement of the paint strokes and color in the upper right-hand corner of the picture, for it is unmistakably a White Rose. As we looked, we saw even more, for the heart of the rose looks like the hooded head of a Light Being and a downward shaft of light forms the body. We all stood in awe and were thoroughly thrilled because of the recent experience with Liebe and her "garden of roses." We were anxious to see if we could receive further enlightenment, so we called other friends and all sat quietly in meditation. We were in very close rapport and a tremendous vibration filled the room. Almost immediately I saw Liebe standing before me in her Light Body. She moved toward me and placed two fingers (index and middle) of her right hand on my forehead, on the Third Eye area, and said, "I am placing My "SEAL" upon each of My Light Bearers, as was mentioned by John the Beloved in his Revelation (Rev. 7:3). This seals us in *unity* and we are *forever* ONE." Then she moved clockwise around the room to each of the group, placing the same two fingers upon everyone's Third Eye. As she removed her hand, I saw on each forehead a WHITE ROSE in FULL BLOOM, and she said, "The full-blown rose signifies the full-flowering of Spiritual Awareness. It means that you are awakened to your Divine Nature and to your Divine Calling, and are ready to accept the reponsibility of bringing the LIGHT of LOVE and UNDERSTANDING to the world. You are now SEALED in ONENESS with me and with all the Masters of Light in this mighty endeavor.!"

I was later to recall a message which had come about three years prior to this in which we had been told that as we moved through the seven steps of Soul unfoldment, and as each of our chakra "Centers" was opened, we would spiritually receive a *Red Rose* for each step, and that as we finished the Octave, the Red Roses would be replaced with a SINGLE WHITE ROSE, which was symbolic of the one who had overcome the Human desires and was ready to give themselves in complete dedication and SERVICE to bring "THE KINGDOM" to ALL of humanity.

After the group had left, we received an additional message: "Beloved, LINKING IS ACHIEVED! I have transcended my mortal identity and now function in My Light Aspect. The Rose is in full-flower! Dorothy, I guided you to the picture. It is my sign to *all* of my presence and guidance. My sign has been placed upon My Light Bearers this night. My Rose will grow in your hearts. My desire lights your LIGHT and My Fire melts away your material and carnal desires. My Flame purifies My Blessed Light Bearers. Malleable now are you, and we forge the CHAIN of LOVE which will draw ALL My Children into the ONE LIGHT. (Again, reference to what I had received many years before.) Mastery comes with this knowledge. Who can doubt his own power when he is identified with SUCH POWER? With understanding, comes Mastery. Believe that Man now moves into his TRUE LIFE, where he will *know* that he is a CREATIVE BEING and that he must create wisely, and uses Wisdom to wield his Power constructively. THIS IS MASTERY! MASTERY OF SELF and MASTERY OVER HIS ENVIRONMENT.

"Keep the Scepter *high*. Light the way for others and LIVE in My LIGHT. My SEAL brings Power and Light. May the ROSE flourish in your hearts and minds."

We were later told that the White Rose was an ancient Egyptian symbol which had been adopted by Moses and taken to the Holy Land to later adorn the portals of the Temple of Solomon.

On the first anniversary of Liebie's transition, we again gathered and received the following: "I once amended a slogan from 'Risen Thinking' to 'Light Thinking,' (in a pamphlet she had published) but now the New Age slogan and activity is to be amended to 'LIGHT BEING'! Henceforth, all Light Bearers are to *BE* the Light in ALL ways and areas of their life. Some time ago, I placed the Seal of the White Rose upon your brows; thus, we were united in mind and purpose. But tonight I move the White Rose from the brow, or from the intellect, into the Heart of each of you, for we are now merged in ONENESS in the Holy Sanctity of the Mystical Marriage to become ONE in purpose and expression. From the heart, the center of Divine Love, will all expression henceforth manifest. The purity of the White Rose is brought into full, radiant bloom through the action of the Divine Spirit within you. Expressing through the heart as Love, it now brings into My world a glorious blossoming of Love in the earth plane. The OPEN Rose, giving its essence of the purity of your Being, makes all things new and lifts mankind into the full stature of his own Divinity. Thus do we move through the earth dimension as builders, as creators of all that is good and beautiful, for in Love are ALL things wrought, all things conceived, and all things perfected."

At another class session, during meditation, I found myself at the open gate of a garden filled with white roses. There was a high arched gateway with two pillars supporting the arch, one black and one white. A white figure stood beside the right-hand arch that I took to be the Keeper of the Flame. This message came through:

"Yes, My Beloved, the Gate stands ajar for all who would enter My Garden of Perfection, but 'Straight is the Way and narrow the Gate, and few there are that find it.' These words were spoken long ago, and they are as true today as they were then. When our mission is completed, many will be so filled with Light and Understanding that they, too, shall enter through the straight and narrow gate.

"I would give you a brief symbology of the Gateway. The pillars, not being the same color may seem like a paradox, for My scribe cannot understand what this means. What she has seen is what must be accomplished *IN* Man, for the two pillars represent the two opposite forces in every man, the forces of Light and its opposite polarity, darkness, which is equally necessary for the support of the arch. This represents the activity which each Soul must engage in to perfect Itself and qualify to join the legions of Light Bearers. In other words, before one can walk in the garden with all of its purity and perfection, they must have balanced the two sides of their nature—the Light and the Dark, and recognize them as being equally important in Soul unfoldment. But, one must connect them with the Arch of Understanding, which then becomes the Arch of Service, as one sees the need of humanity for understanding and love.

"The white Pillar represents that innate purity and spirituality which moves man ever forward, but this is not enough, for Man must also move through the darkness of life and its many experiences and *balance* the two forces, or poles, of his nature. He does this only by his recognition of these two forces and lets them serve each other, rather than oppose each other.

"At a certain point in man's unfoldment, he recognizes that he must do this work *within himself* and he begins to take the necessary steps for its accomplishment. As he proceeds along his Pathway, he realizes that as long as there is imbalance in the world, he is not free to leave it behind without first doing his part fo achieve balance for *all*. So he then dedicates himself to bringing about balance and harmony by service to his fellowman. Can you not see these pillars as supporting the Archway of Service and making the gateway where Light reaches out to Darkness, the Pathway being established for all to move into perfection?

"So, Beloved, as you pass through this gateway, which you yourself erect by your dedication to your fellowman, your Divine-Self and your Creator, you enter into My Garden of Perfection where you can pluck the Rose of Truth, the Rose of Purity, the Rose of Harmony and Peace, the Roses of Light and Love. You can fill your arms with these precious symbols of Perfection and take with you as much as you can carry, and then return into the world and strew them among My Children, that they might be Lighted and lifted and brought to new understanding.

"Fear not, Go forward in Light and I will fill your arms with White Roses to be spread among all of My Children everywhere!"

PART 3

CHAPTER 4

THE CHALICE

I have become increasingly aware of the Chalice as the symbol of the New Age. It symbolizes the individual heart and mind open and receptive to the inflow of the Christ Light and Mind; also, the world as it is suffused with the Cosmic energies that are now being directed to it, that the planet and humanity might be lifted into the Light vibrations. It had been mentioned by John as being the symbol of Christ Consciousness, and one of our first messages from the Keeper of the Flame reads thusly:

"Beloved, I gather unto Myself my own. I come that you might be fulfilled in Truth, Light, and Being.

"I Am the Living Fount of Life; you are my Chalice. I come that you might be filled from the fountainhead of Life. As you commend yourself into my hands, I hold you, an embodied Chalice, to be filled with My Spirit, My Life, and My Love. But Beloved, only if the Chalice is receptive can it be filled with the Living Waters. Should it be filled with 'self' there is no room for the Waters of Life to enter it. So, it is your duty, responsibility, and destiny, to empty My Chalice of all of that which is selfish, egotistical, or material in nature, that you might become the receptacle of My Living Waters.

"This is the full cup of the Living Christ *in* you. You will be filled with My Spirit. This is the Life giving Essence which transforms the human into the Divine. When you empty yourself of 'self,' and become the receptacle of My

Spirit, I will fill you to overflowing, until that which you can no longer hold spills forth as a blessing to all whom you meet.

"I have planted, in the Rose of your Heart, my gift of Love. I have planted, in the Lotus of your Mind, the gift of my Mind. I have planted, in your Soul, the Divine Flame of My Spirit.

"You must allow the Living Waters to bring the flowers of Divinity into fulfillment *within you*. Neither the rose nor the lotus will bloom in the desert; they require the Living Waters. Then the Rose flourishes, and the Lotus, which arises from the morass of materiality, comes into full Flower. This is *MY MIND IN YOU*. I AM the Fountain, Ye are the Chalice. I fill you to overflowing. I water the Love of your heart. I bring into full expression the wisdom of My Mind in you.

"I fill you with the Eternal Flame of My Spirit, that it might burn away all the dross of materiality and refine you, until you become the *Pure Essence of Being*, in *My Image and Likeness*. Truly, I AM IN THEE and THOU ART IN ME. KNOW THIS, live in this awareness, and reveal this Truth to mankind. This is the Light which you must bring to the hearts and minds of Man. The Flaming Scepter of the Divine Infinite Fire must be held aloft, that The Way for all might be lighted.

"I AM FOREVER IN YOU AND YOU IN ME! When Man will grasp the Truth of this and identify himself with ME, he will know no limitation. He will assume his rightful place as the ruler of his Inner Kingdom. Verily, I say unto you, in Truth 'WE ARE ONE!' In Light you walk and are fulfilled. You shall be known as My SON. So shall it be! So shall it be!"

Almost immediately John, the Beloved, came in with these words:

"I add my love and blessings to the wonderful outpouring we have all experienced. The great 'I AM CONSCIOUSNESS' has spoken, and we stand in awe of its Light and Power. As you grasp the full meaning of this Truth, and proceed to fulfill it individually, there will be such a renaissance within the earth plane that the heavens will literally 'open' and all will see the Glory of God.''

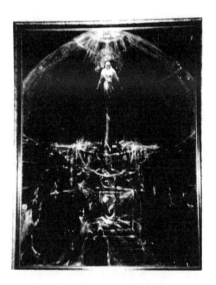

We had been in correspondence with a lady in Denver, Colorado, Anna Margaret Gibbens, who does lovely inspirational paintings. She painted a beautiful picture for us and lovingly donated it to our Center. It is done on black velvet and has a vibrancy that everyone feels when they enter the room.

In the center of the picture is a chalice upon a four-square base, which also holds the Eternal refining Flame. Spiraling up from the Chalice is a shaft of light, atop of which is a Christ figure. This depicts the evolution of the Soul into its Christed state, and the involution of the Light and Christ Mind into Man. Leading up to the base of the Chalice are seven steps, depicting the steps that Man takes as he unfolds in consciousness. Surrounding the entire base are twelve robed, crowned, figures who are carrying lighted sceptors. There are many other symbolic things, i.e. the seven colors, the figure eight in the flame, and an aura of light suffusing the entire picture, suggesting the outpouring from the God-head.

We were very grateful for the picture, but were unaware for several weeks of another symbol in it. Although we had recently been told that ancient Egyptian truths were now to be instilled in Man's consciousness, there had been a certain scepticism in our minds. We had forgotten about the message that had come from Amala ten years before, pertaining to the karmic ties between my husband and myself when we were together in an Egyptian incarnation.

One day, while meditating upon the picture, I suddenly became aware of an Egyptian symbol in it. The way in which the paint has been put on the velvet creates a black background which is the exact shape of a Cleopatra type headdress. In questioning Mrs. Gibbens, we found that she had been unaware of having painted it into the picture. So, we took this as further verification of what we had been told regarding our new assignment, and our Egyptian background.

Different members of our group later purchased small crystal chalices to have in their homes as constant reminders to keep their hearts and minds open to the inflow of Divine Light, Love, Wisdom, and Power. They brought them for a consecration service and we received the following from Keeper of the Flame:

"Beloved, a desire for spiritual understanding is what is necessary for each Soul to burst the bonds of his carnality and move forward upon his Spiritual Pathway. Divine Wisdom awaits the one who gives himself whole-heartedly to the pursuit of his God-Self. Man flounders in darkness and misunderstanding as he seeks answers from his outer world. He starves, with his belly full of the non-nourishing condiments of the outer life. He pursues only the condiments and seeks not the Bread of Life. It is the work of the Light Bearers to help Man understand that his hunger is for the things of the Spirit. Each soul really longs for the bread and wine of the spiritual life, but becomes so involved in the pursuits of the outer world that he does not find what he truly seeks.

"My table is laden with the Bread of Life and the Wine of the Spirit, and it is free for the asking and the seeking.

However, I can only invite you to my table; I cannot force you to partake of it. A vast array of tasty, soul-enriching foods await you that will satisfy your hunger and thirst; a laden table that holds enriching and life-giving substance that nourishes, develops, and fulfills your soul-unfoldment.

"Many are so accustomed to loading their food with spices that they hardly taste the food. This is also true of the Food of the Spirit. They cover it with what they think gives flavor to life, but in so doing they never taste the Real Food. Do not be concerned with the condiments of life; always take the pure Essence of Life and savor it to the fullest. Condiments so stimulate the digestive juices that the food passes through without being fully digested, or its essence extracted. Growth comes to the body only as one partakes of, digests, and assimilates his food. The same is true of the soul as it utilizes each experience with which it is confronted.

"Come to my table and you will find the manna of the Spirit. Bring the Chalices of yourselves and partake of the Wine of the Spirit. Break the Bread of Life and let it enrich you. The Holy Communion of Man and Spirit is much more than just a ceremony in a church. Divine Love and Wisdom is the Essence of Me. As you come to Me and are filled, a new creation is brought forth and the God-Man emerges from the earth-child!"

Consecration Service of the Chalices

"A great love fills and overflows the Chalices of your hearts as you bring the crystal chalices here to be consecrated. A merging of Light as you do this, and holy is the Chalice of your hearts as we fuse in ONENESS together. The crystal Chalice in your homes will bring greater awareness of the Chalice of Life in which all have their Being-ness. So, in this consecration, not only do we consecrate the chalices, but you will find that the feeling of Oneness which you share with each other will expand outward to encompass ALL of Life in its many dimensions, and all of my Beloved children everywhere.

"As we proceed with the Consecration Service, each take your Chalice in your hand and hold it to your heart, as a symbol of your heart being open to receive My Light and Love.

Your Heart is My Heart...
   Your Life is My Life...
      Your Will is My Will...
         Your Love is My Love...
            Your Mind is My Mind...
               My Light is your Light...
                  My Power is your Power...
                     My Peace is your Peace...
Your Body, Mind, and Soul are the instruments through which I may more fully express Myself, My Light, and My Love. I AM *in* You and You are *in* Me and we are totally ONE!

"And now Beloved, as I have filled your Chalices, you in turn will fill mine as you consecrate yourselves to *be* the Light of Me in *all* that you do, say, and think. As you fill my Chalice of Life with your Light and Love, it flows through My Creation, blessing all that it touches, radiating the Light into all dimensions. Light is the fulfilling power of all dimensions, and when you radiate it, each life form receives according to its needs at its specific vibratory level, for the White Light encompasses all of the frequencies within the Light Spectrum. Light is the Essence of Myself in its fullest, the totality of Me which I give to all who can receive.

"Great is the Light as you open yourselves to Me and we become wedded for eternity. Then all is revealed and you find the Love and Wisdom to resolve each task that you are given. The full Light comes only when self-less service is the one desire of the soul, with no thought of reward, self-satisfaction, or glory. Then you become the pure channel for the free flow of the Light, the components of which are Love, Wisdom, Truth, and Power. Seek Ye the

Light and ask for nothing more. Give your total Being in service to the Spirit of all Life and you will feel your At-One-Ment with all. You then become the personification of Love and your radiance is seen and felt by all whom you encounter. You are then My Emissaries of Light and we *shall* light the world!

"As the Master Jesus said, 'Ye are the Light of the world,' and in the Light there is no darkness. So defile not your Light Temple with evil thoughts, or thoughts of negation and criticism, but *live* the Light. *BE* the Light and hide not the Light under a mantle of darkness. The Kingdom of Light is the Soul abode and earthly considerations are the darkness which obscures it. My Light is ever in you. Bring it forth and reveal this Truth to all my children. Reveal to each his GOD-SELF, for each is the vessel of My Spirit. Fill every mind with this realization and mankind will be lifted to a new dimension of life.

"The Chalice of My Being are you. Be filled to overflowing and pour your filled cup into the Chalice of My world, that all might be blessed and raised!

Yojana! Yojana! Yojana!"

THE · PRAYER · OF · THE · CHALICE

Father, to Thee I raise my whole being,
– a vessel emptied of self. Accept, Lord,
this my emptiness, and so fill me with
Thyself – Thy Light, Thy Love, Thy
Life – that these Thy precious Gifts
may radiate through me and over-
flow the chalice of my heart into
the hearts of all with whom I
come in contact this day
revealing unto them
the beauty of
Thy Joy
and
Wholeness
and
the
serenity
of Thy Peace
which nothing can destroy.

This beautiful prayer is available from its author
Frances Nuttall, BM/Flabellum, London W.C.1., England.
It is printed on a 5"x8" card suitable for framing,
@ 20¢ each, plus postage.

PART 3

CHAPTER 5

Proof of Life After Death

In our research we have investigated different instances of psychic phenomena with interesting results. Our account of one such instance was published in the December 1970 issue of Fate Magazine, and read as follows:

On June 26, 1970 we visited Mr. and Mrs. Wm. Nesbit in Newberry, Michigan, after having read in Fate magazine and various newspapers of the phenomenon of the filaments coming from the ring that had belonged to their son Roger who had been killed in Vietnam. We had a delightful visit with the Nesbit's and found them to be very sincere and gracious people. They told us a little about their son and also about the threads coming from the ring and other strange happenings about the home. Because we have had many wonderful things come on the Ouija board in our thirty years of research into metaphysical and occult mysteries, we had taken one with us. After we had talked for some time, they requested that we try the Ouija board to see if we could contact their son. We did this with the following result:

"My Dear Ma and Dad,

"How happy I am to be able to come to you. A wonderful new life for me now, but I am sad to see you feel so bad. It is not sadness for me, Dad, because I am really more alive than when I was there in my earth body. My body now is (made of) Light and I can move it wherever

I think I want to be. Life here is a life of happiness, except that I am sorry you are all so sad.

"I bring the threads (on the ring) to prove that I am living and it will make many people believe that their sons live. So it will be my way of helping the boys here and their loved ones there.

(The following refers to Capt. Robert Moroney, who also lost his life in Vietnam and made his first contact with his mother, Dorothy Davis, through our use of the Ouija board. He had called her Ma-Ma and had given his name as Robin. We had thought we were being fooled, but she then had told us that he had always called her Ma-Ma [French pronunciation] and that when he was a little boy she had called him Robin. We had known neither of these facts prior to his message. Mrs. Davis kept an account of the messages she received from Robert, and they were serialized in six issues of Chimes magazine under the title of 'Robin's Return.' Robert has told that he is now assisting the boys who are killed in battle as they make the transition into the spirit side of life.)

"Nellie and Ed, you will be happy to know that Bob Moroney is helping me. He was there to greet me when I was taken from my body. Bob is helping me right now, because he knows how to use this board."

(Mrs. Nesbit had told us that she also contacts Roger through automatic writing, and that it looks like his handwriting. Neither of them had known of this possibility, or anything about spirit manifestation prior to the beginning of the ring experience. Recently Roger had been telling her when they could expect the next phenomenon to occur. He had said that the threads would be out again on the following Sunday. She now asked if it would be possible for them to appear at this time, since we could not stay that long.)

He replied:

"Maybe. I am learning, here with Bob, and we are helping the boys who are killed in battle. Many of them come in confusion. Sometimes they do not even know where they are, or that they have left the body. Others are sad at leaving their family or the earth. They all have to learn to work their bodies here, and all have to find out the laws of this life. I am being taught by Bob and his helpers. We are all living to help the souls who come here, and to help the people there to realize that when a person dies there, they are born into a much happier and wider life. Death is only death to the body. We are just as much alive as we ever were, and we are no longer held down to a heavy body of earth vibration. We have a body that feels like a balloon and we can move it by wishing it to move. We are all learning the Laws of the Soul and I am finding that life is eternal and that we will go into new dimensions, or planes, or vibrations, by our learning and then helping others. I have learned that life is eternal, growing into a more wonderful knowledge of the universe, and that we will go from class-room to class-room of the Universe. Dad, my interest in (flying) saucers was good because I felt that the universe had life and that this could be (possible)."

At this time Mrs. Nesbit glanced over at the ring, which was on Mr. Nesbit's finger, and excitedly remarked that the threads were out. We stopped the Ouija board and all looked at the ring. The setting is rather massive and made of silver with embossed indentations in a Marine ensignia design.

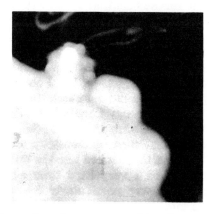

Coming from the ring, on one side of the setting, was a tuft of golden-colored, very fine, filaments. There were at least six of these in the tuft, all being about two to three inches long and standing straight up, with the exception of one which was at least four inches long. On the other side of the setting was a single strand about two inches long. They were all very strangely constructed, being exceedingly fine and almost infinitesimally wavy. We were interested in the explanation of this which a doctor friend of ours, who is a nuclear physicist, gave when we told him of this. His theory is that since the threads are undoubtedly condensed energy, we were no doubt seeing the wave length of the energy. After seeing the pictures which we took, this seems like a logical explanation.

Since many reporters and T.V. people had been having difficulty getting pictures of this, C.B.S. had left a camera and light there. They had asked the Nesbit's to photograph the ring the next time the phenomenon occurred. They now proceeded to do this. Mr. Nesbit placed his hand upon a pillow where the camera was focused and the camera ran for about two minutes. I also took pictures with an Instamatic 134. Because I felt that the pillow was too light as a background, and because I was not sure the T.V. light was right for my camera, I decided to take another picture. I placed my dark coat over the pillow and took a picture with just a flash bulb for lighting. This was my only picture in which the threads showed up, and they look entirely different than to see them with the naked eye. In the picture each filament is obscured by a white filmy substance that looks like the ectoplasm in spirit pictures which I have seen. It is much wider than the threads themselves. At first I was disappointed in the picture, but I am now convinced that, although the camera did not catch the filaments themselves, it captured the energy forcefield around them which we were unable to see with our eyes. So, to me, this is more positive proof of their authenticity as a manifestation of spirit than had they looked like the threads.

Mr. Nesbit has had a very hard time adjusting to the death of his son and was particularly distressed because the posthumous citation had stated that he had died from a wound in the stomach, and that he had stood to fight when others of his party had taken cover. The thought of the agony of such a death was very disturbing, and he wondered if death had come instantaneously, or if Roger had suffered greatly. He now asked that question and received this reply:

"Oh Daddy, don't think of that. It was over so fast that I didn't even feel it. I guess I was in such a state of excitement that I couldn't have felt anything. It was like being under hypnosis when we were in battle. All we thought of was to do the job. My friend Bob was right there, and he made me realize that I was no longer in my physical body."

(Mr. Nesbit then asked why he had not taken cover as some of the others had.)

"I guess it is like I said, I seemed to be like I was hypnotized, and only thought of what we were there to do. But Dad and Ma, it is better this way. I know this is hard for you, but I see the work that Bob and his army of Light Bearers do here to help the soldiers who come here, and I see the work they do to prove life after death; and I am sure that my life now, and the ring, will prove more to people, and make my life more worthwhile, than it ever could have been there. So don't grieve for me, just help me to use the ring to prove that life goes on."

(Mrs. Nesbit then asked if she should publish the things she had been receiving through automatic writing.)

"Oh Ma, that is wonderful. Thank you for doing it. Bob's mother has been so much help to many, and you can be too. We will bring this message to many and it will be a bridge for the many grieving parents and their sons. Can you believe that I TRULY LIVE? Because I am *really* here with you much of the time."

(The Nesbit's had told us that although the ring fits Mr. Nesbit's finger so tightly that he has great difficulty removing it, on three different occasions, upon awakening in the morning, they had found it gone from his finger and out in the dining room beside Roger's picture on the buffet. They had not mentioned that it had always been found around the neck of a tiny statue of Jesus which was in front of the picture, but which we had not seen, so the following answer was evidential to us.)

"Ma, the Light is put around the ring and it moves *to the statue* by my thought. We learn to use the Light. I can't explain it, but I am learning to use it.

"Keep happy Daddy. Please don't grieve for me. We have a lot of work to do together. If I can bring the threads and you can prove that I *live*, think what a blessing this will be to the world. This is my work now, please help me with it. I have no body to work with there, so you can be the body and the voice for me. Believe me, I am *closer* than when I was in the body and I AM LIVING!"

(Early that morning in the motel, I had been awakened with the words, "Take a rose to my mother with my love." I was not sure it had been Roger speaking, but we did take a beautiful American Beauty rose to her when we went to their home that morning. Mrs. Nesbit now asked if he had really asked to have it given to her.) He replied:

"It was for Mother's Day, but a little late. But Nellie did it for me. Keep a rose in the house for me. It is the symbol of love."

(Then Mrs. Nesbit told us that on Mother's Day the threads had come out on the ring and they had been shaped like little flowers. Roger had told her, through automatic writing, that it was a bouquet of roses from him. This again seemed very evidential to us.) We then thanked him for the demonstration on the ring. His answer was:

"Thank you for letting me come. Ma, we will bring this truth to the world and it will be wonderful. My life is going to be a blessing for the world. Your part will be a blessing for you, and for me, and for all who will become convinced of the truth of Eternal Life. Isn't it wonderful that we can give this proof to the world?

"Daddy you can do so much. This is one of the reasons we were all born into the same family. Our love for each other, my death in the physical, my connection with Bob, and now our demonstration (with the ring), will prove that death is only being born into a more beautiful world. Do not grieve for me, but be happy that I came here so we can bring this truth to the world. We are all very blessed. Carry on, do not care if people scoff. But

Daddy, please don't let grief spoil your life. Let my spirit give you strength. We have a wonderful work to do together, don't just grieve. Let us show the world the power of the risen spirit, for I AM RISEN, just as Jesus arose; and we will prove it."

(Ed asked if an Ouija board would be a better way for Mrs. Nesbit to contact him. She also asked if it is truly he who uses her hand for the automatic writing.)

"Ma will get it either way. Of course I do (the writing). I will bring many things as I learn. Remember, I am new at all this and I have to be taught, but I know there are many wonderful things to learn about life in many grades here. As I learn I will try to give it to you. So we will probably have lots of books, Ma. Just keep at it. This is going to be a great experience for all of us. We will probably have many happy years of contact this way. Then, when we are all together again, I hope that I will know enough about things here so I will be able to help you as much as you have helped me. Thank you both for letting me be your son, and for the love we had together. I love you all. The threads will be out again on Sunday the 28th. Thank you Ed and Nellie."

As we were about to leave there was a very loud rap on the wall near the stairway. We could not be sure that it was Roger, but the Nesbit's told us that at one time they were all in the kitchen and the record player had started by itself in the living room, playing a certain record that they associate with him. They also said that at one time he had appeared to his father, in a muddy combat suit. They had embraced and Roger had placed his head upon his father's shoulder, and they had both cried. When he had disappeared, Mr. Nesbit's shoulder was wet. On the previous Sunday, while Mr. Nesbit was taking communion in church, the threads had appeared. The priest had noticed them and commented about it as they had left.

With our picture as evidence, and having seen and felt the deep sincerity of both Mr. and Mrs. Nesbit, we are firmly convinced of the authenticity of this remarkable phenomenon.

Mrs. Nesbit has since written a book entitled "Roger's Phenomenal Ring." She tells us the threads still occasionally appear on the ring.

At other times we have been able to establish contact with the departed loved ones of some of our friends, bringing words of comfort and proof of the survival of the personality after so-called death. One dear friend, who knew very little about our work, lost her husband and needed proof that it was he whom we were contacting. She questioned him about what she did before retiring each night. He replied, "You kiss my picture." She said that was true and asked what else she did. She received the answer, "You also kiss my pillow." A fact that she then confirmed, about which we had known nothing. In one communication he gave the following words of wisdom:

"Love is the great power for good which lifts souls into higher frequencies. The more love you have and share, the greater help you are to the souls who need to grow.

"If the people of earth could see the effect of their loving thoughts and the effect of their hate-filled thoughts they would be amazed. Love in the heart and mind gives off a beautiful vibration which we can use for strength. It is a beam that is filled with Light and is very powerful. It seems to be an energy that we can enter into and use.

"Hate looks like a dark tornado and it swirls and twists and seems to destroy whatever it touches. Those who are caught up in it are like they are in a whirlpool from which they cannot seem to get out. They just go around and around in circles and get twisted and battered by the forces of hate. It if terrible to see the ones who are caught in hate, they suffer constantly. Hate is violent, but Love is healing and helpful. There is a big difference between Love given unselfishly and love which binds and holds. It is like pulling the wings off a butterfly if you hold the soul of a departed one in grief. The soul must be free to live and learn in its new dimension."

When contacting another departed friend, he told that

his two weeks of being in a coma before passing on had been a blessing, for while his physical body had lain in the hospital bed, his spirit had left the body and been thoroughly oriented in his new dimension. So, when he severed all connection with his body, he was able to function very effectively there.

My mother returned to say that at the time of her transition she had had a happy reunion with all of the loved ones who had preceeded her, and she stated, "I was also greeted by a company of white-robed Masters who walked with me into the Light. She says that her work now is to be a substitute mother to the very lonesome and homesick boys who have lost their bodies on the battlefields and are longing for their mothers, with whom they cannot make contact. Most of them, having left home when very young and it having been their first experience away from their mothers, find it difficult to adjust in their new dimension. She says she is "mothering" them until they are joined by their real mothers.

Recently my brother passed into the next dimension very suddenly. A few nights later he appeared at the bedside of my brother-in-law, who saw his face, very plainly, and the upper part of his body as a mist. He asked to have his love conveyed to all of the family and assured my brother-in-law that he was fine and that, "Everything is exactly as it is supposed to be." He also left a personal message for my other brother that referred to a boyhood joke they had shared.

My husband has also had the good fortune of clearing up three haunted houses. In one of the houses the rappings were so loud, and the manifestations so extreme, that the owners were going to let the house revert to the mortgage company and lose their equity. In each instance he was able to exorcise the invading spirit immediately by invoking the Christ Light and Presence and asking for Master Teachers to take the invader away and instruct it in the laws of soul progression.

PART 3

CHAPTER 6

QUOTATIONS FROM YOGANANDA

We have occasionally received messages from Yogananda and feel the following are especially beautiful and enlightening:

"Beloved, my love is as the dew that descends upon the flower at twilight and imparts its essence to the absorbent flower. All dear disciples are feeling my vibration, and I am helping you all to unfold the lotus of your hearts and minds. A great vibration of love I send to you and I am in the midst of your Being, for in the ocean of Oneness we are totally One. My vibration is a ripple being sent out which moves through each when he is attuned to me. Holy is the Divine Chalice of your being and it is filled to overflowing as you attune to the Spirit of Life and respond to it. All is Motion and Response in the Oneness and no thought is thought that is not felt by all. Give an impulse of love to Life, send its vibration throughout all Being, and you will harmonize all of creation. Thank you for seeking my Light and for responding to my love. Continue and we shall all be instruments of peace and harmony, that the Father-Mother-God can use to bring Man to his divine fulfillment as he is made aware of his Oneness and his mission. The fragrance of the Incense of Truth and Love I leave with you, my Beloved."

Yogananda explained that he had been assigned to one member of the group as his personal teacher. He stated

that when such an assignment is given it is binding upon
the teacher and he cannot leave the pupil until the pupil
has reached the state of Being that the assignment requires.
So, at times he lovingly chided and gave instructions as to
what must be done.

"Make love your most vital concern. You will understand love by being more loving, for love reveals more of
itself as you open yourself for giving and receiving it.

"Do not wander alone through the maze of life. You
can weave a web of love to encompass as many as you
wish to share in your life. You can weave a web of love,
or one of hatred and condemnation, and each will be equally binding but not equally pleasant or advantageous. You
have the choice.

"Prepare your heart and mind with understanding and
goodwill for everyone and love will follow."

"Have love and you have the key.

"With love you raise your frequency. This creates an
avenue for the Masters to come to you. When you indulge
in anger, resentment, criticism, or fear you keep your frequency at a low level. Spasmodic flashes of love are not
enough because the greater part of the aura is still impregnated with negative vibrations. The emanations from the
aura are the vibrations which attract forces from other dimensions to you. If your aura is filled with high, loving
vibrations you will attract highly advanced souls, but if
your aura is filled with negative vibrations you will attract
low grade entities who will confuse and impose their misunderstanding upon you. You must provide a clear channel if you would commune with the Masters. Your every
thought is registered in your aura and you create your
own channel of communication.

"I hope this will show you why there is sometimes difficulty in holding a Master teacher in conversation. The
others, you might say, slip in through the weak spots in
your auric field. You are making much progress, but I am
unable to fill your aura with enough love to neutralize the
power of your own mind's activity. You are required to

make a way ready. This is the job of the pupil. Then, when the line is open, we can instruct you. Remember, you must dial the phone before you can speak to your party. Love, compassion, understanding, kindness, and patience will fill your mind, soul, and aura with light. Then you will be in tune and you will have much revealed to you.

"Auras become murky and distorted when you allow yourself to become disturbed. Light will stabilize the aura. If you are loving and wise, you will open your minds to the Light. God's light perfects and heals all conditions but you must ask for it and be receptive to it. If you could see your auras when you are disturbed, you would be more careful. The aura becomes as a dark swirling cloud when all of the bodies are out of balance. The meshing of the bodies with each other is as necessary as the meshing of the gears of your car. You know how the gears would be destroyed if they were tearing each other apart. Your bodies, out of gear with each other, are also destroyed. Violent upheaval of the emotional body will strip the gears of the mental and physical bodies, chaos ensues and one becomes mentally, physically, and spiritually ill. Harmony comes only with love. The color of the aura must be kept favorable or you will attract demonic forces. They thrive in the violence within a murky aura, and they stimulate it into greater disturbance. Casting out demons is not a myth; it becomes very necessary if you have been unwise enough to allow them to attach themselves to you. Only the Light, which comes through love and understanding and wanting to live for the Divine, will insulate you against their power. Light dissolves darkness and promotes growth."

(Question by pupil—"How long will I be in the doghouse?")

"No one is ever kept from his Light any longer than he allows himself to be. Your teachers never punish by withholding their light or presence, but you are required to furnish the beam over which contact is made with them. If there is no beam from the heart, man is trapped in his own aura."

PART 3

CHAPTER 7

THE TEMPLE OF THE LIVING GOD

The experience in which I "became the Temple" kindled an interest to know more about the mystical significance of the temples which mankind has erected throughout the ages. I found that most of them have held much symbology, both in their structure and in their furnishings. Probably the most elaborate and symbolic was King Solomon's Temple in Jerusalem. I found the *Metaphysical Biblical Dictionary,* published by The Unity School of Christianity, Unity Village, Missouri, most helpful in understanding its symbology. There are two approaches to studying the Bible—the literal and the metaphysical. Undoubtedly the latter helps us to relate more personally to the stories we find there, and we can see the Bible as an account of "soul unfoldment" as well as an historical record. Most of the names and events have deeper inner meaning which is not generally recognized.

The pyramids, Moses' Tabernacle, Solomon's Temple, and many others, all depict the "inner" work of the Soul of Man as he journeys along his evolutionary Pathway to Christ Consciousness.

Paul wrote to the Corinthians (1 Cor. 6:19—2 Cor. 6: 16-19 and 7:1), "Know ye not that ye are the Temple of the Living God, and the Spirit of God dwelleth IN You." Man is a three-fold Being—body, mind, and Soul. Each aspect has its existence only in and by "The Spirit" which gives it life and being.

238 MYSTERIES OF LIFE

The body, with its various systems and organs, is a marvelous "unity of life." The mind, with its perceptive and creative faculties, its memory, reason, will, etc., has its existence in Divine Mind. The Soul, with its qualities of love, service, compassion, and appreciation of beauty, is an individualized expression of the Spirit.

Man has always sensed his own divinity, which has led to the erection of the great temples, but it is the requirement and the privilege of each individual to find his own "Inner Temple."

Preceding the building of Solomon's Temple was a long chain of events, with various people involved in them, all being symbolic of Soul unfoldment.

Moses (the drawing-out process, or the Law of the evolution of man's consciousness) led the Israelites (spiritual thoughts) out of the land of Egypt (a material state of consciousness) through the Wilderness (confusion) to the Promised Land (Christ Consciousness). Moses' Tabernacle was a tent (the transitory state of consciousness before one becomes established in Christ Consciousness). Moses went up onto the mountain (a high place in consciousness) for forty days and nights (a time for fulfillment). Here he made a Covenant with God and was given the Tablets of the Law (rules by which to live and the Divine Law of one's own Being) and specific instructions about the Tabernacle and how to build an Ark, which was to be the receptacle for the Tablets of the Law; the Pot of Manna (God's ever abundant supply), and the Rod of Aaron (the animating Spirit which had brought forth the "Living Waters" when used to strike the rock. The regeneration of all of man's faculties). The Ark was to be carried with the Israelites wherever they went (The Law, abundant supply, and the Spirit are everpresent *in* Man, no matter where he might be, or in what state of consciousness). Moses never reached the Promised Land; he only led the way and saw it from afar.

After a long series of rulers, among whom was Saul (personal Will), the Israelites came under the leadership of David (the Love Principle, Shepherd of the sheep, or materialistic and animalistic thoughts). David had been called, anointed, and taught by Samuel (spiritual discernment).

His great desire was to build a beautiful temple as the permanent abiding place (stabilized love consciousness) for the Ark, but his human characteristics often prevailed and he was beset by wars (inner conflict and confusion). He did not succeed in building the Temple, for love is not enough, but he did draw up the plans and he instilled his desire into his son Solomon (the intellect, wisdom, the ruling faculty that is established in peace).

When Solomon ascended to the throne, he ruled with intelligence and justice in a peaceful way. He (the Intellect) took the plans which had been given by Moses (the Law of Soul unfoldment) and David (the Love Principle), and proceeded to build the Temple (a regenerated state of consciousness.).

He called the Twelve Elders of the Tribes (man's inner forces and faculties) to work on the project, under the direction of Hiriam (the Christ Spirit). Together they built the most magnificent edifice ever erected. It covered 3/4 of an acre of land and cost over one billion dollars. Only the best of material was used; Cedars of Lebanon (pure thoughts and deeds), rare gems, etc. The entire structure, inside and out, was overlaid with gold (the Soul gives its best to the building of the Inner Temple).

When the Temple was completed, the Ark was brought from where David had kept it in the City of David, or Zion (the subconscious) to Jerusalem (the heart center and conscious awareness). Here it was placed in the Holy of Holies within the Temple.

The way in which the Temple was laid out is also symbolic of soul progression. One first enters into the Outer Court; the Gentiles (sensual and materialistic thoughts) can go only this far. Next comes the East Gate (seeking enlightenment). One also passes through the Pillars of Boaz and Jachin (to establish—by being receptive and obedient to the things of the Spirit). When reaching Solomon's Porch (a place of judgement and evaluation) the faculty of discernment is established and order is brought into one's life.

In the next courtyard one approaches the Sacrificial Altar (the burning away of material, sensual desires and emotions; transmutation; changing of the mind; obliterating

the carnal, animalistic consciousness). In Solomon's temple
this altar was thirty feet square and seven and one-half
feet high.

The Soul then proceeds to the Brazen Sea, the Laver for
cleansing. This contained 16,000 gallons of water and stood
upon a base of twelve brass Oxen (Man's twelve faculties—
Faith,Strength,Judgement,Love,Power,Imagination,Under-
standing, Will, Order, Zeal, Purity, and Life). All souls are
required to wash in the Laver before they can proceed into
the Inner Sanctum, using the "water of the Spirit" to cleanse
the consciousness they must accept spiritual ideas, and with
spiritual Desire wash away all of the contamination of the
outer world. One must prepare himself for greater spiritual
experiences.

Beyond the Laver is the first veil. It parts and the prepared Soul approaches the altar where the incense is burning (the rising Essence of Being, holy thoughts, prayer,
spiritual desires and aspiration).

To the right of the incense altar is the table upon which
are the twelve loaves of shewbread (man's five senses and
seven psychic centers, all spiritualized and divinely prepared to be partaken of and assimilated into the consciousness). To the left is the candelabra holding the seven candles
(the seven notes of human expression). When the Soul has
learned all of the lessons of the Human Octave and has
become purified, it BECOMES the LIGHT upon each note.
With all of the candles lighted, the chamber is filled with
Light and one is ready to enter into the Holy of Holies.

The Sacrificial Altar, the Laver, the Incense Altar, the
Table of Shewbread, and the seven Candles have formed a
cross, the top of which is Golgotha (place of the skull),
where the material mind and the intellect are transcended
and the Soul ascends into Christ Consciousness.

Now the Second Veil is parted, by ILLUMINATION,
and the Soul enters into the Holy of Holies. Only the High
Priest (one's highest level of consciousness, the Christ Self,
the I AM) may enter here. In this holy sanctuary the Soul
finds the innermost recesses of its Divine SELF, for upon
the Sacred Altar is the Ark of the Covenant. The Ark contains the Divine Promise and Law of one's Being (to bring

forth the I AM). This is the fulfilling of the Law and the Covenant, for God's promise to Moses was everpresent Manna, Regeneration through the "Waters of the Spirit," and the Law.

Surrounding the Ark is the Shekinah Glory (the Eternal, Divine, Fulfilling, Light; No more darkness). Here the Soul may always come to be enlightened, renewed, and fulfilled. This is all watched over by the Golden Cherubim (Omnipresence, power, and protection of God). The Soul is finally sealed in the Divine Covenant and stands in the radiance of its own Divinity. Jeremiah 31:33—"This shall be the Covenant that I will Make with the House of Israel (the spiritualized consciousness) after these days; saith the Lord. I will put MY LAW in their inward parts and write it in their hearts, and will be their God and they shall be my people."

Man is the Master Builder of his own divine "Inner Temple" as he purifies his consciousness and identifies himself in total At-One-Ment with the "Father within." As evolving souls we are building a "Temple not built with hands," in which we can always find the answers to our problems and the necessary strength and love to solve them, no matter in what dimension we may be functioning.

Temple of the Living God

Father, I thy Temple art,
For thou abidest in my heart.

This Temple, beautiful beyond compare,
Was built by Thee, with love, so fair.

Within this ARK will ever be
Thy wondrous Covenant with me.

Bathed in Shekinah glory I now stand,
Perfected by thy loving hand.

Purified by thy great Light,
May I be perfect in thy sight.

Body, Mind and Soul, all three,
I dedicate, in love, to Thee.

Amen.

PART 4

CHAPTER 1

MORE PERSONAL MYSTICAL EXPERIENCES

Since our contact with Keeper of the Flame, I have had several mystical experiences which seem to have Cosmic dimensions. In these I seemed to be projected into situations in which I was either shown, or experienced, great revelation. They follow, just as they were taken from tape recordings made during class where I experienced them.

TO *KNOW* IS TO *BE*!

Nellie relates what is being shown:
I seem to be in a beautiful garden. There is a pool with a lovely tree beside it. The tree is laden with golden fruit, like apples, except for the color. I think it is symbolic of the Tree of Life.

I have a very strange sensation. I feel as if I were taking all of this into myself and then being compressed as I find myself being pulled into a spinning vortex. Now I seem to BE the seed of the fruit. I FEEL the consciousness of the seed as the Life Force begins to move within it. Now there is a feeling of expansion, a doubling and redoubling, but the same "knowingness" is within each segment as reproduction takes place. There is an irresistable "force" which seems to be propelling this.

Now a root system and stalk is extending, which grows and grows, sending out branches and bearing fruit. I am feeling each individual part of this, yet it is all One. It

243

seems that this is the "Divine Principle" causing what was my "innate knowingness,"as the seed, to come forth into manifestation. While this is happening, an assimilation process is also going on. As my roots go down and my tendrils go up, I absorb moisture and minerals from the soil, and light and energy from the sun. This is all absorbed, synthesized, and transmuted, so this too is ONE. There is a tremendous sense of ONENESS, and KNOWINGNESS, and BEINGNESS. It is as if I were the very heart of LIFE. As I merge with the water, which is being absorbed, I *become* ALL water, I *become* ALL minerals, I now go farther and become the hydrogen and oxygen molecules as they feel attracted to each other to become water, yet I am still ONE with everything else. I am the energy of the SUN, and that from which it came. I AM LIGHT, I AM ENERGY, One and the same with ALL LIFE, EVERYWHERE. I AM Energy, yet I AM the MIND which formulates energy into its various expressions. I AM the KNOWING FACULTY, and *BY* the *KNOWING, I AM*. It is by the very fact that I KNOW that I AM. Whatever I have the consciousness of *knowing*—I AM. So, *I AM* ALL things, I AM the seed of All, I AM the fulfillment of All, I AM THAT I AM! Wherever I pinpoint my consciousness, *That* I AM!

Now there are swirls and swirls of pure light energy. It has no color, just white. When I take on the consciousness of the seed, that consciousness is clothed in this energy, and the seed comes into manifestation. When I assume the consciousness of the tree, or the sun, the energy forms itself into these. Whatever I seem to pinpoint my consciousness as, the energy forms into that around me and I AM that. I feel that I can be anything, or ALL things, just by the KNOWING, for Divine Energy molds itself around that which I KNOW, and that becomes manifest in the world of form.

Keeper of the Flame:

"Beloved Lights, you have been shown this picture that you might understand that whatever is in the consciousness is indeed brought into manifestation. Whatever one is, *in consciousness,* whether it be in the human form, the Christed state, or the lesser kingdoms, becomes manifest. So, if you would change your lives and grow in understanding, you must first *become* the new *in consciousness.* Then the energy of the universe forms itself into that State of Being. This is REALITY, this is the whole crux of BEING! That which you KNOW becomes manifest for you, be it positive or negative, wittingly or unwittingly, it is *your* creation. There is but ONE Life, ONE Mind, and you are ONE with it. Whatever portion of Divine Mind you identify with, THAT is what you ARE.

"This is the 'Knowingness' which we would have you understand and attain. KNOW that you ARE divine. KNOW that ALL power IS yours. KNOW that there is no place for inharmony or negativity in the Love Consciousness, for it is Love that fulfills all life. LIFE MUST conform to whatever pattern is held for it. Therefore, *you are the creator of all which you hold in consciousness!* Your state of Being is that which *you* have conceived and created. Catch the vision of the Divine Life, and use it as the mold to be fulfilled *in* you. Beloved, you ARE the Creator of your own environment and circumstances, but, you are also UNIVERSAL and you can experience ALL that is within the universe as you grow in understanding and in your ability to KNOW AND IDENTIFY. You move through many cycles; as you unfold you catch the broader vision, and this then becomes the pattern for the next step.

"This *KNOWING* is a true mystical experience which it is hoped each of you will have, for when you have perceived and experienced that 'the KNOWING *IS* the REALITY,' you will be able to use this knowledge in bringing about your Divine fulfillment which only comes into manifestation after it has been established in the consciousness.

"In your quiet moments, identify yourselves with something, as we have done this evening with the seed. *FEEL it so completely that you become* it. This is an exercise in Awareness. As you use this exercise, you will find that you can grow from the awareness of lesser things into the more advanced states of Christ Consciousness and Being.

This will be a gradual unfoldment but it can be done. This has been shown that you might learn the process of IDENTIFICATION and its consequent expanding into greater KNOWING and BEING.

"As you learn to *BE* the outer expression of your true DIVINE SELF, you will ultimately know that you *ARE* Divine Energy, Divine Mind, and Divine Creativity Itself!

"Yojana! Yojana! Yojana!"

CHART

THE SOUL'S PROGRESSION
NUMERICALLY, GEOMETRICALLY,
AND IN STATES OF
CONSCIOUSNESS

THE SOUL'S PROGRESSION NUMERICALLY, GEOMETRICALLY, AND IN STATES OF CONSCIOUSNESS

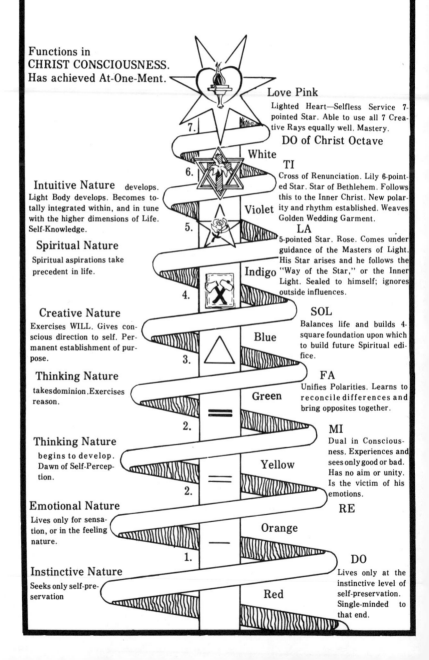

Functions in
CHRIST CONSCIOUSNESS.
Has achieved At-One-Ment.

Love Pink
Lighted Heart—Selfless Service 7-pointed Star. Able to use all 7 Creative Rays equally well. Mastery.

DO of Christ Octave

7.

White
6.

TI
Cross of Renunciation. Lily 6-pointed Star. Star of Bethlehem. Follows this to the Inner Christ. New polarity and rhythm established. Weaves Golden Wedding Garment.

Intuitive Nature develops.
Light Body develops. Becomes totally integrated within, and in tune with the higher dimensions of Life. Self-Knowledge.

Violet

LA
5-pointed Star. Rose. Comes under guidance of the Masters of Light. His Star arises and he follows the "Way of the Star," or the Inner Light. Sealed to himself; ignores outside influences.

Spiritual Nature
Spiritual aspirations take precedent in life.

5.

Indigo

4.

SOL
Balances life and builds 4-square foundation upon which to build future Spiritual edifice.

Creative Nature
Exercises WILL. Gives conscious direction to self. Permanent establishment of purpose.

Blue
3.

FA
Unifies Polarities. Learns to reconcile differences and bring opposites together.

Thinking Nature
takes dominion. Exercises reason.

Green

2.

MI
Dual in Consciousness. Experiences and sees only good or bad. Has no aim or unity. Is the victim of his emotions.

Thinking Nature
begins to develop.
Dawn of Self-Perception.

Yellow

2.

RE

Emotional Nature
Lives only for sensation, or in the feeling nature.

Orange

1.

DO
Lives only at the instinctive level of self-preservation. Single-minded to that end.

Instinctive Nature
Seeks only self-preservation

Red

PART 4

CHAPTER 2

THE SOUL'S PROGRESSION NUMERICALLY, GEOMETRICALLY, AND IN STATES OF CONSCIOUSNESS

Nellie is shown the Spiral and symbols.

Keeper of the Flame:

"Beloved: As you grow in understanding and are able to encompass more of Truth and Light, there are facets, as yet untold to you, of the symbology of the Life of Man as he travels through the Human Octave of Expression. There is a direct relationship in Man's nature to all that is in the universe, for all moves in numerical and geometrical progression, even in the unseen areas upon other planes of life. Numerical and geometric order is ever present, for it is the Divine Law by which ALL things progress, unfold, and move into new vibrational rates and states of Being.

"As Man embodies and works upon the first three notes of the Human Octave, he functions upon the first note in a purely instinctive way, through his Instinctive Nature, seeking only self-preservation. On the next two notes he functions only upon a two-dimensional level. In other words, he knows only duality. He considers all things as either good or bad by how they seem to affect him. He finds no compromise and no unity between these two aspects of his nature, his environment, or his experience. He sees only these two facets of himself and functions in his emotional nature, therefore he is dual in his consciousness. Although he is a part of the ONENESS, his dual consciousness makes him numerically two. Geometrically, he is also two, for his nature is such that he sees only in two straight lines, good or bad, and the two are destined never to meet as long as this is his level of consciousness and his attitude toward life.

"As he experiences Life in the complexity of his duality, he begins to analyze his experiences and develop another quality. Where he previously had functioned only in his Instinctive and Emotional natures, now his Thinking nature is stimulated. He begins to try to unify the opposites in his life and directs his thinking to bring the opposites together in some kind of workable and happy combination. He then becomes a three-fold Being numerically. Geometrically, he becomes triangular as his new line of direction brings the opposites together. He now moves into the note of FA upon the Human Octave.

"Gradually, as he analyzes and reasons upon his experiences, he achieves a more balanced life. He begins to exert his WILL to build a firmer, balanced, foundation for his life. Thus, he becomes a four-fold, four-square Being, and moves into the note of SOL. He then lays the foundation for that spiritual edifice which he begins to erect as he moves on in understanding and in States of Being. He becomes 'The Builder' and his Creative Nature comes into domination.

"When he has exerted his WILL to build a firm foundation and has balanced his life, he starts to build upward. He then becomes a five-fold Being. He builds the Pentagram and becomes the five-pointed Star. Now, on the note of LA, he starts to concentrate on his spiritual unfoldment. He catches a glimpse of the 'Higher Self' and begins to direct his energies to becoming a 'New Being.' He assumes the 'Way of the Star,' for he will now follow the 'Inner Light' which has come over the horizon of his consciousness, and it will lead him forward into new areas of expression and new States of Being. He begins to consciously utilize his Creative Faculty to build purposefully and enduringly. He now realizes that he is a Creative Being and, by his own direction, he will build his new spiritual edifice, using all of his creative powers to this end. He becomes the five-pointed Star and is no longer subject to that which comes to him from the 'outside world' but follows the 'Inner Light' and knows that this is his course from now on. It is at this note that he comes under the guidance and tutelage of the Masters of Light, for they recognize that he is now dedicated and sincere. He develops a 'Love Consciousness' which becomes his 'Light' and which he begins to radiate. From him emanates love, peace, harmony, purity, and service, for he realizes that he no longer lives for himself alone, but to serve a nobler purpose, and that there is a Divine Principle within himself which he must bring forth and serve. As he works consciously in this direction, he gradually becomes the six-pointed Star, the Star of Bethlehem, the Human and Divine integrated into ONE. He has become sealed unto himself, open and receptive to only the higher nature of himself and to the Divine Messengers of Light. He has formed the avenue by which Divine in-pouring and total At-One-Ment can take place. He is now on the note of TI. His intuitive faculties and nature develop and he is able to 'tune in' at will to the higher vibrational levels. His physical nature, mental nature, and emotional nature, all become ONE with the Spirit WITHIN. Geometrically, he becomes the six-pointed star, and numerically, he becomes six, with all of his bodies active and functioning in perfect alignment with each other. He has now woven the Golden Wedding Garment, or Robe of Light, and becomes ONE with his Divine Self. His Star glows ever brighter for it is 'The Star of Bethlehem' which beckons all of his lower nature forward in search of 'The Christ,' or 'The Buddha,' or 'Atma'—it matters not what term is used. It is that DIVINE SELF that is totally wedded to the Divine Creative Principle, which now brings forth only Divine offspring of thought, word, and deed. This is Man's final note of Human Expression, the note where he becomes ready to function as a 'Christed Being.' Mastery is achieved!

"Now he has established a new focal point for his rhythmic cyclic pattern. He has completed the Human Octave and now comes a more rapid and intense frequency—He has raised His vibration into that closed "inner circle"—No longer is his consciousness circulating in a wide orbit, encompassing the mundane and negative aspects of life. He is focalized in the 'Indwelling Mind and Spirit.' This vibration is of such intensity that it carries great power—healing power, mental power, and power of abundance and peace, for he is a Master. By establishing himself in his new vibration, he becomes the Seven-pointed Star. He then functions as a 'Christed One' in total realization of his At-One-Ment, with all the powers of that At-One-Ment. Here he is in command of, and unified with, the Seven Creative Rays and moves freely upon any Ray in which he chooses to serve. Therefore, he becomes a seven-fold Being. This is the note of DO of the Christ Octave.

"This, Beloved, is the Divine use of Divine Power. Can you not see how it is impossible for one to have this power until they have first 'Become' it within themselves? This is what happens 'within' Man, not outside of him. It is his own unfoldment, his own 'BECOMING.' He moves through and BECOMES each new facet of 'Being'—ever more comprehensive, ever greater, until he becomes that beautiful 'Diamond of Perfection,' a many faceted GEM which reflects the Light of the Divine into all areas of life.

"This is your destiny! Become so totally sealed to the Divine within you that your Star arises. Then follow it until it leads you to the 'Indwelling Christ,' your Star of Hope, Star of Love, Star of Light, and Star of Life. In this you are perfected and raised until your Light becomes a beacon to all.

"Yojana! Yojana! Yojana!"

At the next class session more symbology was given.

Nellie relates what she is experiencing:

I find myself back in the beautiful temple where I have been before. All of the rainbow colors are again scintillating between the enormous pillars and the whole place is suffused with their light. Each color is shimmering, dancing, and sparkling. The only word I have for this is LIVING LIGHT, because it is not like the light to which we are accustomed. Now I see the same altar where I knelt before. Perhaps I should tell a little of my former experience here. As I knelt at this altar before, it seemed that I WAS the temple of the Living God, yet I could see, within this temple of myself, the Soul of myself kneel at the altar and receive a benediction as I knelt in obeisance to the Divine of Myself.

I am here at the same altar, but this time it is different for it is shaped like a cross. Growing up in front of it comes a beautiful, full-blown Easter lily. The cup of the lily almost covers the arms of the cross, although I can still see the ends of them. A great shaft of light now comes and illuminates the whole thing. It floods down and all of the colors seem to merge into one pure white light focalized on the altar. Now I seem to be moving into the heart of the Lily........

Keeper of the Flame:

"Beloved: You are being shown the initiation of those who become totally merged with the Divine SELF, and have renounced the ego 'self.' The Lily is the Cosmic symbol of total renunciation, and of the giving up of the lesser self into the service of the Divine, or Universal.

"You have experienced several initiations, for initiations come as one travels the Pathway to perfection. As you have gone through the many facets of your life there have been different initiations of a lesser nature perhaps, and you have not always been aware of them as being initiations. But, each time the Soul attains a realization, in such measure that it changes its attitudes and the course of its life for the better, initiation takes place on the Cosmic level of one's Being.

"At your last meeting you were given the numerical and geometric symbology as you move up the spiral of unfoldment at its different levels and keynotes. Tonight you will learn of more symbology.

"The Lily has six petals and is the symbol of the Soul who has become the six-pointed Star, or has made the complete integration of the human with the Divine Self. You were told to follow the 'Way of the Star'. Many years ago you were given the symbology of the five-pointed Star and you received the 'Initiation of the Star' as the Rose elongated to become the Star. When one is on the level of the five-pointed Star, he brings into flower the Rose of Love and Understanding, mostly for his own unfoldment for he still has much work to do within himself to become the Personification of Love. As the 'Rose' grows and gives of its perfume, and as he dedicates himself in loving service, he brings the six-pointed Star into manifestation and moves into a new keynote. Always, as he moves through the various notes, his vibrational frequency of Being increases, and he adds faculties which were not there previously. As one becomes totally integrated into the six-pointed Star, his intuitive faculties open, and he establishes the route for direct communication and impregnation from the frequencies of the Christ Octave. As these energies, or vibrations, combine with his own he is raised in consciousness, in his vibrational rate, and in his state of Beingness. He becomes totally integrated, the human with the Divine, nevermore to be separated.

"Each initiation is merely the beginning of a new state of activity. Whether you accept the challenge and do the work required is entirely up to you. As you cultivate the Lily of Renunciation this does not mean that you will step out of the human realm, or withdraw yourself from human activities. In fact you will undoubtedly become more involved; but you will give all of your activities and associations the benefit of your selflessness in love and understanding, without thought of recompense or spiritual gain. He who becomes the purity of the Lily lives only to serve, and it is only in this service that he becomes a 'Christed Being' and is able to 'graduate' from the Human Octave of Expression.

"The floral symbol of the five-pointed Star is the Rose, full-blown and giving of its perfume of Love. When you have achieved complete At-One-Ment, the Lily blooms upon your cross, for you will have walked the 'Way of the Cross,' you will have surrendered yourself totally in self-renunciation. Henceforth, you live only to serve, with no thought of self. A Master does not live to revel in his own Mastery; he lives only that the Power, Light, and Love which he has become might be freely given to all whom he meets, in total service and humility.

"To complete the symbology: We spoke earlier of the seven-pointed Star of the 'Christed Being,' those who function in the Christ Octave of Expression. There are those of this quality who have chosen to inhabit a physical body to be of greater service to humanity such as the Master Jesus, Buddha, and many others. The seven-pointed Star has for its symbol, the Heart with the Flame of Love burning brightly within it. This is what you are moving toward as you accept the Initiation of the Cross with the full-flowering Lily upon it. The work does not end here. As you prove your diligence and serve with the Masters, the heart becomes ignited with the Fire of Divine Love, and you move into the beautiful expression of a 'Christed Being,' who is crowned and henceforth carries the LIGHT through all future dimensions *within* yourself, for you will have BECOME the LIGHT. The heart is the Life-Center, and when it is aflame with Divine Love, one moves rapidly into the higher dimensions of life.

"May the Lily of purity so bloom that all who see your actions, hear your words, and feel your presence, are aware that you are an integrated Star of Light, Love Personified!!

"Yojana! Yojana! Yojana!"

PART 4

CHAPTER 3

THE RIDDLE OF THE SPHINX

Nellie relates what is being shown:

I am back in ancient Egyptian times. I see great temples and palaces. All kinds of people are running hither and thither. They seem to be extremely materialistic minded. They are furiously pursuing materiality and there is a great deal of sensuality among them.

I see huge, ornate palaces and temples with high arched, columned doorways. Beside the columns of each entryway stands a carved statue of a full sized lion. This is not very pleasant and I am not happy in this environment. I do not understand the significance of the lions except that they seem to represent strength and power. I do not know the moral of this, except that it is a very earthy, materialistic society that I seem to be in and I do not want to stay here.

Now I find myself walking in the desert. This is strange, because I seem to see myself walking ahead of myself.

I see a lonely, solitary figure in a long white garment walking and leaving each track in the sand. I see this objectively, and yet I know that it is I. Still it is not only I; this is every man on his lonely trek through life, for each walks alone in spite of how many may surround him physically. This figure is now surrounded by swirling sand as a great wind comes up and erases all of the foot-prints. I realize that as I walk this way there must be no living in the past or retracing of footsteps, only a pressing *on*. This is a very lonely pathway which each soul walks as he leaves the realm of materiality behind and steps out into the wilderness, not knowing exactly where he is going. I do not seem to know where I am going, I only know that I have this awful feeling of aloneness. I know that I had to leave the city, for I was not happy there, but I have not found whatever it is that I am looking for. In spite of the loneliness, I know that I must search on.

Finally, in the distance I see the Sphinx. As I approach it I realize that here too is a LION, but with a human head. This seems to be a lioness, the female of the species, which must have some significance.

I recognize this as the bestial lower nature of Man. It seems to crouch, ready to spring. It seems to be portraying its protective attitude toward its offspring. I remember that it is the lioness who catches prey to feed her young. It is she who guards and protects her offspring against all who would molest or destroy them. I interpret this to mean that Man's materialistic mental and desire natures, which have brought forth his cherished material possessions and his sensual revelry, fiercely stand guard over their offspring. They protect and nurture them, and prey upon others to sustain them. I recognize that these are my own characteristics, as a materialistic human being, as well as those of most of mankind. I realize that the "desire nature" will do most anything to keep the seeker from entering into the "Inner Temple," which can be entered only by passing the Sphinx and recognizing its significance. I know that this lion is also a symbol of great POWER, which must be converted into constructive, rather than destructive use. I must pass this creature if I am to enter the Great Temple which lies just ahead.

Again, I am in the "Inner Chamber of the Ghizeh Temple." Again, I see the altar with its twelve steps which I, as Man, must climb. I realize again the symbology of this. On the three lower steps I must overcome the lower aspects of my nature, then I must move into Self-realization and finally, into the higher levels where I become the personification of Love and Service. Again, the lighted brazier stands on top of the altar. I see this as the Divine Fire of Purification. It seems that, if I am to become totally perfected, I must place myself upon this brazier. Again this is an objective experience, for I see myself placing the "Lion" of myself into the brazier. Upon this pure altar, the epitome of which is Love and Service, is now burned away all of the bestial, materialistic, lower tendencies of the human nature. The Lion Power is now transmuted, by the Divine Fire, from the lower into the higher. When it is finished, I am free of carnality, materiality, and earthly desire.

I now descend the twelve steps, but I go in a different awareness and understanding. I now know that although I walk through various levels of human consciousness I am not a part of them, but I have no revulsion for those who still function there, only love. I understand that whatever they are doing, or going through, is all a part of their unfoldment, and that those things must be experienced to bring them into Divine Awareness.

I find myself again in front of the Sphinx. This may sound facetious, but I am laughing in its face, and saying, "You have no secrets from me now, I know your 'riddle.' You have kept your secret over these many centuries, but I know your secret. You are only the facade that Man has erected before his own eyes, which causes him not to recognize his own Divinity, but IT IS THERE, he only needs to overcome his lower nature to find it." In the *overcoming* he grows in spiritual power. Now the power, which the lioness represents, is to be utilized just as ferociously as before, but it now guards and sustains the spiritual aspects of Man.

I now return to the city. I see the people still coming and going, apparently still bent upon their same pursuits. But now, as I see the lions at the entrances of the temples and palaces, each of them has a *pair of wings*. I recognize that for me, as Man, they are now *spiritual* power, rather than merely power as they once seemed to be. I can now go through any portal, and it is guarded by spiritual power.

I know that this is Man's great work, he *must* come to this realization and, when he does, he can walk anywhere and doorways are always opened and guarded for him.

Materiality has no power over him, but he can use it constructively for the good of all, and he can translate his mental powers into activities that will be helpful and uplifting to all.

The LION has taken on great symbology. Now *winged*, it is the POWER of SPIRIT, to be used by all who are aware of it.

There are those who will not see, who are blind to the wings on the lions. They will use their power materially or destructively, but for the one whose eyes are open, all the portals are guarded and ALL Truth, Light, Love, and Power becomes *his*. He moves into ever new, ever expanding, understanding and use of his Divine Power.

Keeper of the Flame speaks:

"Beloved, you have been shown the symbol of the power that comes to the one who earnestly seeks understanding. Each must follow the lonely pathway to find and overcome *his* Sphinx. Another cannot do this for you. The Sphinx gives up its secret to all who will fearlessly face the materialistic, the bestial, the carnal within himself, and overcome it. Then he has the power to move fearlessly, with the 'Winged Power of the Spirit,' to do all that is necessary on his upward journey.

"Yojana! Yojana! Yojana!"

The preceeding, and the following, are almost overwhelming in their significance. In spite of much verification of guidance and revelation, I never cease to be amazed and elated when something as obvious as this occurs.

As soon as this meditation period was over and I was back to my normal state of awareness, Julia Norgaard, a member of our group, handed me a beautiful Egyptian medallion on a heavy gold chain. It is about 2x3 inches in size and made of hammered brass with greenish overtones. On it is the very thing which the entire lesson had been about, a WINGED LION! Julia had been sitting with it in her hand during the entire transmission but had said nothing to me about it, since she had arrived just as the meeting had started, and we had not had time for any conversation.

She said that while shopping the day before she had a few minutes to spare so had stepped into the art museum. There she had been drawn to the counter where objects were for sale. She had been fascinated by the medallion and felt a great rapport with it, even sensing that it might be meaningful about a previous lifetime. She said she just *had* to have it, so had purchased it. She had wondered about its symbology, so had brought it to class, thinking that if she held it she might 'receive' something about it.

Later the same evening we received the following from the Keeper of the Flame:

"Julia was motivated to the medallion as another bit of proof. Proof of my presence and thereby proof of my Linking, and the work to be done. Wings of Power will be yours for *I am with you.* With the transmutation of the power from the material aspect to the spiritual of Man, he flies into spiritual heights. With Wisdom and Love he then raises all who will accept his Light."

We had been so excited about the Winged Lion that we had given little thought to the symbol on the reverse side of the medallion, but had casually interpreted it as being symbolic of the unfolding of consciousness. It is somewhat abstract, like a set of wings, a fanned tail with seven feathers, and a crowned head. In the next class session we received this interpretation of it:

"You were given the symbology of the 'Winged Lion' which is the 'Power of Spirit.' The opposite side of the medallion bears the symbol of the 'Winged Spirit,' or 'Winged Soul.' This is the ancient symbol of Osiris. It symbolizes what is called the 'BA.' It represents the Soul ascending on wings. Those of the ancient Order of Osiris know this symbol well, for it represents the 'everlastingness' of the Soul which arises to ever new heights. It is the symbol of the Phoenix which arises from the ashes of itself as it is transformed into the new. The BA, Phoenix, or Soul, moves on into ever new experiences and expression, leaving behind all that it has outgrown, discarding all that is irrelevant to its New State of Being, pressing forward into more glorious expressions of life.

"How wondrous to recognize the eternally unfolding NEWNESS as being always ahead of you. How could one be bored with life, or claim to have reached the epitome of life, if they understand this FACT of life? Life should be a JOYOUS ADVENTURE! Remember the joyousness of your youth, when you were always looking forward to exciting new things? If man could only have this same exuberance, the same joyous sense of expectancy about his eternal unfoldment, he would be able to dispose of the lethargy, chronic disenchantment, and disappointment which he now suffers. You are not limited to a few years upon the earth plane, you are ETERNAL BEINGS, moving forward into glorious and wondrous experiences which can be very exciting if you will but look forward to them. TAKE HOLD OF LIFE AND LIVE IT JOYOUSLY!

"Yojana! Yojana! Yojana!"

PART 4

CHAPTER 4

REVERSING THE POLARITY

About two weeks prior to this experience I had been awakened in the middle of the night and had been asked if I would like to be taken into a different dimension. I had expressed the desire to do so but in the excitement my heart had begun to pound. I was then told that the time was not right, but that I must learn to "Reverse the Polarity." I had pondered on this but was unable to understand what it meant.

Nellie relates what is being shown:
I seem to be in the same temple where I witnessed the procession of Egyptian-like figures bearing lighted scepters. Again they are moving down a gradual incline and are walking in double file away from me.

I feel that I must join them. We move down a long corridor. I follow them but I walk alone. As they move to the lower level they separate into single file, one line going to the left, the other to the right. As I reach the place where they separated, I am confronted by a huge door. The same figure stands here who handed us the lighted scepter, the Keeper of the Flame. He opens the door, and we enter the chamber.

I see what seems to be a coffin, but I am told, "Fear not, I have told you that I am with you. For the Soul to arise, the material must be laid aside. Fear not, to leave the material is to ascend into the glories of Light. My peace attends you!" Now I place myself in the coffin—he touches my hand and I seem to float. I look down and see that I am leaving the material world. I am as light as air. There is an opening at the top of this room. A long shaft of light comes down, and I ascend through this shaft. I go up and out, then continue up and up. I feel that I am only Light and I am free—Free—FREE! I move OUT—a ball of Light seems to be approaching, first a pinpoint then larger and LARGER. We seem to be on a collision course!

Keeper of the Flame speaks:

"Beloved, you have just witnessed the 'Ascension of the Soul' into the ONENESS of the Light of the Universe—the small self lost in the Divine SELF, where you become AT-ONE with Me. Together we then traverse the universe, revealing its laws that you might know more of the great wonders that are yours to explore.

"Great is the Light, great is the Truth which is revealed. Engaging in the operation of the LAW helps one to understand what takes place in the ONENESS. Each of you must accept the Scepter of the Flame. You must accept the Light and Truth that is to become manifest in My world, and you must help others to understand; for Man cannot work consciously *with* the Law until it is revealed *to* him. You must understand this Divine Principle:

"Life is Power! Life is Light! Life is constantly projecting facets of itself into the cyclic patterns of creation and involving itself in form. Spirit moves through all of creation, descending into ever lower frequencies, serving a time in matter, or form, and returning through its various dimensions into its ONENESS where it adds to the great Cosmic Body of Light that which has been learned in its sojourn through the many planes, or densities.

"Within the ONE Life is the activity between the two polarities of Life, the Masculine and the Feminine. The Masculine moves itself upon the Feminine, that out of that union might be conceived and born the various manifestations of Life in all densities. It makes its descent into the lower levels of vibration in a spinning, spiraling fashion. As it comes to a point of rest, or union, impregnation of the Feminine Principle takes place and various forms are brought into manifestation, depending upon the frequency level at the time of the arrestment and union with the Feminine aspect. Within the Feminine Principle is the seed, or pattern, of that which is to be brought into manifestation. The Eternal Flame impregnates the seed pattern to bring forth *all* manifestation.

"This is *one* arc of the cyclic pattern which the Life Force takes.

"It then continues through the period of gestation, Becoming, and BEING, and completes a *second* and a *third* arc.

"Having moved through the world of form, it makes a final, or *fourth* arc through the higher vibrations to return itself to its undifferentiated state. It has now completed the *figure Eight*, and becomes the TOTALITY of Being, for it has been consummated by its own inner unification of polarities. It has descended, conceived, matured, and moved through the entire cycle of Creativity.

"Beloved, you do this also. As Soul, you descend into the world of form, moving through its many phases and learning its lessons. You then return into the ONENESS of ALL, but bringing with you a completeness, a fulfillment, a knowingness, which could be gained in no other way.

"Having come into the world of form, it is only through DESIRE and WILL that one raises himself back into the higher levels of consciousness. Many are trapped, because of the lack of Desire and Will, and should they leave the body in this state of consciousness they are confined to the Astral Plane, held there by their Emotional Bodies and their earthly desires. It is only by Spiritual Desire and Will that the earth plane is transcended, and one moves into their unfoldment in the higher dimensions.

"Knowing this LAW, you can understand the operation of Polarity in all dimensions. The Masculine force of Life, the Fire of God, the Divine Atomic Flame, the ETERNAL FLAME, seeks consummation in union with its opposite polarity, the Feminine force of Life, the Divine Mother, and engenders ALL of Creation. This LAW is equally in operation upon the physical, mental, and spiritual levels.

"There is another aspect of this which you should understand:

"While this power is Masculine in its descent, it is dual—in that it has within itself ALL of Beingness. Therefore, it can be Feminine as well as Masculine simultaneously. This is also true of you! The Soul, involved in form, is feminine in nature, regardless of the body sex. The Activity of 'Spirit' upon it then engenders Desire and Will, to bring about Soul fulfillment. Having achieved Desire and Will, the Soul can then assume a Masculine role and become the impregnating power upon the Feminine Principle of Creativity. Then by THOUGHT, WILL, and DESIRE, *YOU* BECOME the vibrant power which directs itself toward the WOMB of LIFE of the higher levels where the SEED of all that you can experience awaits your impregnation. IT IS ALL THERE, but it MUST BE ACTIVATED. You are the generating factor. The womb of Life has the seed of ALL within it. Whatever seed your desire impregnates, *THAT* will become manifest in your life, be it good or bad.

"This is REVERSING THE POLARITY, as you were told you must learn to do.

"So remember, at all times: YOU ARE NOT ONLY FEMININE in nature, YOU ARE MASCULINE AS WELL, YOU ARE THE CREATOR of that which becomes manifest in your lives. The womb of Life is FULL of seeds that are waiting to be impregnated by your THOUGHT and DESIRE. When you understand the great Law of Polarity you will have the Key to ALL Power and Life upon all dimensions, for you will understand the Law of Creativity, and you will be able to consciously utilize it. In all dimensions, Life gives forth its fruit according to the pattern of the seed that has been impregnated and the pattern of the impregnating power. The offspring bears the mark of both parents. So, if you would have the perfect life, you must impregnate the Perfect Seed Pattern with your highest Desire and Will. According to the pattern which you give to Life, SO IS IT DONE UNTO YOU! *That*, and *only* that, can come into manifestation for you! If you take the wonderful Seed of Life and impregnate it with ugly or hateful thoughts and desires, it can bear only ugly offspring; but, if you conceive in Love, you will bear Divine Fruit.

"LIFE IMPREGNATED ITSELF and brought forth YOU. You impregnate Life and bring forth whatever *you* think and desire!

"Beloved, Creation is in your hands. You have been Divinely conceived, now take the power that is yours and engender Divine offspring in thought, word, and deed. Conceived in Love, Purity, and Perfection, they will move you forward upon the Stream of Life in the knowledge that you walk in the Light and that you are proceeding into your Divine fulfillment. Love is the magic key. Light is not given to those who would misuse its power. It comes only to those who will use it to SERVE.

"My Peace, Light, and Love attend you.

"Yojana! Yojana! Yojana!"

PART 4

CHAPTER 5

The Soul Moves Symbolically Through
The World of Form

Keeper of the Flame:

"Beloved: We move into a very special work, a special time in the unfoldment of the Consciousness of Man. Those who carry the Scepter of the Flame must give themselves in complete dedication to the furtherance of this great Operation.

"We now present an experience for each of you if you will move with us in what will be portrayed through my instrument.

"Several of you were present to witness the experience through which she was previously taken in Reversing the Polarity. Tonight we reveal more of what the Soul experiences in its sojourn through the world of form, while encased in a physical body. This will be a symbolic experience depicting the struggles and the overcoming which each Soul must experience. Again the picture will be projected to the channel and she will move through the experience. Know that this is for *each* of you, not for just one individual. Identify yourselves with this experience as it is shown.

"Light! Light! Light is the understanding Mind. Light is the receptive heart. Light is the Soul's intense desire to move forward in its progression. LIGHT moves *into* you, revealing TO you that which it holds FOR you. As we proceed, be unafraid, for those who walk in Light have already passed through much of what will be revealed. However, the Light Bearer, to be an effective teacher, must have an understanding of that which all Souls experience in their progression. Having witnessed this picture you will better understand the great trials, tribulations, and misunderstanding through which mankind goes. You will therefore be better equipped to help others in their struggle."

Nellie relates what she is experiencing:

I seem to be in a ball of Light, descending toward the earth. I see a great mountain and I am approaching it. It is a beautiful mountain, with its head covered with snow. The sun shines upon it, and it seems majestic in its grandeur. I know this mountain is what I must pass through, as well as surmount, for it is symbolic of what I, as SOUL, must achieve. I must pass through all of its inner recesses and I must reach its summit.

As I come to the base of the mountain I see the entrance to a cave and I know that I must enter it. As the Soul comes from the realms of Light to be encased in earthly flesh and form, they seem to have the solidity of a mountain, with rugged beauty, but also formidable, and with a treacherous nature to overcome. This is an experience which I do not seem to want, yet I know that I MUST have it. *I must pass through this,* for it is a part of what must be learned and incorporated into my Being. Only by this experience will I master the corporeal phase of Eternal Being.

As I move into this cave, I seem to have a staff in my hand, the kind that shepherds use. I sense that this is the Divine ever-present Power and Wisdom that is innate within each Soul. It is the only thing I may take with me.

I am in a huge cavern which is completely filled with stalactites and stalagmites. They are beautiful to see, but I know them to be solidified, absolutely *crystallized.* I know they represent the crystallization within my consciousness. The Soul often becomes crystallized in various states of understanding. Crystallized into the patterns which it has become through previous incarnations and past experiences; crystallized in its misunderstanding, its hatred and its greed; crystallized in its unawareness. I am aware that I am CRYSTALLIZED in most everything. I see the moisture dripping from the stalactites, and I know that this could have been a flowing stream had it not been caught in the crystallization process. I realize that I must move out of this. I MUST MOVE! I do not wish to stay in this state of awareness. There *is something more,* and I must break through this crystallization. I must move into a different area of awareness and experience, so I climb laboriously over these sharp, jagged obstacles and find myself at a small opening which apparently leads into another cavern.

This is even worse! Here I am confronted with all kinds of slimy, creepy creatures. There are serpents and lizards and all of the denizens of the deep, but I MUST PASS THROUGH THEM. I know this to be the PIT of DESIRE, where the Soul is spiritually unaware, motivated only by its lusts, hatreds, and sensuality. In its lower levels of progression it is trapped in materiality. The Desire Body has full sway, and the Soul is shackled to its desires. These creatures writhe around me and literally strip the flesh from my bones. Surely this is being trapped in the ABYSS in the 'bowels of the earth,' the lowest of Soul experience!

In this combat I have lashed out with my staff, for I know this staff is the Power of God within me. Some of the reptiles and creatures have been destroyed and the floor is strewn with them; others are wounded and dying. A vulture appears and devours all of this. There are only two serpents left; they come to me and coil themselves around my staff, forming themselves and the staff into the symbol of the Caduceus. They represent the dual powers of the Soul, the positive and the negative, now combined in ONE UNIFIED endeavor to bring the Soul into understanding the fulfillment. This is the regeneration which takes place in the Soul and frees it to move into new dimensions. I am now free to move out of this pit, and I again go through a small opening into another cavern.

Here I find ore. Thin layers of a shiny substance run through the various strata surrounding the wall of this cavern. I start tearing at this with my hands, for I know

I must extract this gold from the surrounding ore. As I tear away the wall I uncover a vein of PURE GOLD. I know this is the GOLD OF SPIRITUAL UNDERSTANDING and TRUTH and LIGHT. I realize that I MUST glean this and take it away from this cavern, so I fill my robe and my hands with it and carry as much as I can as I go through another opening into another cavern.

This, too, is surrounded with ore. I see nothing but the ore, but I KNOW that it contains something of great value and that I must dig here also. I start to dig with my hands, but suddenly I realize that I need other tools, so I take the gold which I have and fashion it into a shovel. This seems to be a magic shovel, for when I touch the ore with it, it cuts right through the rock as easily as one would cut through butter. The ore falls away and reveals a PERFECT DIAMOND. This is the treasure for which I have been digging, the PERFECTED STATE OF BEING! I pick this up and hold it in my hands. It is very large, very heavy, and also very BEAUTIFUL.

Now an opening appears in the roof of the cavern and a bright shaft of light strikes the Diamond. Through the opening and down through the shaft of light a large eagle descends. He picks the Diamond up in his talons and, as I cling to it, he raises us up through the opening into the sunlight above. We go up and up, now on the outside of the mountain, until we reach the very summit where he sets me down and flies away.

From the summit of the mountain, I look out on the vast panorama below, and above. I see it as a vast stage where the drama of 'THE LIFE OF MAN' is portrayed, and I realize that it is all wonderful, beautiful, and perfect. It is all a part of God's Great PLAN that Man might work his way through the darkness of Crystallization, Desire, and the torturous Search, for when he has done this, he reaches a Perfected State of Being and comes into a new AWARENESS. This is a new dimension of consciousness, where he sees that ALL which he has experienced was only a means of revealing to him the PERFECT GEM of his DIVINE SELF!

Now I know that the vulture who ate away the dross in the cavern, and the eagle that brought me to new heights are one and the same, for now the eagle returns, but it has become the PHOENIX!

Again I cling to the Diamond, and again I am lifted, off the mountain-top and back into the Ball of Light, where I move UP and OUT into UNLIMITED BEINGNESS from whence I came.

I now know the meaning of the words, 'Ye shall mount up with wings, as eagles.' For, I know that the vulture, the eagle and the Phoenix are all the Innate Light, Love, and Power of God, which impels the Soul forward and brings it to its fulfillment.

So I return from whence I came, but now BEARING THE GEM OF PERFECTION, for I have traversed through the world of form, and I am now ready to rise to new heights by what I have learned. Only by this sojourn have I become qualified to take my place in the great work of teaching, or in the arts of Creativity.

Peace, Joy, and Thanksgiving. Holy art Thou, O Father-Mother God!!

Part 5

LESSONS FROM KEEPER OF THE FLAME

1— At-One-Ment and Duality

Think of the word 'atonement'; it really means At-One-Ment. When confusion reigns in your life, think and *feel* your at-one-ment with the Divine Source of your Being, and rest in the knowledge that the Divine Plan *is* being unfolded for your life. This is the great lesson that the Master Jesus attempted to reveal to Man when He said, 'The Father and I are One' and 'Know Ye not that Ye are gods?' This is also the lesson He tried to give when He said, 'If thine eye be single thy whole body shall be full of Light, but if thine eye be evil, thy whole body shall be full of darkness.' If your eye is single to the realization that you *ARE* Spirit, if there is no duality in your consciousness, if you live in the realization that Form and Spirit are ONE and that form could not exist except as it is animated by Spirit, then the body is full of Light. But, if the eye is not single and sees duality, and if you identify yourself with the world of form with all of its inharmonies, then the body is filled with darkness and you will suffer all the experiences of that darkness. As long as the 'eye' perceives in duality you will experience all that is within the dual consciousness. This, Beloved, IS THE CRUCIFIXION! This is Man hanging upon the Cross of the world of Form. It is only when he lifts himself above this and makes his RESURRECTION into total AT-ONE-MENT that he attains Mastery.

Throughout the ages much fallacy has arisen in Man's interpretation of age-old Truth. The biblical story of the Garden of Eden is a symbolic analogy of that which happens within the consciousness of Man, but Man has translated it in a literal sense and lost much of its meaning. Arising from Man's dual consciousness has come the concept of good and evil, heaven and hell, God and Satan, etc. He has believed in 'two powers' rather than keeping his 'eye' single and adhering to the Divine Principle of the ONENESS of BEING. Therefore he has lost sight of his own innate Divinity and has pictured God as being separate and apart from himself. He has thought of himself as a 'dual Being,' spirit and body, and most of the time he has not thought of himself as 'spirit' but has centered his consciousness upon the form, or body, of himself and identified himself *as that*. Ask the average person who they are and they will almost invariably identify themselves by their name, their profession, or their relationship to family members, or in some outer way. Few ever think of themselves as being Eternal SOULS, or of their bodies as being the vehicles for themselves, as Souls, to use as a mode of expression while in the earth dimension.

What fallacy has been perpetrated upon Man in the name of religion, for the churches have failed to make Man aware of his At-One-Ment. In fact, they have denied Man's divinity and made him feel sharply separated from his Divine Source by telling him that he was 'born in sin,' and 'a worm of the dust' with no hope of redemption except through a 'vicarious *atonement*.' The true meaning of the word was lost long ago.

The Jewish and Christian religions, as well as many who have taught Ancient Wisdom, have been equally guilty, for they have misinterpreted the true meaning of the story of creation. In attempting to help the unlearned better understand the Masculine and Feminine Principles of creation, the analogy was given of the Garden of Eden, with Adam and Eve representing these two principles. Instead of recognizing this as being but two aspects of the ONE POWER, the idea of duality arose and was foisted on succeeding generations until Man lost all realization of his At-One-Ment. In reality there is but One Power and it is ever present in ALL dimensions, regardless of whether it is the world of 'form,' or more etheric realms. Man is so closely identified with 'form' that he fails to realize that there is an eternal cyclic pattern which is being fulfilled as the One Power expresses itself in its myriad manifestations. This power manifests in different vibratory frequencies according to the sensitivity and response, and the level of consciousness, of the vehicles it has created. Within the consciousness of everything that has been created there is a sensory apparatus which accepts and reacts to the vibratory impulse it has received which determines its nature. It is similar to the human nervous system which picks up mental impulses and proceeds to carry them out.

You too have a soul 'Sensor,' or 'Receptor,' through which you can receive impulses for Soul unfoldment, for there is a 'Divine Magnetism' which draws every Soul to its Divine fulfillment. So realize that your TRUE BEING is not the form that you inhabit for a particular embodiment. *YOU* are the Spirit that animates the various forms which YOU will use as you move forward in your Soul Progression.

Man constantly becomes polarized in his thinking and feels separated from the WHOLE. A better vantage point would be to think of all of Life as a circle of everlasting ONENESS with oneself standing at the center. From here all the radii are equal and it can be seen as one great WHOLE connected to the HUB of the universe. Everything then seems equally necessary and equally true, with no up or down, or good or bad, or better or worse, or beginning or ending. Find your Divine Center and then encompass all of creation within the Divine Circle of yourself.

Release the Mirage of Duality and live in the Eternal ONENESS!

2— The Karmic Board

The Karmic Board is a group of Karmic Angels who meet together to examine the karmic threads of individuals and best determine how they can be interwoven to be the most helpful to embodying souls. Each soul has a Karmic angel, although one angel has charge of many souls. When souls are ready to embody, they meet with their angel to determine what lessons are to be learned, what Karmic obligations are to be worked upon, and under what conditions this can best be done. The Karmic Board and Angel then confer with the Guardian Angel of the individual and arrangements are made for the Soul to enter the earth dimension through the proper parents, in the proper culture, and with the proper physical and mental equipment to fulfill what it has agreed to work upon during that embodiment. So each life is predestined to a degree, but one also has a measure of free will and can, if he chooses, neglect to fulfill his soul commitment. However, in doing this he finds himself confronted with the same obstacles until he has taken the proper steps and completed the required work.

The Akashic Record

The Akashic Record is written in the etheric substance of the higher frequencies. This substance is magnetic, and just as the magnetic tape of your recorder receives and retains the impulses which are impinged upon it, so does the etheric substance receive and retain any force of thought or action which causes it to vibrate. These things are *fixed* upon the substance, just as sound vibrations are fixed on tape, and are available to one who is able to 'read' them.

(Question) "When we receive messages, are they from entities, or are we touching the Akashic Record?"

It can be either. By being sensitive you attune to various vibrations. Many of the teachings of the Masters are recorded on etheric substance and are available to whomever is able to attune to them. But your personal Master is always attuned to you and comes at your call. If you attune to Astral levels you receive from there. YOU CHOOSE FROM WHAT LEVEL YOU WILL RECEIVE, for YOU DO THE ATTUNING!

(Question) "Is the Akashic Record a continuing record of each Soul and is it subject to time and space?"

You place limitations where there are none. Etheric substance is the ALL-PERVADING essence, without limits! Each Soul leaves its imprint at each stage of growth by every thought and action. Before rebirth this is evaluated by the Soul and the Karmic Angel, and/or Karmic Board. What is to be accomplished in the forth-coming embodiment is then determined.

(Question) "Who is able to read the Akashic Record?"

Some are able to read the record for themselves and for others, but for most people this is neither possible nor wise, for until the Soul is highly evolved, to learn of past mistakes could be disastrous and might chain them to the past through feeling guilty. At the time of death, one is allowed to 'see' and then distil from earth experience what will be carried forward into future incarnations. Anything irrelevant to Soul growth is left behind, unless one is 'earth-bound.'

(Question) "Is the Soul's growth as rapid after death as while in an earth body?"

It depends upon the individual. Many long for, and seek, only sensual satisfaction. They are earth-bound. Others seek Light and soul-growth, they are taught as rapidly as they can assimilate and use new understanding. Again, IT IS A MATTER OF PERSONAL DESIRE!

(Question) "Is what is learned in the etheric realms between incarnations retained in the consciousness?"

It is all indelible upon the soul-fabric, but it is veiled to the conscious mind until it is recalled through some experience or is needed in some situation. This is why, when you have a question, you should turn it over to your soul-self as you go to sleep. The answer may come as in a dream, or in a flash of intuition. The answer will invariably come if the Soul has had a similar experience. If not, the abiding teachers will try to give the answer.

(Question) "Is 'Judgement' then, only a matter of one's conscience?"

Judgement is not an act of God, and to say that it is your own conscience is equally wrong. Conscience is a matter of preconditioning according to one's background and culture. One man can kill and feel no conscience, another can cheat or rob; and so it is with all that you might call 'sin.' But in the etheric vibrations each thought and deed is recorded and is on eternal record. Then as each Soul begins to realize that it must love and serve, it is given access to the Akashic Record to decide what aspects of its character it must work upon. You might call this judgement, but it is not judgement in the sense that one is punished by God for his sins.

3— The Aquarian Age and the NEW Man

Just as the earth moves through the twelve signs of the Zodiac and is influenced on a monthly basis by the other planets within your solar system in a yearly cycle, so does your solar system move through a galactic pattern in a 26,000 year cycle. This comprises twelve Ages, the Aquarian Age being the next to influence the Earth planet. This new galactic relationship will bring much stress to the planet and its inhabitants as it, and they, are bombarded with new Cosmic vibrations of a higher order. Man will be confused and will seek help and answers concerning what is happening.

Many old and wise souls have embodied at this time, and many more will come, to help mankind through this time of transition. The Masters of the White Brotherhood are also working from their dimensions to raise the consciousness of Man so he will learn to live harmoniously in the new vibration. This is also to be the work of my Light Bearers who take the larger view and see it as a time for the purging and cleansing of the Earth.

When the New Age has weathered its 'birth-pangs' it will be known as the 'Golden Age,' for the masses will be brought to a new awareness of the power of the MIND and to a greater understanding of man's OWN *SELF* and his relationship to the Creative Mind and Power of the universe. Each age has raised the level of Man's consciousness and brought with it a new concept by which he can live. Moses, of the Aryan Age, brought the revelation of the *One* God. Jesus, of the Piscean Age, tried to teach that Man can be 'AT-ONE' with the Father but the people did not grasp his message and they deified Jesus, rather than claiming their own divinity, as He had tried to make them understand when He said, 'Know ye not that Ye are gods?'

However, His message of Love has been somewhat effective. Consider the profound changes during the past Age, even though it suffered the dismal coercion of the church, which, in the name of Jesus, nullified much of what He came to reveal. But, He comes into his own in the New Age, through the 'Christ Mind' of his enlightened emissaries.

Man is already feeling the Aquarian vibration, although the Piscean Age is not completely finished. But, each Age is felt before the full vibration is manifest.

The time of transition will not be easy, for old social and economic structures will crumble from their own decay since they were not built upon spiritual foundations. Greed, lust, and power were their underpinnings, and they will fall into the dust of destruction before the new edifice can be raised, for the world MUST be transmuted! The new Cosmic vibration of the earth will be greatly intensified and Man *MUST* raise his frequency in accordance. That which does not vibrate in harmony with the new Cosmic vibration will simply disintegrate.

The old order was built upon the premise that Man's strength gave him license to exploit his brother. The New Age will bring him to the realization that all are brothers in one spiritual community and that all must be equally respected and revered. Many will panic as they find themselves involved in the chaos, for material possessions will be stripped from Man's grasp. All who have been possessed by their possessions will find themselves stripped of possessions, but those who realize that possessions are loaned and to be used for the good of all will be able to have and use material goods.

Material technology will emphasize the exploration of outer space, but the Light will come only to those who begin to explore *inner* space. Man must come to know himself as a Divine Being, and let *that* manifest through him. This is a new concept for Man and it takes much time and inner devotion for him to come to this *realization*. But when he does, he will transform his world and he will reach new heights of Mastery over himself and his material world. When he *KNOWS* himself to be a Divine Creation and a Divine Creator he will bring untold wonders to pass. He will find the secret of CREATIVITY and nothing will be beyond his ability. The new man will be MASTER OF HIS FATE. He will *WILL* and produce his mental image into manifestation. An understanding of the Law of Vibration will give him power over all matter. He will CREATE by MENTAL VIBRATION! He will TRAVERSE the Universe by THOUGHT. He will HEAL by IMAGING, BUT BETTER STILL, IN TIME HE WILL REQUIRE NO HEALING, for he will learn that inharmony is his own creation, and he will learn to use Creative Law divinely and for the good of all. This is hard to imagine, but you will be amazed at the rapidity with which it will come, for the earth is being prepared and the old order falls very quickly.

(Question)—"Can you give us a specific time?"

Time is not measured in days and hours, as you know it, but according to the PLAN and its outworking. It is hoped by the Hierarchy that much destruction can be averted if man can be brought quickly enough to a new awareness. If he can be awakened and transmutes his hates, and greed, and intolerance, before the new planetary vibrations are in full control, he can function in the new vibration without experiencing the full impact of it as a destructive force. These conditions are not being 'visited' upon mankind as punishment, but are the natural consequence of planetary progression, which also brings a new vibrational level in which hate and animosity and material consciousness can have no place. The old falls of its own weight and those who are trapped in it will experience the chaos of it, but those who arise in Love and Light will know that it is The Great PLAN and they will let Love reign in the new order.

(Question)—"Will Light Beings continue to embody to help in this work?"

Yes, many of the children now embodying are highly enlightened souls who will lend their Light and Love to this endeavor. The earth's frequency can only be harmonized with the Cosmic vibration through a mass raising of the individual consciousness. All mankind are potential Gods, and in time we will bring forth the God-Man. Then will my world be cleansed of all imperfections and will take its place in the Galactic Federation as a planet of Light with the Guardians of the Universe, rather than as a place for the laggards to be taught. The earth plane has been as a school to prepare souls to function in other galaxies and dimensions. Many souls have rushed into embodiment before they were completely ready because they wished to have experience in the earth vibration before its vibration was raised beyond their capacities. This is one reason for the population explosion and for the violent and hateful characters of many people.

(Question)—"What happens to such people if they do not qualify?"

They will be relegated to the proper vibrational level in a different galaxy until they can qualify. Man must move with the new vibration or fall behind the Race unfoldment. My present Light Bearers are forerunners of the 6th Root Race and are here to reveal Man's Divine Nature. The 6th Race will develop the Mind and the Intuition and harmonize the physical and spiritual natures by developing the Love Nature. Love will become the hallmark of this Race and Man will be aware of his creative power. The present consciousness of mankind has demonstrated that when his creative faculty is used negatively, or for personal gain or glory, he has produced only destructive monsters which have destroyed him. But this has served its purpose, for as Man reaches the brink of annihilation he becomes spiritually awakened and seeks a better way of life.

(Question)—"It must be very frustrating to the invisible Masters to see how indolent mankind has been."

It is Divinely ordained that Man be brought to his full Divine Stature. Each Age and Root Race succeeds in lifting the human consciousness to some degree. This is a cyclic pattern through which humanity constantly moves. As Light descends into the earth vibration, it motivates Man to seek higher Truth. It has always been the work of the Guardians of the Planet to reinforce the progressive galactic vibration by lending their Light and Love and inspiration to aspiring souls and to the planet. There seems to be a time of Man's assimilation and practice of the truths he learns, but a corresponding drifting away on the part of many. Then crystallization takes place and a new release of Light and energy is needed to give a new impetus to mankind. All life and unfolding consciousness moves in cyclic patterns, and it is as much a part of Man's growth to have a time of dormancy as it is to have a time for flourishing. Life and Intelligence are eternally evolving, but all growth comes in its proper season. Just as a seed lies dormant in the winter months to strengthen its inner power for later release, so does mankind have its season for unfoldment. To call mankind indolent in his growth is not really factual, for the Cosmic Release is timed to the Galactic Rhythm for human unfoldment. Just as a tiny tendril breaks through the shell of the seed, so is Man breaking the shell of false understanding, and coming forth into a new state of expression. Do not underestimate the Power of Life to bring forth the new, for the Tendril of Truth *will* break forth and Man *will* become the God-Man. To be disturbed because it takes time for Man to grow into new concepts of Awareness would be as foolish as to be impatient if a seed did not come to full growth and flower when first planted. Be patient and loving, and BE Light for My Children. This will act as a catalyst for their growth, just as the sun activates the seed's growth. Incubation time has been fulfilled. The flowering MUST follow!

The Aquarian Age is the beginning of the earth's transmutation, in which each Soul finds his True IDENTITY and purpose, and then lives to be the Perfect Channel for the Expression of Divine Light and Love. Man will come to know himself to be an Eternal, ever progressing, Soul who is not limited to the earth's frequency, but is a Universal Being, who will find himself expressing throughout the ages upon an infinite number of planets and galaxies as he grows in consciousness and in vibratory frequency. Man is but an infant in the Cosmic Scale of Being, and he must traverse the many pathways of Life to reach his fulfillment. This can be a glorious and happy experience if it is approached in the spirit of adventure. But if one does not catch a glimpse of the Great Adventure, life can be very dull and frustrating, and much time can be wasted in the mundane pursuit of materiality and satisfying the sensual nature. Seek the Kingdom of Life and Light. Keep your feet steadfastly on the Pathway of Eternal Soul Unfoldment and be enraptured with the beauty of Life as it unfolds itself IN you and reveals more of Itself TO you!

4— Astral Entities

The law of communication with other dimensions is in operation and is utilized by the Lower Forces as well as by the Masters. Do not mistake the ability of contact as always being with the highest levels. Many of lesser spiritual development know, and use, the law and can even densify their bodies so they appear in solid form, but often without good intent. They are from the Astral levels of consciousness and many are 'earth-bound.' They have no desire for spiritual progression but seek only to satisfy their sense desires.

The astral body is that which houses the emotions and sensual nature of an individual, and it functions after the physical body has been left behind. Desires are not left behind at the time of death, for one moves into the next dimension in the exact state of consciousness he has attained while in the physical body. If he is filled with sensual desires, he will attach himself to an earth person with similar tendencies and try to vicariously satisfy those desires through him. His desire is often so strong that it influences the earth person to fulfill the act. Many excessive drinkers, and sex deviates, and even murderers, are being controlled by astral entities. It can be noted that during, and after, great wars there is an upsurge of murders in the civilian population. This is because soldiers, leaving their bodies in the heat of battle with a great emotional desire to kill their enemies, have created such a strong thought vibration of 'Kill' that it is often picked up by an earth person who then proceeds to carry out the act in the earth dimension.

There are countless cases of 'obsession' where the earth person has allowed an astral entity to 'take over' his mind, and sometimes even move into his body. Whenever you indulge in any negative thinking you open the doors of your mind to these demonic forces, for they await that kind of vibration to utilize. They will continue in acts of obsession, haunting houses, and all kinds of mischief until they are awakened to the realization that they must choose a better way. When they show that desire, they are helped by the

Teachers in the higher dimensions and are gradually taught the Laws of Soul Progression.

These Beings are not to be confused with your loved ones who seek to contact you, although they too are no different than they were while on earth until they are taught more of, and work upon, their soul progression. To try to hold them to you is to hold them in bondage to the earth vibration. They should be lovingly released so they can be free to move forward on their Eternal Pathway. There are legions who are seeking understanding, yet are so held by their earth loved ones, that they find it difficult to break completely with earth ties and enter into the Schools of Light that await them.

There is hope and inevitable growth for every Soul, but it comes only through their own desire and through doing the work required for its accomplishment! To be bound to the Astral level is the 'Hell' that Man has been told about. But IT IS NOT ETERNAL! It can be transcended!!

5— Birth—Death—Abortion

Before conception the Soul has been directed to its proper forthcoming environment and parents by its Karmic angel, with whom it has predetermined what aspects of Soul unfoldment it will work upon during that particular incarnation. It then awaits the moment of conception, at which time the Soul Seed Atom is placed in the heart genes and is the blueprint for the new body and new life expression for the incarnating Soul. The Soul is the architect and oversees the building of the body, but does not take up permanent residence until birth. Prior to birth it can function in the body or in the etheric dimensions.

Life in a physical body is the means of giving the Soul a vehicle for expression and growth in the earth dimension. Earth is but one of the many classrooms for the Soul's unfoldment. Do not discredit the body, for it is also the vehicle for My Spirit and is as holy as any of My creations. To give it proper care and honor is wise and good, but remember that the outer vehicle is not the Real YOU, and no matter what frequency YOU are functioning in, your body of that dimension will always be of My Essence.

Death is a great balancing experience for it gives the Soul the opportunity to review all of its past human experiences and distil the good from them. Leaving the body is only discarding the old and taking on the new. Life constantly moves every soul into more exalted states where old concepts and inhibitions are released, and new expanses are opened. So it is an opportunity for growth and one should not grieve for the one who has passed on, but rather should rejoice at the good fortune of the loved one, who then can go forward to his new work.

To cling to the earth vibration is to deny oneself the opportunity to move forward. Many do this after earth life has little to give them. This usually stems from fear of the unknown. To try to keep the body after it has outworn its usefulness would be like keeping a caterpillar in its cocoon and never setting it free to use its wings or experience the expanded existence of a butterfly. The function of birth and death is to give the Soul varied experiences by which it can unfold more rapidly. Think how jaded one's attitudes can become when they reach a point in years where life holds little that seems new and exciting. It is in the challenge of life that it is exciting, and this can continue throughout one's entire life if they approach life with expectancy and think of every experience as an opportunity for soul unfoldment. But most elderly people find little of interest in life and simply await their release. When this happens the experience of death is advantageous for the Soul, for they will find new interests and means of expression in their new environment.

For those who understand the eternal unfolding process death is considered a 'graduation,' and they calmly step out of their physical bodies and take up their work in the next dimension. It has been one of the failures of the Church to have advocated fear of death rather than telling their people of Soul Unfoldment. Consigning people to 'eternal damnation' was the greatest hoax ever perpetrated upon the human race and it has held man in bondage for centuries. The veil of ignorance MUST be lifted from Man's eyes to reveal the Truth.

Give your finest efforts to your soul growth while in the body, for you take nothing with you when you leave the earth plane except that which you have BECOME in consciousness. If you leave in the consciousness of materiality and injustice, you find yourself abiding in the same conditions in the new dimension. If you have transcended materiality, hatred, animosity, criticism, and all other limitations that are of the human plane, you will find the 'Father's many mansions' of Light to be your abode. However, do not expect pearly gates or harps, and an indolent existence, for you will find that you will only go to a new 'workshop' where you will learn more advanced lessons and become a more highly advanced Being. Mastery becomes yours as you fill your heart with desire for the greater life. Aspire to become a more perfect expression of the One Divine Life!

You question reïncarnation:

Man must experience life in all of its aspects, but he usually does so in a sense of duality, or separation from his innate God-Self. When he completely identifies with the INDWELLING SPIRIT, he will have no further sense of separation or dividedness. Then ALL experience is a part of the great NOW and he no longer thinks in terms of past, present, or future lives, but lives to serve the Divine in the realization of the ONENESS of life in *all* dimensions. He becomes universal in his consciousness, with no barriers of time, space, color, creed, or any of the limitations he has imposed upon himself while functioning in a consciousness of duality. Reincarnation is a product of man's dual consciousness, but as long as it seems the Reality to him, it serves him well in his unfolding spiritual realization.

You question abortion:

There is a reason for the great influx of souls to the earth dimension at this time. The Cosmic Tone was sounded that proclaimed a New Age and new vibration for the Earth planet. Since the earth is one of the schools through which all souls must move, and since many souls are not sufficiently developed to function in the earth frequency after the establishment of the new vibration, they have answered the Cosmic Call and have entered into embodiment now, that they might have the necessary experience to qualify them for the New Age. Planets, as well as humans and all life, are cyclic in nature, and when a planet is accelerated its inhabitants must be of the proper frequency to live upon it. To abort a soul is to deny it this opportunity.

While the ecologists might consider it necessary, by the Cosmic Design it is not necessary or proper. LIFE is of the Cosmos and the Great Design is beyond man's comprehension. This is not given from the standpoint of religion but from the standpoint of Cosmic unfoldment for the New Age. Of course, each mother will follow her own inner consciousness in this matter. To not become pregnant is a reasonable choice, for, viewed from the standpoint of the world situation, one could easily be reluctant to add to the earth's population; but, after conception has taken place, to abort is denying a soul its Cosmic right.

(Question—"When does life begin?")

Life is always seeking for channels through which to express. Life exists before conception because LIFE is Cosmic Mind and Power awaiting a vehicle for its expression. LIFE *IS*, and always has been; and SOUL *IS*, and always has been. The act of conception merely begins to provide a body for Life, or Soul. To say that life begins at conception is not true, for it is eternal.

(Question—"Is not prevention also denying souls entry to the earth dimension?")

When a soul has found a channel through which to obtain a body vehicle, and all the plans are worked out on the etheric levels, to be aborted delays its progress for all karmic and environmental decisions must be re-evaluated and worked out in other ways. The mother must then assume the responsibility of denying its entry. However, to prevent pregnancy is more general and not as personalized as abortion.

(Question—"What of abortion before there is a heartbeat?")

Abortion ejects a soul from its physical vehicle at any time after conception.

6— Criticism and Negation

Overcoming negation is the key to Soul unfoldment!
Do not belabor negative news or circumstances!
The practice of engaging in disparaging conversation belittles the Divine. When you see only the outer aspects of a person or situation, instead of the Divine of it, you call forth more of worldly action. The masses are the vessel for ribald actions and thoughts, but you are endowed with understanding and you betray your God-Self when you engage in negative thought and actions, such as criticizing and seeing error. My Light Bearers must SEE no evil, HEAR no evil, and SPEAK no evil. Behold the Divine in all and call it forth, and LOVE all regardless of seeming actions and inharmony. My world IS in Divine order. My children *are* working out their destiny. All is well! Find your true Light in Me, and question not the ways of the world. Live in My Light. Behold my perfect Plan bringing all of my children to Me in their own way, and at their own time. You have your own Pathway to tread. No one walks it for you, and you walk the Way for no other.

(Question—"Did not Jesus criticize the hypocrites and money changers?")

Yes, but He did it with love, not disgust, and while He condemned the actions He still loved those who performed them. There is no place in Divine Consciousness for condemnation. When your criticism is invited, and you offer it in love, it is different than when it is done in anger. Nothing is ever accomplished by angry criticism.

When you see something you would like to criticize, put yourself above it. Otherwise you will become trapped in a whirlpool of inharmony which pulls you only downward. You know how the lower point of a whirlpool spins much faster than the speed at the outer rim. As you are pulled deeper into a negative vortex, more and more negative things are brought to you, and it becomes harder and harder to extricate yourself. Only more inharmony can come until you bring Love into the situation.

Your purpose in life should be to help others, not to push them further into the mire. What you SEE in others is sometimes a reflection of yourself. Rise above it and BE the Light!

7— The Church, Jesus, the Bible

The Church has been used as an instrument to present Truth to mankind, but it is significant to the Soul only as one becomes illumined by the Inner Realization and Light. So it has served many well, but it can never reveal the full measure of Truth to anyone, for until the Inner Fire is ignited and the Inner Light established in the individual, it is like trying to view the wonders of the world by the light of the moon, rather than by the bright light of the sun. It is the INNER LIGHT that is the REVELATOR.

Much wisdom has been lost to Man by the imposed doctrines of the formal church. As a consequence Man has lost much of the inner realization of the Spirit of himself. For ages the dogmatists have down-graded the Spirit of Man and have caused him to think of himself as a worm of the dust with no possibility of salvation other than through the blood of Jesus. This has been a grave injustice, for Jesus came not to shed His blood as an atonement for Man, but to demonstrate that God dwells IN Man. The early church put the emphasis upon Jesus' crucifixion because it lost sight of the true purpose of His earthly sojourn, which was to demonstrate that the Spirit of God was within Him and within every man. He made the total IDENTIFICATION

with the INDWELLING PRESENCE which He called
'The Father,' and He said, 'I and my Father are one.
It is not I but the Father that dwelleth in me that doeth
the works.' He had no sense of separation and He tried to
make His followers aware of the same Presence within them.
The Church has forgotten this part of His ministry and
emphasized His death and resurrection, and has disregarded
what He said about the Spirit of Man. It has deified Jesus
but defiled Man. It was never the wish of Jesus to be deified.
He only wanted to demonstrate the Spirit Within, and He
tried to make the lives of others meaningful by recognizing
and calling forth their 'Indwelling Presence.'

Blood sacrifice was an ancient rite that was carried into
the Christian religion by pagan converts. When Jesus was
crucified, as was the common practice of the day, He
became 'the sacrifice.' The idea of atonement developed
from this. You will recall that Abraham was willing to sacrifice his son, as an earlier religious requirement. Sacrifice
was a symbol of devotion to the gods. This was accepted
by the early Christians as natural, and Jesus' death became
the sacrificial symbol.

It would have been wiser if the early Church had emphasized the Cross as being the symbol of that which every
man experiences as he goes through the trials and tribulations of human existence, and finally overcomes, or cross-
es out, his carnal instincts and desires. The Cross is an
ancient symbol which predates Christianity by many centuries. Its upright shaft depicts the grounding of Spirit in
the earth dimension; the crossarm depicts the physical and
mental aspects of Man. Put together they comprise Man's
three-fold Being—body, mind, and spirit. As one overcomes
the Cross of Materiality, he raises his consciousness to his
Spiritual Nature. This is his RESURRECTION!

The New Age will help Man transcend the limitations
imposed by the Church and allow the Spirit of Man to
raise him to his own Christed state. This is by far the greater Truth than that which has dominated the thinking of the
people of the past Age. It has been a case of the blind leading the blind in most churches. So when Light comes,

LET THERE BE LIGHT! They will find their way out of
the maze of dogma, creed, and secularism, but it will take
time and time grows short. Organizations are always limited to the consciousness of those who make the edicts, and
the Church has long suffered this limitation and lost much
of its ability to serve humanity rightly. It needs revitalizing,
so you can serve as the 'leavening in the lump.' However,
the only real Salvation for anyone is his *total* IDENTIFI-
CATION with his own INDWELLING PRESENCE and
then *LIVING* to *BE* ITS PERFECT EXPRESSION!

(Question—"If the Church has been so misleading should
the Bible, then, be taken literally?")

The Bible is a compilation of the writings of men. It is
contradictory and not infallible, but it contains much Truth
if considered rightly. As Man has grown in his knowledge
of the universe his concepts have changed according to his
understanding. To say that ALL Truth has been revealed
would be limiting the Spirit, for Spirit has been constantly
revealing itself in new ways to Man's mind. ALL has forever
been in Spirit, but it is Man's consciousness which evolves.
Ancient Man worshipped the elements in fear and, as he
formed a society, he worshipped a tribal God. Then he
came to know there is ONE God, but he made that God in
his own image, giving God a body and a particular
dwelling place. Now the time has come for Man to know
that God is *innate within himself,* and in ALL of creation.
He will thus recognize his Oneness with all life in all dimensions.

The Bible is an historical record of Man's conception
of God, and the activities of the people of its day. It is only
as true as the author's consciousness revealed to him. However, Truth is revealed therein, but Truth is also IN you,
so accept only that which seems right to you. When reading
the Bible, seek for the *inner* revelations contained in it,
for those men told their revelations in the language of
their day and with illustrations understandable to the people of that time. Therefore, seek the *inner truth* which re-

lates to you *now*. Consciousness unfolds and mighty is the Power of Spirit as it moves you into ever more glorious dimensions of the ONE Life!

8— Holy Communion

Come to my table, Beloved. Feast, and fill your cups with the nectar of Love and Joy, for I bring you together in a mighty purpose for the enrichment of your souls. The glory of 'The Kingdom' is yours as you sup with Me this night.

Your cup runneth over as you drink from the Fountain of Wisdom. Wise is he who seeks the Light. Blessed is he who eats of the fruit of the Tree of Life and Wisdom. The Tree is My Spirit, full grown and mighty, bringing forth the Fruit of the Spirit that each of My children might partake of the fruit of Love, Life, Peace, Harmony, Joy, and Power. Great power comes with the release of the Spirit Within, power of which the world knows not.

Man seeks the hidden power within the atom, not realizing that he has a much greater power within himself which, if he would only allow it to be released in the world, would transform the world and all that is in it. With his recognition of the innate power within the atom, he is beginning to sense the power within himself. You stand on the threshold of a wondrous day where Man moves into this realization. Those who have been fortunate enough to have experienced this 'Presence' are richly blessed. You must now be the perfect example of this power as you portray it in the world, that others, catching a glimpse of its mighty power in your lives, will seek it for themselves.

This is the time for the separation of the wheat from the chaff. A mighty threshing is taking place, and it seems that all the world is in turmoil and strife. This is the threshing floor upon which the grains of Truth are separated from the chaff. Those who would gather the grain must cast aside the chaff of Life. All must go through this great milling process. So, when life seems hard and all seems lost, know that from these experiences comes the rich grain of which the Bread of Life is made.

The Cup of Life is filled to the brim, and it is for the passing of this cup to all, that you are called into service. As you pass the Cup of Love and Truth to your fellowman, they are blessed and lifted to new states of awareness and Being.

So tonight, at My table, you drink from My Chalice of Love and Truth, and you partake of the Bread of Life, as it is being made from the grains of Truth which are being separated from the chaff as you seek understanding and learn to serve in Love and humility.

THE BREAD OF LIFE, together with the FULL CUP, I PASS TO YOU THIS NIGHT, AS WE COMMUNE IN HOLY AT-ONE-MENT!

May you *know* that henceforth WE ARE ONE in Spirit and in Truth, that I AM *IN* YOU and YOU ARE *IN* ME! If you seem to walk a lonely way, you have only to turn your thoughts to the INDWELLING PRESENCE to know that in our ONENESS all things are possible, and that you never walk alone. My Mind is your Mind. My Life is your Life. My Love is your Love. We are eternally ONE, and that which is Divinely joined together, let no man put asunder. No man can separate Me from Thee. The only separation is in *your* mind. When you KNOW that we are ONE, you will walk forevermore in that realization, expressing My Light, My Love, and Truth in the world. Give your heart to the truth of the INDWELLING PRESENCE and *feel* the flow of Life and Love moving *in* you. This will bring peace of mind and health of body. Freedom from all restricting ideas comes as you accept yourself as a beautiful soul who lives only to be the channel of Divine Life, Light, Love, and Wisdom.

Practice this realization with deep breathing exercises in this manner: As you breathe *in*, say to yourself, "I absorb the Light, Love, and Wisdom of the Great Cosmic Mind. Its love and power suffuse my every atom, cell, organ, and muscle. My bloodstream carries the Life of God through my total Being and I am Divinely sustained and perfected. I *GLOW* with Divine Life. My body is perfected. My Mind is at perfect Peace, *BUT* ever alert to the new and beautiful. My Soul is in harmony with *all* of creation, as the Song of Creation *RINGS* through my body. I am in harmony and Resonance with ALL Life, everywhere.

As you breathe *out,* let your breath be a praise to your Creator and a blessing to the universe!

It is the task of the Light Bearer to become so perfectly At-One with Me that he is the living, breathing Essence of Me, and breathes beauty, peace, and love into the troubled world.

Beloved, we are ONE. Your only separation, and your only confusion, is in failing to be aware of it at all times.

Come unto Me and I will give you rest and fulfillment! Fear not the world and its limitation, for IN Me do you live and move and have your Being!

9— Christ Consciousness

Conversation had been about the Christ Consciousness and whether that implied the same consciousness in which the Master Jesus functioned:

The many steps of Christ Consciousness are the notes of the Christ Octave. Christ Consciousness can be at many levels. Just as the human Octave is composed of Beings in all levels, so is the Christ Octave composed of those in various degrees of Christ Consciousness. Many are highly evolved souls who are Light personified, while others are operating in the lower notes and work to serve Man on corresponding notes of the Human Octave. It is a matter of resonance with the harmonics of the keynote of individual souls. Masters serve those who are vibrating with their keynote.

Christ Consciousness is that level of consciousness which all great Masters have attained. Jesus, Buddha, Mohammed, and all the others made their complete identification with the Spirit within. When you make this identification you are in 'Christ Consciousness.' Your work is to so closely iden-

tify that you live in this state of awareness at all times.
Then you become a Christed Being, and live to serve mankind, and all life. Mastery is then yours, but you will
develop greater powers as you move through the Christ
Octave.

(Question—"Are the different levels of Christ Consciousness,
then, just different degrees of awareness?")

Yes, different degrees of awareness, but also different
vibratory rates. Awareness is consciousness, and it varies
according to the frequency of the entity. Each note of the
octave is of a different frequency and the Masters must progress through every note, just as each human must progress through each note of the Human Octave.

Masters help those who are in the harmonics of the keynote in which they are functioning at a particular time. As
Man progresses, he comes into a different keynote also,
and therefore is in resonance with different Masters at different stages of his progression. Every soul, in both octaves,
is moving into higher frequencies as they work upon the
various notes.

Just as the human finally becomes 'Christed' and grad-
uates from further human expression, so do Christed Beings
move through the Christ Octave to become Lords of Creativity in the next octave. Eternally upward do my beloved
children move, until they have become the *totality* of
Being, through understanding and service.

Love is the motivating force that fulfills *all* Life. My
Love lives in each of my children, just awaiting their recognition of My Presence. Blessed is he who finds and accepts
my Love as his way of life, for he then moves into the
fullness of his God-Self.

10— 1970 Christmas Message from Keeper of the Flame:

Beloved Lights, My Mantle of Light and Love enfolds you
and we are One. My Light goes before you in all your ways.
Holy is the Light and holy are you as you fill the Cha-

lices of your heart with Love and Light. Know that Divine Light is ever present with you. Invoke the Light and be filled with the Light, for Light is the Essence of Myself in its fullest. Light is the totality of Me which I give to all who can receive. As you grow in Love and Light, you encompass more of Me and we become wedded together for eternity. Great is the Light for you if you open yourselves to Me, for in that Light are all things perfected and fulfilled. Desire and work will intensify your Light. Be my Light Bearers and it can be said of you, "Ye are the Light of the World." Go in the Light and carry the Light to my hungry children. Joy comes to the world in the Christ Light as each heart becomes the manger for the borning of 'The Christ' *within*. Only in this way does peace come to the individual and to the nations. This is the Christmas season. Let 'The Christ' be born in all hearts and light the world.

Peace, Light, Love, and Joy to all Dear Light Bearers.

Yojana! Yojana! Yojana!

1971 Christmas Message from Keeper of the Flame

Beloved Lights, My mantle of Love and Light enfolds you and we are One.

Listen for the Inner Voice and you will receive much. For too long you have given entities credit for that which is really the Divine *within* yourself. God in *you* is as great as God in any other. Claim this and call it forth, and seek no man or entity as your teacher. God in *you* is your *real teacher,* and this is true of all men.

It is time now for the world to be awakened to this realization and bring forth the God-Man from the swaddling clothes that have held him in the manger of Christ Consciousness. The birthing time was 2000 years ago. Man must now leave the manger and the swaddling clothes and begin to walk and grow into his Godhood.

This is the Christmas Season. My Christmas Message for Man is this:

Tarry no longer as a babe in the manger, for that was

for mankind 2000 years ago. This Christmas must see the bringing forth of the God-Man, not the Christ-Child, for the New Age is for men of Light and not for infants swaddled and coddled by institutions and creeds. Each must come into his Divine Man-hood and become a responsible Bearer of Light who is ready to assume the responsibility for his own thoughts and actions, and who desires to serve his fellowman. This is not the attitude or action of a child, for a child must be nurtured and fed and instructed. If Man is to be raised to his new estate, he must become *Responsible* and find expression for his manhood in *manly* activities. This means that he becomes a *provider* rather than a *dependent*; a provider of Love, Truth, Light, Joy, Wisdom, and Peace. He leans not upon others, but is a pillar of strength for others. This is the Birthing Time for the GOD-MAN and the swaddling clothes must be left behind as he takes on the Robe of Light!

Carry this message to my beloved children, and let this be the most Joyous Christmas they have ever experienced.

Spread the Glad Tidings. Rejoice and be Glad, the God-*Man is* being born and a New Age comes as surely as the Christ *Child* came 2000 years ago.

11— Children

Life is a miracle of Law and Love. Every child that is born is the incarnated Spirit of God. Always remember this in dealing with your children, and also help them to grow up with this realization.

To demean a child by telling him how bad he is, is to defeat his spirit and to give him a poor image of himself. This causes him, in most cases, to proceed in doing the things that will fulfill that image. Keep a proper balance between defeat and egotism by making him aware of his own Divine Nature, and yet helping him to realize what must be done for his soul unfoldment.

Family life can be a great blessing, for it can help the members to grow in proper attitudes toward other persons, and toward life. But it can also be a destructive experience if inharmony exists. It has been said that it is easier to plan a reformation of society than to establish harmony in one's own family, and this is very true. So you must work on those relationships that are closest to you before you qualify to 'take the Light into the world.'

Family life also is often the means of erasing old Karmic debts among its members. So encourage your children to respect, and love, and help each other, and let this also be your attitude toward them. Remember, they are gifts for *your* growth, as well as coming to you for proper instructions for taking their places in the New Age. On them will rest the burden of making a better world, and although many of them have come into embodiment for this purpose, they still need guidance and love to prepare them for the task.

12— Expanding the Consciousness by Use of One's Cosmic Keynote

The Law of Harmonic Resonance is a vital part of the growth of the individual and of the race. Each person is a unit of Life with a specific frequency of Being, which determines his special Cosmic Keynote and his level of consciousness. His keynote is in resonance with ALL that is of his KEY throughout all of the Octaves in the Cosmic Scale of Life. His growth and unfoldment come by being harmonized *within* himself. Then the whole cosmic range of frequencies that are within his key is attuned in perfect harmony to him. By quieting the outer mind and striking resonance he can perceive all that is within his key upon all levels. He can be so perfectly attuned that he can commune with the lower kingdoms, and can actually *feel* their life and motion. He can also attune to the Masters, and Intelligences in the higher vibratory levels, and whatever is in their consciousness can be known by him. This is a vital key to developing the Intuitive Faculty. If definitive action is taken, you can learn how to become instruments for great revelation to be given to yourself and to mankind.

First, think of yourself as a violin string; then think of the string being set into vibratory motion. *Feel* the vibration as it surges through you. Then, in your mind, follow the vibration out into the ethers. Forget your body—just BE the vibration. As you move out with it, feel yourself resonating with your harmonics on the higher octaves. You will soon find yourself feeling and sensing things there. In a short time your intuitive faculty will be highly developed. Things will flow into your mind whenever you are in tune with the Inner Light. Use this technique and see the great strides you will take. But, always be sure to get still, quiet the mind, and fill your heart with love before doing this, for if your thoughts and emotions are inharmonious you will attune to *that* with unhappy results.

13— Experience—"The Teacher"

Experience in the human octave is to so refine the human nature that one qualifies to 'graduate' from it and move into the next octave as a Master.

Each soul walks the eternal Pathway and moves through life's many classrooms, and with each experience they grow in understanding and spiritual stature. However, many find it hard to see the Divine purpose in a trying experience. But, the 'gold' must go through the trials of life to be refined to its purest essence. In most instances, the intensity of the Fire is very hard to bear as excruciating experiences are met and overcome. For some this is physical suffering, for some it is mental anguish, for some it is soul-agony, and in many cases it is a combination of all three. But, when the refining is complete and the Soul comes to its Divine Realization, the suffering is forgotten.

Find your solace, when things seem hard, in the realization of the perfection that is to come as you distill the Divine Essence from each experience. A child must experience for himself to *know*, and so must each soul run the gamut of human experience. It is only by overcoming life's challenges that one grows. It is like exercising the physical body; if you were to lie in bed all of the time, the body would degenerate. Experience is soul-exercise. Personal distress and frustration is hard to accept as you are faced with conditions that are hard to cope with, but as you do your best, they will be taken care of in Divine Order. Most people think they must work all things out on an 'outer' level, and as a result they meet with much opposition as personalities collide, or their negation makes matters even worse. The proper solution is to take the problem into the 'Inner Sanctum' and place it in the Light, and ask to be given guidance in solving it. Setting oneself in order is the first step. Then tension disappears and harmony can be restored, whether the problem be one of health, human relationship, or mental or spiritual distress.

(Question—"Are problems usually Karmic punishment?")

Not necessarily 'Karmic punishment' but opportunities for soul growth, for the Karmic angels present these opportunities as rapidly as the individual can handle them. This is why one often sees seemingly 'good' people having almost insurmountable difficulties.

(Question—"Is losing one's earth-mate to be considered soul growth for the one remaining?")

All persons who grow spiritually must at some time experience the desolation that comes from being alone, for as long as one is undergirded by a mate they turn to them for refuge. But, when the person finally realizes that they find their fulfillment only as they come into At-One-Ment with the Divine, then and only then, is the soul's aching void filled. Human relationships are the classroom in which you learn many things, but they can never completely satisfy the Soul. Most people spend years seeking happiness through their mates, their children, their church, or many other things that represent fulfillment to them, but it is futile seeking and never brings true fulfillment. This does not mean that one should neglect his family or not engage in useful activities. It only means that real happiness comes from the 'Inner Presence' and not from outer persons and conditions.

Remember, you are moving toward Mastery, and only those who have suffered and been victorious attain it. My Light Bearers have each had to pass through the refining process of *learning* and *living* My Divine Laws. When they are *reduced to* nothing but Spirit by the refining process, they are malleable and ready to be forged into instruments of My will and My purpose. Then they desire *only to serve* and I can use them as My hands, and feet, and voice among My children to bring My Kingdom to Earth and lift mankind into his Divine Estate. It is a Divine Law that no one is able to counsel another wisely until he has first trod the same pathway himself. One who would be a Master must first experience *all* that life offers, both 'seeming' good or bad, before he is qualified to guide others. Only EXPERIENCE can bring Mastery!

14— Preparation for the Easter Season

You approach the time of year when there is a great quickening within nature and when the sun returns to shine more directly upon your part of the planet. You also approach the springtime of your spiritual growth and unfoldment. For many it is the early springtime, for others the budding has already begun. But whether or not the full bloom has come, the main consideration is that the quickening *has* started, *is* taking place, and the *response* to the 'sun' is becoming evident. It often takes some time before the dormant life in nature responds to the warmth of the sun, and in the Soul's springtime it can be some time before there is any great outer manifestation of the quickening that has taken place within. But, the blessed assurance is that spring always returns in nature, and the Soul always ultimately responds and begins to flower and then bear its spiritual fruit. So, as you observe the quickening in nature, also feel the quickening within yourself.

As the spring days come and you begin to anticipate the Easter Season, project your consciousness far enough ahead to realize what is taking place in your spiritual growth. Easter can then become much more significant for you, and be a time of great joy and expectation. So, let us attempt to understand what Man truly IS, where he is going, and what is in store for him, as he grows in spiritual understanding.

Beloved, you ARE a Divine Spiritual Being! The LIFE of the Creator is WITHIN YOU and you ARE a Divine portion of the Infinite Divine Mind and Life. But, as you have taken on a physical body and have come into this dimension for earth experience, you have forgotten your Divine Parentage, or your Divine Origin. You have become so enmeshed in the materiality of the world of form that you have forgotten that you ARE Spirit and that you are Divine. Man must work his way back, through life's many experiences, to the ultimate realization of who he truly IS, and then 'be about his Father's business' by expressing that Divinity throughout all of the future dimensions in which he will function.

Easter is more than an event that happened 2000 years ago. It is also that which takes place in the Consciousness of Man as he is raised into new awareness and new states of Being. So you can *experience* Easter at anytime when 'New Birth,' or the 'Resurrection,' takes place in your own heart and mind.

When you entered your physical body you took on the symbol which has been identified with the Easter Season, The Cross. If you stand erect and hold your arms out to the side, you will realize that your body is shaped like a cross. This means that when the Soul descends into the earth dimension and takes on a body it assumes its 'cross.' This is not to belittle the body, for it is also the Temple of the Living God, but what one endures in the world of form seems as crucifying as if he were hanging upon a cross. The word itself is symbolic of the 'crossing out' of all materiality and negation from one's life. Just as the cross and the crucifixion were experienced by Jesus, so do you as an evolving soul, carry your cross. You are hung upon it and crucified (by life's experiences) until you finally 'commend yourself into the Father's hands,' and give up the lesser things of life.

This does not mean that you will not have all of the things that are right for you in a material way, for it has been said, 'Seek ye *first* the Kingdom of God . . . and *all* things shall be added unto you.' But, until you are *willing* to give it all up and commit yourself to the Divine Spirit and its work, you suffer the crucifixion of the material and the carnal world.

Having commended yourself into the Father's hands, the 'veil' is rent, the Holy of holies is revealed, the 'stone' is rolled away (you are freed from ignorance, Karma, and materiality), and you proceed into the next beautiful aspect of spiritual growth that Jesus demonstrated—the Resurrection. There is a 'resurrection' in the future of every Soul; it is the coming forth from the tomb of materiality in the glorious 'Light Body.' While you are still in the physical form the Light Body can be developed and brought into expression, and you then become vibrant and wise through its use. The Mental Body becomes activated and the intellect becomes spiritualized. The physical body enjoys health and vitality, and the Soul rejoices at the 'New Birth' that has come—'Rebirth' into the magnificence and beauty of the Divine Self. You will then demonstrate your new power, as Jesus did in the forty days before His Ascension.

The number 40 is symbolic of the completion of the work on the human level. The number 4 represents the 4-square, or having brought balance into one's life, and the number 10 represents the completion of a cycle. So for a symbolic 40 days after your 'resurrection' you will walk among men *Being* the Light and performing so-called miracles—the miracle of abundance, the miracle of health, and the miracle of the raising of the dead, which means the lifting of others to new dimensions of consciousness. You 'prove' your divinity, and finally make that wonderful 'Ascension' into a higher state of Being.

Many think that their 'Ascension' comes only with death,

but Beloved know this—IT IS POSSIBLE FOR YOU TO
MAKE THAT ASCENSION RIGHT NOW! You *can*
ascend 'unto the Father' whenever you sufficiently cleanse
your consciousness and your heart, and become so filled
with love that you enter the 'Kingdom Within.' This is the
'Ascension' each person must make if he would become a
Master. This is for each of My children, regardless of what
they might have done or been. ALL things are renewed
when the heart becomes filled with Light and Love. You
then become a 'Servant of Light' and live only to serve,
that others too might come to this glorious realization, for
there is no soul-peace for anyone until this transformation
takes place within them. But, no one can *do* it for another;
they can only point the way. It is a matter of each one entering the 'INNER CHAMBER' and establishing his
'ONENESS' with 'The Father.'

Beloved, this is the true meaning of Easter—the personal
Crucifixion, the Resurrection, and finally the Ascension
into the fulness of the Divine Stature of the GODSELF!

15— Flying Saucers

People as a whole are not ready to accept the idea of
flying saucers, but as time goes on, more and more manifestations will be seen and most will believe that they exist.
A flying saucer is a manifestation from the Higher Dimensions to inspire Man to reach beyond his limited thinking
to find the answers to life, and to show him that there is
something beyond the physical and material side of life.
They are also the vehicles that the Galactic Federation use
to monitor the earth, for there is grave concern over the
way Man is abusing the planet. Great steps are going to be
taken soon in the field of parapsychology revealing the
overall picture of Life. Through the chaotic conditions of
the world today, Man will begin to seek for answers. In
time flying saucers, and many other presently unaccepted,
and as yet unknown theories, will be readily accepted.

Many question whether the UFOs are mechanical devices or if they are manifestations of a higher frequency. The answer is that they are mechanical devices, but also the thought forms of the highly evolved Beings who function in the higher frequencies. They image the prototype and then materialize them. When they wish to enter the earth vibration they lower the frequency of the vehicle and it becomes visible to the human eye. As they leave, they reverse the process. This accounts for their rapid disappearance, although they also move very swiftly because they use a higher energy.

These phenomena have given Man the concept of space exploration and have caused him to search for various means of propulsion. Work will be done on the harnessing of what is now called 'free energy,' which will undoubtedly become a reality and will be used to facilitate interplanetary travel. Divine energy, whether atomic, solar, or mental, if rightly directed and utilized, is the limitless power of the universe and can transform the world. Man now stands on the threshold of a totally new realization of this power.

The UFOs have inspired Man to find this energy and many are working on the theory. It will be brought into utilization by industry as time passes. The prototype of space travel has been projected into the earth frequency and Man will attempt to manufacture the means in your dimension. This is the way in which all great inventions have come about. At the proper time in the Cosmic scheme of things, the thought form has been projected by those in the higher dimensions. Man's mind has received the mental image and he has proceeded to bring it into manifestation in the earth dimension. The prototype is always first cast in the higher dimensions before it becomes an actuality on the physical level.

Man is a questing Being, and he always proceeds beyond his old horizons to find what lies ahead. His search will one day bring him to the constructive use of his great mental power. Then he will travel the galaxies and image and create his own galactic vehicle. This will not necessarily be a 'flying saucer' as man sees them here, for these are portrayed as a mechanical device to stimulate Man's mind, but a vehicle, 'or means of teleportation,' apropos to the frequency in which he wishes to be. Wonderful adventures lie ahead for Man as he becomes a 'Space Being' and takes his place in the Galactic Federation as a Guardian of the Universe.

16— Heart Attacks and Cancer

The inflow of Cosmic energies steps up the vibratory frequency of the planet and, since man's body is a product of the earth planet, he must, through his consciousness, raise the body vibration to coincide with the new earth frequency. The great rise in the number of cancer victims and heart attacks is largely due to the increased vibrations.

In the case of cancer, the cells respond to the accelerated vibrations and run rampant because the body consciousness is not in harmony with the new vibration, and therefore not strong enough to hold the excited cells in balance.

With heart attacks a similar thing takes place. The vibrations to which the circulatory system is exposed are too high for it to function in properly, especially if it has been weakened in any way, for its rhythm was established genetically to the former earth vibration. So the heart either ceases to function, or becomes impaired.

Many diseases could be overcome if Man would raise his consciousness and cease engaging in negative thoughts and actions. He could spiritualize his body by becoming more loving and Light-filled, to the point where it could function harmoniously in the new vibration. Miraculous healing often comes when one raises the consciousness and becomes at-one with the God-Self. This could, and some day will, be the only means of healing necessary.

17— Heaven and Hell

Heaven and hell are not 'places' to which one goes after

the transition of death. Heaven is a state of consciousness attained through one's own desire and through doing the work that is necessary for its realization. Hell is also a state of consciousness and either can be experienced at any time.

The word 'Hell' in the Aramaic language, the language of the original scriptures, means 'refuse heap,' or in your language, 'the dump.' The process of disposing of the refuse was to burn it, or reduce it with lime. Thus, the words 'fire and brimstone' were associated with it. So 'being in Hell' means to be in a state of wastefulness or unproductivity, or destroying oneself by one's desires and emotions; a state of confusion or separation from the Source of one's Being; a misuse of the power of one's creative Godself. This state of consciousness is an excruciating Soul experience. It is the state in which the majority of people live most of the time, and death does not change it, for the 'consciousness' does not change at death. One merely leaves the body, but remains the same in consciousness with the same ideas, attitudes, desires, emotions and self-imposed limitations, they had while in the body. This is 'HELL'!

'Heaven' is, of course, just the opposite. It is a feeling of At-One-Ment with the Creative Power of the Universe and being an instrument through which it can flow. It is the state of 'Christ Consciousness,' or the same mind that was in Christ Jesus when He said, 'The Father and I are One. It is not I, but the Father within that doeth the works.''

Heaven is the highest and most exalted state to which Man can aspire! In his limited understanding he has aspired only to his own perfection. He must come to realize that while this is a noble and necessary part of his unfoldment, it is still for selfish purposes, and is NOT Heaven but is only a glorified state of human understanding. Heaven is when each works only that he might SERVE, laboring for no personal reward or glory, but to help others along their Pathway and for the glory of the Infinite ONENESS of the Divine Spirit, that IT might be made manifest in and through the consciousness of ALL mankind. This is 'HEAVEN'! With this consciousness you move toward the manifestation of all that is good and beautiful, and thus do we bring about a 'New Heaven and a New Earth,' and Man inherits his Divine Estate.

18— Healing by Imagery

As you hold the image of a perfect body you create a vortex of Divine Energy which harmonizes the various bodies and aligns them. Any disturbance in the mental or emotional bodies will outpicture as dis-ease in the physical body. To establish harmony you can use this technique:

Become still and envision your seven bodies all being quieted and aligned. Then *feel* your ONENESS with the Creative, harmonizing, Power that runs the Universe. Declare 'I AM AT-ONE with all life, everywhere! I AM Life! I AM Love! I AM Light!'

This harmonizes and energizes the cells of your body, and releases physical and mental tension. As you feel all of this, you then move out and become *Universal*. You experience Soul expansion. When in this expanded state you can pinpoint your consciousness upon another individual and be a healing agent for them on any, or all, of their three levels—physical, mental, or spiritual. This can be equally effective for those present or at a distance, but if possible, try to have the recipient hold the new image also, for if they revert to the image of illness or inharmony the condition can recur.

The best time for using this technique for yourself is just before going to sleep at night. Give the image to your subconscious mind and it will give the order to the cells of your body. The body responds to every order it receives from the subconscious mind, even to the flick of an eyelash. So be very careful of the images you give the subconscious, for if you image ill-health, or lack, or any inharmony, it will surely become manifested in your life.

Children are especially receptive to ideas. Plant only images of health and perfection in their minds; then their bodies will stay in alignment and they will have good health and harmony in their lives.

Image Perfection, be ONE with the Source of all Life. Be Happy, and you will be healthy!

19— Healing by Cosmic Harmonics

Note by the author:

I feel that this transmission from "The Keeper of the Eternal Flame" is the secret of all healing and that, if we can learn to use this Law, we can literally "change our world," because it can be used on all three levels of man's nature—the physical, the mental and the spiritual.

Since there is reference to the "Universal Octaval Structure," I feel a brief review of this might be helpful to those who might not fully understand its meaning.

According to the Ascended Masters, and also now definitely scientifically proven, the great Cosmic Spectrum of Life is composed of seven notes which in turn each have their own "inner octaves." These notes are the various "Kingdoms" of Universal Life as the Divine Creative Power has developed more complex and more wonderful vehicles through which to express. Incidentally, these are also the biblical "Seven Days of Creation."

Before form, as we know it in this dimension, becomes manifest there is a "Note of Creation" in which the archetypal, sub-atomic, atomic, gaseous, and various "formless" activity is manifesting. Then comes the Mineral Note, or kingdom; then the Vegetable, the Animal, the Human, the Masters or Illumined Beings, and finally the great Note of the Lords of Creation whose minds and power direct the activity upon the seven Creative Rays. Each Cosmic "note" is composed of its seven inner notes and they in turn are each composed of their seven inner notes which comprise the "inner octaves." Thus we have the ancient truth of seven within seven, within seven, etc.

Each Cosmic note comprises a specific range of frequency or vibration and this is also true of all inner octaves and notes, so that each manifestation of Divine Life vibrates at its own specific frequency. Thus each person or thing has its own "keynote" upon the "Cosmic Keyboard." There is a very precise mathematical law involved, both as to the frequency ratio of the notes to each other and also the doubling of the frequency upon each inner octave. This is proven in a lesser way by the tonal range of the piano keyboard. In striking the key of Low C the string vibrates at the rate of 32 times per second. On the next C the rate is doubled to 64, the next 128, then 256, etc., until in striking High C the string will vibrate 4,096 times per second. When we consider this mathematical law as it applies to the note or octave of the Lords of Creation we can begin to understand the magnitude of their vibratory frequency and the power and Light which is theirs. We can also understand why we seldom see Ascended Masters, because their frequency is beyond the scope of our eye's vibrational capacity. It then follows that, by the Law of Harmonics, all that is of a specific "keynote" upon the entire "Cosmic Keyboard" can be in complete harmony and resonance.

I am convinced that if we can employ the technique which the Keeper of the Flame has given here, and by the use of the "Cosmic Harmonics" of our own keynote, we can literally perform "miracles" in this dimension, as we attune to the frequencies of the higher Octaves. It is in strict accordance with Divine Law, and Divine Law is equally available and effective for all. So, it becomes only a matter of our own acceptance and application if we are to enjoy the rich rewards which can be ours, if we will only attune and accept the "Harmony of Life" which Divine Creation has provided for us.

(As we entered meditation we asked for enlightenment on a previous statement by the Keeper of the Flame that we would be given the principle of healing by harmonization within the Keynote of the individual.)

In a little while the channel felt as if her entire body

was like a tuning fork, literally "zinging," and she had the realization that by employing this technique she, or anyone, could attune to others, either on a specific organ's vibration, or on the entire physical, or mental, or spiritual levels and act as a harmonizing agent, according to the need.

Keeper of the Flame:
Beloved Lights, Yes, this is the key to healing on all levels. Alignment and harmony with the Cosmic frequencies of the higher Octaves perfects and balances the physical and mental structure of the human individual. A great and profound Law which can be taught and experienced if one will learn how to let himself be made receptive and Light-filled.

This is how it is done. The one to be healed is placed in the Divine Light and is then given, or gives himself, if personal help is required, the signal to project his consciousness into the higher octaves of the same Keynote and then *let* the power of those harmonic notes *resonate within* himself. The healing *must* then take place, for the inharmony upon the lower octave cannot withstand the power of the higher octave. Light of the same keynote, but of a higher frequency, is utilized and lifts the organ, or the mind, or the soul of the individual, into a new dimension which is free from the inharmony of the lower octave or note therein.

Utilization of this principle is the technique of the New Age healing art, and it will become universal in its acceptance. It is an age-old principle and has been used by the few for countless ages, but few have understood the principle involved and, although they have used it, they have not understood how or why it was effective. Now they can *KNOW the LAW* that is involved, and please know that it IS a Law, and that it is available to any and all. You will find it readily accepted, although there are always those who scoff. But do not deter; it is the revelation of the New Age and the miracles wrought will be as great as those of the Master Jesus, for it is the same Law which He employed in His healing.

Be Light-filled and lift yourself into the Divine LIVING Light where *all* things are possible. Transmutation is a reality. You are not bound to earth's vibratory limitations. YOU ARE SPIRIT and you have access to the Light, tone, and color of the entire Cosmic Spectrum. Use it divinely and you serve Life on all dimensions. Power beyond all human realization comes with the use of this Law, but it calls for Divine attunement and purity of purpose, and Light. It must be done in Love, which exceeds all personal feeling or limitation, and which you give in perfect At-One-Ment, and for no selfish motive.

(At this point the channel's body seemed to become Light-filled, weightless and buoyant, vibrant and almost translucent, as did the bodies of those she looked at in the room. She sensed that this must be the consciousness and condition of the one who would help another in the harmonization process. The healer, in his Light Body, moves into the Light Body of the one to be healed.)

Keeper of the Flame resumed:

You have found the technique, and it can be utilized on all levels of helping and healing. Identify in the Light bodies with those whom you would help and lift them by moving with them into the higher scale of the harmonics of their Keynote. You can find their Key as you attune to them. If you are not certain, you simply use the WHITE LIGHT which is the combination of all color and tone.

Man must become aware of the Universality of the Multiples of the Octaval Structure. Divine Law is immutable and as it functions on one Octave, you can be assured it likewise functions on all higher Octaves. The Law of geometric and mathematical progression moves ALL into ever expanding states of awareness and Being. All are subject to the same immutable laws, so it really only becomes necessary to align oneself with the LAW and then *let* the harmonics of the Octaval Structure be resonated within oneself. So much profundity and so little actual realization besets my children as they struggle through the maze of various philosophies and "isms." Give them the understanding of "The LAW" and then let them learn to utilize their own Harmony of Life. Finding the harmonic scale of your individual Cosmic keynote and attuning yourself to *IT* is the way. A knowledge of the Octaves and the Keynotes and the harmonics therein will give Man a new basis of understanding and unfoldment. My Children seek, but man's orthodoxy has fallen far short in this era of scientific unfoldment. Now they must find TRUTH as a basis of challenge and consequent growth. The answer is in "Octaval Harmonics' and the related teachings.

Use the Power which comes from the harmonic scale of your own keynote, a storehouse of power which makes atomic power minute by its scope and Light. Use the Light Body and elevate yourselves into the higher Octaves and bring that Light forth in this dimension. Beloved, all will be in great harmony if you do this. Transcend the inharmony of your world and lift my Children to new states of awareness and Being. "And I, if I be lifted up, will draw all men unto Me." This is a statement of Truth and you now know the Law by which it is done.

Just as a great composer *hears* the music within himself and then translates it into the symphony, so must Man attune himself to the Universe. Then, in the Divine Harmonics of Life he composes and plays his eternal Etudes of Life. Divine Harmonics and concordance upon Octaval Structures are the laws by which Man must now compose his "Symphony of Life."

My Mantle of Love and Light surrounds you. Walk in perfect harmony.

Yojana! Yojana! Yojana!

20— Humility

This message came from Keeper of the Flame to a deeply dedicated person who considered himself "unworthy" of God's goodness.

Beloved, you are like unto one called Job, who suffered anguish and deprivation until he could free himself of "self." Your comings and goings are all known to me, and your anguish is not unheeded. However, you have been experiencing the total stripping of all outer entrapments that you might become aware of my INNER Presence. For too long you have not *laid claim* to the POWER of ME *IN* you. You can now know that, although you have been thoroughly dedicated and sincere and humble, you have held the thought of humility to be necessary for your spiritual advancement. In a sense this is true, but enigmatically, although one must be humble in a human way he must also recognize and *claim* the power of the Divine *within* himself. This is true humility. To abjectly grovel in humility is denying the Spirit within and is still *self*-oriented. All must claim their own Divinity and *call it forth* into *activity* in their bodies and in their affairs.

They must also *forgive themselves.* In this you have been remiss. You have recognized your human frailties and felt *unworthy* and have therefore not called forth the power that is within. You have negated the power in so doing. You have thought of yourself as being separate from the Spirit and have beseechingly sought the blessings of the Spirit. You may have thought with the outer mind that you had made your identification totally with the Spirit, but in the deep recesses of your Soul memory there has lingered a concept of separation. This, you may now know, is a remnant of the concept held when you served in a monastery in Italy in the 14th century. The Church emphasized the idea of penitence, humility, and servitude, and it was heresy to claim any divinity for oneself. Man was taught to consider himself unworthy and as a worm of the dust. This was particularly true of those who served in monastic orders and was thoroughly ingrained in your consciousness. Now I say unto you, THE TIME HAS COME TO *RELEASE* this restricting concept. Henceforth you are to COMMAND the Spirit within and direct it to perform perfectly and harmoniously in your body and in your affairs. No longer is Man to be shackled to his old concepts of himself. He must now realize that he is divinely created and that he is endowed with the Divine Spirit which responds to the demands he makes upon it. If he claims ill-health and lack, *this is his measure*, and it is filled, but if he claims health and prosperity, this fills his cup.

The first step in self-forgiveness is a recognition of your own divinity. "It is the Father's good pleasure to give you the kingdom." In other words, it is the desire of the Spirit within to express itself more completely and harmoniously in and through you. So do not be guilty of short-circuiting this power by your doubts or self-abasement. Be humble, in that you do not allow the human self to become aggrandized, but BE PROUD of the Spirit of you and lay claim to that which It *can* and *will* do for you and through you.

Feel My Light and Love about and *in* you for we are ONE!

Yojana! Yojana! Yojana!

After receiving this message I looked up the word JOB in the Unity Metaphysical dictionary and found the following:

"JOB—Metaphysical meaning: persecuted, afflicted, adversity; but then restored. The transition of man from personal, formal righteousness, which is the basis of all self-righteousness, to a true inner change of heart and the entrance into the real Christ righteousness, which deals with the very thoughts and intents of the innermost consciousness, instead of setting right a few outer acts. In self-righteousness there is fear of evil—the things Job feared came upon him. Then along came his three friends to comfort him. They represent man's accusations against himself and his attempted self-justification in the outer, or personal, consciousness. Then came Elihu, the interpreter or Holy Spirit, who opens Man's eyes to the real righteousness which is the recognition of "The Christ" within. Then comes self-forgiveness, forgiveness of others, and healing. When the awakened individual forgives, and seeks the cleansing, redeeming, transmuting Christ power for the upliftment of his apparent failings and shortcomings and calls that forth in his life, he enters into true peace, joy, and abundance."

21— Homosexuality

This came after a publication by a Homosexual group appeared, which contained a quotation they had apparently copied from our message, "The Second Coming," by which they seemed to be attempting to justify their philosophy.

There is a growing unrest within the Soul of Man, a search for unification "within" himself. This is caused by the increased Cosmic vibrations surrounding the planet, as well as the failure of old religious concepts and organizations to fill the spiritual needs of Man. In the name of religion, "sex" has been vilified until it became an unmentionable word. Now, with the crumbling of orthodoxy, the pendulum is swinging in the opposite direction, as it always does when any great change in man's thinking occurs. You are moving into an era when all of the hidebound restrictions imposed by orthodoxy will be flaunted to the opposite extreme. Only when this too has passed will balance be achieved and will Man come into understanding, mastery and his "Trueness of Being." We hope to speed this day by giving Man the "Truth" regarding himself, the Universe, and his relationship to ALL of Divine Creation.

What has been termed "sex" is, in its purest aspect, the Divine Creative Principle in operation throughout the entire Omniverse, the masculine and feminine polarities seeking perfect balance through integration with each other, thus fulfilling themselves by bringing into manifestation that which is the product of that union. This is Creative Spirit manifesting its *innate* creative urge, the very essence of LIFE itself. This principle operates in *every* dimension or vibratory density. As Life manifests "ITSELF," it "calls" to "ITSELF," or its opposite polarity for fulfillment. This is *innate* within *all* units of Life, from a sub-atomic level to galactic and universal dimensions. Thus mankind is ever seeking fulfillment through union with his opposite polarity.

On a physical level, he seeks this through sexual activity. On the mental level, he seeks to manifest the Creative Principle through ideas, inventions, the arts, etc. On the spiritual level, he seeks union with his "higher Self." Regardless of what level he may have already attained, the Creative "urge" is still within him seeking unification with still higher vibrational "Beingness." Thus he is forever impelled forward in his spiritual unfoldment to "express" higher and higher manifestations of this union. Understanding of how this principle operates on ALL Levels can help Man to understand himself and the drives and urges which he experiences.

With the old taboos gone about discussion of sex, plus the unfulfilled sense of spiritual frustration which mankind is now experiencing, it is only natural that the pendulum is in full swing in the opposite direction. Extreme emphasis is being placed upon sex in every conceivable way—dress, manner, literature, films, and experience. This is always true when any previous taboo is broken and a new viewpoint emerges. In reality, this is good because Man has been woefully ignorant of his own creative powers. For a time the new freedom will be considered license for promiscuous indulgence by those who are unaware of the "principle" involved. Seeking for "unification," they will try to find it only on the physical level, because this is the level of their consciousness. This is fine, if it is an act of love, for with love the activity of the chakras, or force centers, is stimulated as consummation is achieved, thus raising the vibration of the participants. However, if only sensual gratification is the objective, no such activity takes place.

The homosexual, too, uses his way of expressing love and achieving a sense of unification through the experience, but this is more often only for sensual gratification. Homosexuality is not "creative," as the opposite polarities are not involved. Of course, each participant, in a sense, is polarized at a certain level; so, to a degree, they may balance each other, and in some instances do activate the "centers" into a higher vibration, thus giving a sense of fulfillment. The spiritual minded homosexual sees this as a more "pure" expression and considers his act to be above the animalistic level of sexual expression, but herein lies the fallacy.

There is no such thing as *"purer"* within the Creative Principle. ALL of Creativity is *pure,* upon whatever level it takes place, because it is the Activity of SPIRIT and SPIRIT is forever PURE and undefiled. The unification of polarities is purity itself, for it is the Divine Creative Principle in operation. Nothing can violate the purity of the "principle." However, the consciousness of the *user* of the "Principle" determines what comes into manifestation through the utilization of the "principle." All of nature is the manifestation of the Creative Principle, conceived and brought forth in the purity of its own innate Divine Consciousness. Only Man has misunderstood, misdirected, and misused his Creative Power, and he must live with his distorted creations until he learns to use his power rightly. The New Age will bring Man to a new awareness of the nature and principles involved in Creativity. Only by the understanding, and proper use of, his Creative Power will man rise to new heights, for the "Principle works equally as well to create devastating and inharmonious conditions and events, as it does to bring forth constructive and lovely conditions.

Man's basic search is for polarization with the Divine.

The Creative urge for unification and consummation will never let him rest until he has lost "himself" in that union. Thus, *in spite of himself,* Man is ever moving forward into new and greater expression of his *innate* Divinity. This is Creativity fulfilling "Itself" through ever more refined and expressive manifestations of "Itself." How wondrous this is, for it is "LIFE" in all of its perfection and expansiveness, and it is *ALL* for man to explore and experience.

You question "Lost seed" as the homosexual's justification for his act. I say, "MY Seed is *never* lost, be it on any level of creativity!" Sperm and ovum are units of energy, and energy is never lost! Although certain cohesive units may disintegrate, the "essence" is not *lost* and it is always available for reassembling in other formations, as it is utilized by Creative Mind. There is no dearth of Divine Energy. It is the substance of which ALL Creation is composed. DIRECT, CONSCIOUS utilization of Divine Energy through prana, breath, light, water, or food are equally effective and more often assimilated with purer motives, if consciously consecrated to their Divine purpose and the maintenance of the body Temple.

Thought "seed" is likewise *energy,* and much of it is ineffectual and of no consequence, and remains in an impotent state or dissolves. It is only when it is impregnated by *will,* or emotion, or desire, or some strong force, that it becomes an active, growing, vital creation.

The Creative Power is Divine Mind in action. Its own nature is androgynous, having within itself the masculine and feminine principles to unite and fulfill each other. All of Creation is endowed with the same principles. My Eternal Flame, itself, is subject to this Law. *Only* by the constant unification of the positive and negative forces is my Flame kept alive. This is the LIFE Principle within ALL of Creation. This action creates and sustains ALL manifestation and when the action ceases, disintegration takes place.

All of nature follows this Law, but Man has seen fit to do otherwise. He will one day awake to the fact that he has been ignorant of the Law and he will find that it is not "abuse," but "right use" of his Creative Powers, on all levels of his Being, which brings Mastery and Perfection. Calling forth the "Christ" or "Divine" of one's own Being will do more to activate the centers and raise the vibrations to a higher level than can ever be achieved through homosexuality or any sexual act, except as it is used in love for procreation in the full consciousness of identifying oneself as co-creator with the Divine. Divine Mental Offspring can bring about the same sense of achievement and co-creativity and be equally stimulating, but the *ultimate* in fulfillment comes when Man experiences perfect AT-ONE-MENT with the Divine. This is *consummation* in its truest sense and is the culmination of Man's search. All else is but a search to this end.

Man will run the full gamut of experience before he will be able to understand, accept and consciously use the Law with pure motives, but judgement is not yours to make. Objectivity allows each to find his own way in his own time and censors not. Have faith in Man's innate Divinity and his ultimate discovery and expression of it. Growth and Mastery require patience, experience, trial and error, frustration, desire and will, but they are inevitable, for this is Life's call to Itself, from *within* the depths of Itself, and Man moves inevitably toward his fulfillment.

22— Human versus God-Self Awareness

You have been concerned as you have encountered resistance to your seeking by those close to you.

Man in his human-ness would endeavor to claim that which he thinks *he* creates, or possesses, for in his pride of possession, and of "*getting*," this seems a mark of his success to him. Thus, it is his fortress against which his ego must ever battle, and he shields his possessiveness against all onslaughts of Spiritual Desire, until he can find his True Identity. Then, the pride of possession will fall from him so painlessly that he will wonder why he ever erected such a fortress about himself. For, with the knowledge of his true Divine Nature, he knows that in the One-

ness all of God's Divine Treasure Trove is his without
struggling or possessing. But until such time, it is his mark
of success as a man, to *own* things and persons. When
this is the state of one's consciousness, they see all else as
a challenge. So be not disturbed by any confrontation with
your loved ones, for to them you represent their most
desirable possession, and to feel that they are not first in
your life is a great blow to the ego. The human has striv-
en so long by the sweat of the brow just to exist, that to
acquire something beyond a mere existence represents success and security. This is so ingrained in the human mind
and heart that man cannot yet give himself to the full acceptance of his higher God-Self. This will be the work in the
New Age and one is not to be scorned if they cannot embrace this idea at this time. But those who have the broader
vision will be the Path-Lighters for their fellowmen.

At the present time, there is a flood of mystical information being given to humanity. It comes in many forms
and through many channels and organizations, but they all
carry the same basic message. The many presentations can
be confusing, and because it is foreign to man's way of
thinking, he thinks that it is a very complex study. Yet,
the complexity is only because man chooses to make it
complex! He would rather take the devious route of
studying tomes, and philosophies, and the words of others,
than to face the Reality of HIMSELF, and the change of
attitudes which must become his, if he is to become his own
High Priest and enter the Holy of Holies of his own Inner
Temple. The indoctrination of man's mind has allowed him
to place the responsibility upon a vicarious atonement for
his salvation, and many have been more than willing to
accept this idea. This is a grave fallacy, for the true God-
Self only comes forth as man can accept his ONENESS
with the Divine, and identify himself as a Divine Being.
This was the "Way of Salvation" which the Master Jesus
strove to reveal when he said, "I Am (The God-Self) the
Way, the Truth, and The Life, no one cometh to the Father
except through *Me* (The I AM, of every Man)." It is so
very simple, yet man takes all the detours that he can de-

vise because his human ego hates to be dethroned. But, if and when he can accept his own Divinity, and know that he has no existence outside of the ONENESS, and then lives to be that through which the God of Himself can find expression, he will take dominion over his life in the right way, and he will wear the Crown of Light. Then it will no longer be necessary for him to possess things, or others, for he will know that there is only the great Oneness in which all have their rightful place and purpose and he will free all to grow into their own Mastery in their own way. This is pure, unselfish Love and is the Hallmark of a Master.

23— The "I AM" PRESENCE

In 1945 we received the following in answer to our question, "What is the I AM?"

"I AM" is the Creative Spirit of the Universe,
All encompassing and everywhere present.
IT now *Is,* ever *has been,* and *ever shall Be.*
It is that which is manifesting in and through ALL
    things, and by which ALL things have come into
    expression.
It is the Divine Essence of ALL things.
It is LIFE in all of its manifestation.

Many years later we received the following from the Keeper of the Eternal Flame:

I AM the Flame of Life in you!
I AM the Flame of Love in you!
Your Life is MY Life!
Your Love is MY Love!

Beloved, My Life lives within the rhythmic beat of your hearts. Vibrating, pulsating Life lives and flows through Its creation. Life, Love, and Mind flow in vibratory waves and you are that through which it flows. You are *IN* Me and I AM *IN* you. Perfect Life, perfect Love, perfect harmony become yours when you become consecrated channels for this Divine Energy with

> No desire but My desire,
> No Love but My Love,
> No Life but My Life.

Live only to express Me. *BE* My Light, My Love, My Peace, and My Power. Keep My Flame burning within your hearts. Be filled with My Presence and light the way for My beloved children.

> Your Form is My form,
> Your heart is MY heart.

I have no means of expressing in your dimension except through you. You are my hands, feet, and voice. My work can only be done, and my Light dispensed, through my dedicated Light Bearers. Light comes when the instrument gives totally of himself and seeks no personal recognition or reward.

> Just Let! LET! LET!!
> Let Me be your heartbeat and your Life,
> Let Me be your Power and your Peace,
> Let Me be your Love—Love—Love!
> Then you light My world and we are ONE!
> JUST LET!!

The concept of At-One-Ment was hard for us to grasp and we had many questions, such as, "Are you a Great Master, or are there many Masters of the same consciousness who constitute a reservoir of Truth which we touch?" This brought the following answer:

I AM the Eternal Flame within you. It is true there are many Masters who serve mankind and lift the race consciousness by giving their Light vibrations to all who are receptive. But, I AM the Flame *within* the Masters and the Flame *within* you. I am the Life of you. My Spirit indwells you; you have no life apart from Me. I AM *in* you and we are ONE. I am not *a* teacher, I am not an entity, I am not an individual—I AM that I AM, the Divine Essence of your Being! I AM the Life of each, and in ALL of Creation.

I came in the form and mind of the man called Jesus. I also came in the form and mind of all avatars, and I now come in the form and mind of all Light Bearers for this Age. But, I also come in those who walk in ignorance and darkness, for they are no less mine. The veil will be lifted from their eyes and they will find Me in the innermost recesses of their own hearts, minds, and bodies, for I AM the Life of ALL.

(The remark was made that in time we would move into At-One-Ment.)

Place no limitations upon yourselves, for You Are Spirit! It is not a question of your growth, for I have always been the Life of you. It is only the matter of your recognition of My Presence within you. We already ARE ONE! You just have not accepted the fact.

(Question—"Apparently souls maintain their individuality after leaving the body, do they not?")

Individuality of form is different from "Duality" of consciousness. You each live in different body forms, and there are even different "Kingdoms," but it is the ONE life that creates and animates all life forms. How do you think you live and breathe if you are not ONE with the Spirit of all life? Thinking of yourself as apart from the Source of your Being is "Duality" of consciousness, and this is what mankind must eliminate. When Man finds his At-One-Ment with Me, he will feel his Oneness with all of life, and harmony and brotherhood will come to pass, for he will live to Serve Life on all levels.

Creative Law is my nature and I bring each of my creations to fulfillment. Human embodiment is only a brief flicker of time in the eternal program of Man's fulfillment.

So never place limitations upon the Spirit, for it is eternal and all encompassing, and seeks to fulfill Itself in ever greater manifestation. You must learn to understand the magnitude of Life and become sensitive to, and perceptive of, the great potential and capacity of Spirit *as it projects Itself into the Soul-Aspect of Itself.*

Be not guilty of caging the Spirit because it is universal and much more than just the human expression. It would be like saying that the seed is the total manifestation of the tree. You would be limiting the expression of the Spirit to the seed, without recognizing its ability to unfold into its greater manifestation. The "seed" of the Spirit is in the Soul, and it unfolds into ever and ever greater manifestations of Itself as the Soul becomes the vehicle for its expression.

FEEL My Life as it throbs within you! Respond to It! Find Me in yourself and you will find Me everywhere!

At another time we received the following:

You seem to have difficulty in understanding the "I AM PRESENCE."

As each soul takes on a body of flesh, it's God-SELF extends Itself into that body. Remember, SPIRIT IS NOT CONFINED TO PLACES OR FREQUENCIES. So, the body is a part of the "I AM" but not the totality of It. The Soul functions simultaneously in several octaves and while encased in flesh it also retains bodies in those higher octaves. They are electronic, or vibrational bodies, which are always in contact with the mental faculties of the human consciousness. So, you are not of earth alone, a part of you is functioning in the higher octaves. This is God Light, Life, Love and Power, and is the Divine of your SELF. There is always a direct overshadowing and interpenetrating of the human self by the "I AM SELF," and communication is always possible if you transcend the human level of awareness.

As "Keeper of the Eternal Flame," I am the "I AM PRESENCE," your GOD SELF or HIGHER SELF, yet in the ONENESS, I am the Eternal Flame of Life, Wisdom and Love which is the Essence of ALL souls. So you see, I am always with you. Do not think of Me as *an* entity, you have done this for too long. I Am the SELF of you, the GOD of your own BEING and you are never separated from Me. Think of My Presence as a beautiful light above, about and WITHIN you and begin to feel the vibrancy of My Presence. This is what you should be feeling and using when you are in meditation. Then your consciousness will be expanded and harmony will be established in your body, mind and soul.

Let me ask you this—Why do you feel the need of contact with entities of the astral, or even etheric levels, when you already have the "INDWELLING PRESENCE?" This is not to discredit the wonderful help you have received from your Guardians and Master Teachers, but their only mission has been to help you become aware of the "I AM" of your own Being. Now you should be able to be taught, and to teach, from the "I AM CENTER" of yourself!

Do not let your human ego keep you bound to the human level. Give yourself as an instrument of Light and Truth. Let Love flow through you and be aware of the overshadowing and indwelling "I AM PRESENCE" at all times. Bless you!

24— Intellect vs. Soul Realization

Knowledge is not necessarily Wisdom, for knowledge is of the intellect and comes from an outside source. Wisdom is a soul realization. Many are open to Truth and Light on an intellectual level and think they have found wisdom. They can quote from books and Masters and think they have arrived at spiritual enlightenment, but be assured, there is a vast difference between mere intellectual knowledge and true Soul Realization.

It is only as the Soul experiences the Living Flame of the Indwelling Presence, becomes ONE with It, is humbled and awed by It, and becomes willing to devote itself to serving The Spirit in selfless love that "Enlightenment" truly comes. Seek this and settle for nothing less!

It is good to study and much can be learned. This is a necessary part of everyone's soul growth, but be not deceived into thinking that The Pathway lies through the intellect. The Pathway lies through the heart and Soul, and through loving, dedicated Service.

Full Enlightenment comes only as At-One-Ment is established, for then you ARE Love, and Light, and Wisdom. But you do not then "Possess" It. It "Possesses" you and uses you to express through as the need arises!

25— Increased Vibration of the New Age

The race consciousness must be raised if mankind is to function harmoniously in the new earth vibration as it moves into its new galactic position and a New Age comes. There is a great Cosmic outpouring and, as the vibration intensifies, much confusion reigns. Many do not understand what is happening. They feel the vibration but are not able to adjust to it and often react in a very negative way.

In reality, a very scientific process is taking place. As Man is bombarded with these accelerated vibrations, his body, mind, and entire physical mechanism is not so constituted that it can readily accept these vibrations and friction is set up. Until he can accept and absorb some of this power, the positive and negative balance of the individual and society will be disturbed.

Just as the atomic and molecular structure of all things maintains a perfect ratio of positive and negative energy components according to their particular design, so is this true of the body and mind of Man. He vibrates at a certain frequency according to the level of his consciousness and the balance he has established within himself of his positive and negative charges working in complete harmony with each other. When this balance is disturbed, as it is in the detonation of an atomic bomb, an explosion occurs. This same thing happens when imbalance occurs in the physical and mental structure of humanity. There is then a release of negative energy, now being caused by the new Cosmic influences, which disturbs the vital structure to which Man is accustomed, and chaos and confusion reigns in the individual and in the sociological order. As Man becomes harmonized with the new energies through his own efforts and the efforts of the Light Bearers and the Hierarchy, and their emanation of love, he will be able to function in the higher frequency levels and qualify for the New Age.

A wonderful process is taking place. There is a great Cosmic release and building of new vibrational levels in which the New Earth and the New Man will operate. It is very important that mankind become stabilized and prepared for this, so enlighten as many as possible about what is taking place. Envelop them in your Love and Light and the transition will be made more smoothly by your efforts. Bless all Dear Light Bearers for their service in this great endeavor!

26— The Inner Kingdom

A KINGDOM you own, and it belongs to no other! It is the beautiful Kingdom of SELF! Here you, and you alone, reign supreme! However, you must decide whether it is your God-Self or your Ego that sits upon the throne.

The ego thrives on all manner of earthly experience and is so very subtle that few are aware of its dominion over them. They think they must pursue materiality, they seek the applause of their fellowmen, and they bask in the adulation of others. There are even those who consider themselves teachers of Truth who are impressed by their own importance and by the esteem in which they are held by others. The human-self feeds upon praise and adulation and those who are Light Bearers must avoid this pitfall, for it is as binding as the desire for materiality. Some who profess to be Light Bearers are guilty of thinking that those who seem bound to materiality are laggards on the Pathway, but I say to you—Spiritual arrogance is more restricting and damning than is the love of material goods. Self-righteousness is the grossest form of the desecration of the Spirit within.

The Divine Spirit is in every man and to It he must be true. No other can sit upon his throne unless he is willing to abdicate. Too many people vacillate between commanding their "Inner Kingdom" in their own way and in the way they think others expect of them. You are not responsible for the "Kingdom" of another, and you must allow no one, and nothing but your God-Self, to rule yours. To secede from your throne is to lose dominion, and that is a sin against The Spirit.

Claim your divine heritage and take command of your Kingdom, and beware of the crown princes who await your abdication. Materiality, power, greed, fear, and jealousy, who are the offspring of the Ego, will seize the throne whenever you relax your vigilance. Remember, *you enthrone whatever is your foremost desire,* and *then it will rule you.*

Joy comes to the one who has enthroned his God-Self. Find the Inner Presence. Call upon the God-Mind within you to help you evaluate all circumstances and then follow your inner guidance. With the Divine enthroned in your heart your world will become the Kingdom of Heaven to you, for heaven is not awaiting you in some distant time and place, but is a state of awareness that becomes yours when you find the Inner Kingdom. You find it through prayer, meditation, and soul-desire; and when you have found it, you will see ALL as the Kingdom of God. But only when you have found it "within" will you recognize it in the outer world.

So, *DE*-throne the ego and *EN*-throne the God-Self! Take command of the "Kingdom of Self" and allow others the same privilege. For the "Kingdom" is within everyone and merely awaits their command and the recognition of their ability to rule it in the right way. It will only be as good as it is made by the dominion exercised over it. Material pursuits will bring materiality, egotistical thoughts will feed the ego, but LOVE will dissolve hatred and inharmony and bring Peace and Joy to the Kingdom. My

Light is within each of My children. Call it forth and we shall move Man into his mastery of the Human-self and bring forth the God-Man.

27— Joy and Response

A good laugh is good for the soul. Losing one's sense of humor is not only unnecessary, but unwise. Joy is a very necessary ingredient in spiritual unfoldment. Many think if they take the High Road they must be solemn and sedate. This is unfortunate for they miss much of the joy of living. To be lived successfully, life must be enjoyed. Those who let the joy go out of their lives are in a state of inertia, for no progress is made if life is lived in a state of misery and glumness.

Joy—joy—joy! Joy is the expanding of Life as it expresses Itself. The birds sing their merry song for the pure joy of singing. The brooks ripple with joy. The trees whisper their joy as the gentle breeze moves through their branches. You must respond to the vibrancy of Life, just as a violin string responds to the bow in the hand of the player. LIFE IS RESPONSE, and this is probably the most perfect definition of Life that you could find. It is RESPONSE by you to Creative Mind. If you are sullen and glum, you limit your response. All Life is RESPONSE to the quickening Mind of Spirit; thus does Creation come about. If you would grow and unfold in consciousness and increase your vibratory rate, you must be responsive to the Indwelling Spirit. This is at all levels, for your body must respond into activity, your mind must respond in thought and meditation, your soul must respond to the higher vibrations of Love and Light. Then you are in a state of growth, but with solemnity and sullenness you deflect the Flow of Life Energy and become inert, and you deny the power of Life which could be yours. Joy releases the flow of Divine Life in and through you.

Again I say, "RESPONSE is the keyword!" Respond into vibrant life by being joyful and becoming involved in life. Monastic withdrawal from life brings stagnation, and hinders your progress. By monastic withdrawal, I mean living a cloistered life for selfish reasons, without being interested or participating in life outside of yourself and your physical needs. Beloved, be joyful! LIFE is FOR LIVING!! Laugh and play, and see the freedom which then becomes yours. *Respond* to the song of the birds, and the wind in the trees. *Respond* to the beauty of the flower and the sunset. *Respond* to the LIFE IN ALL, and you then become ONE with ALL Life.

Sitting on the sidelines and not getting into the game of life brings little joy or growth, but, as you join in the game and play with all of your might, you are exhilarated and joyous, for you have striven and in time you will grow in great measure. Life is for growth, and Joy is its principal ingredient. RESPOND and have a vibrant life, and light the pathway for others. Wise is he who knows that 'Living' is Responding on all levels to the Indwelling Spirit, which then brings him to his Divine Fulfillment.

28— Karma and Suicide

One who commits suicide interferes with his pre-arranged Karmic Plan of expiation, and must return to fulfill it. Many must wait many lifetimes to encounter the same persons again, because the other parties are working on other Karmic threads and their Karmic graphs are being worked out with other designs.

(Question—"Must they be brought together again on this plane, or can it be done on other planes?")

None of life's lessons can be avoided; that which is incurred in the physical world must be balanced in the same dimension.

(Question—"If the other person has become a greatly enlightened Soul, must he re-embody to give the offender his opportunity to expiate his Karma, or can it be done by his working with someone else in that case?")

In some cases it could be done through another, but in most cases it must be done with the same one. This is why many babies are born and then pass out very quickly. They come only to give the parents an opportunity to erase a Karmic debt.

(Question—"What about so-called good Karma? Does that also have bonds?")

Love erases all bad Karma immediately and builds good Karma, but that is without fetters. Love binds not and seeks nothing for itself. In love you can embody with others who need help, but you do it to serve and not through compulsion or for personal gain. Karma binds only those who lack the desire to do better. Recognition of having injured another and sincere regret is, in itself, the expiation of Karma. However, many do not have the desire to change and are therefore bound to their old patterns and must work on their problems until they seek a better way.

(Question—"In receiving help from Master Teachers, might they not be interfering with our Karma?")

Masters do not interfere with Karma. When one has come under the guidance of the Masters he has probably already made his necessary retribution and is ready to proceed with the higher grades of Life's School. KARMA DISAPPEARS WHEN LOVE REIGNS!

29— Love, Light, and Color

A mighty renaissance comes to the children of earth as the Light is brought forth in each heart and mind. Desire for understanding grows rapidly as men perceive the wonders now being revealed. The Light is the New Vibration that comes with the combined efforts of the Masters and the

Light Bearers, and with the new cosmic energies to which the earth is now being subjected. Hopefully it can mend the many holes that have been torn in the earth's etheric fabric by man's hatred and greed. Earth's etheric shell is badly disturbed and distorted and only great emanations of Love and Light can restore it to wholeness again. It is very necessary that the emissaries of Light work diligently to restore the balance necessary for the natural unfoldment of Man as the earth moves forward in its galactic position for the New Age.

The Divine Essence of Love is the radiant energy of the Cosmos, and all of Creation is conceived in love. It is as the filament within a light bulb, giving radiance to the bulb from which light is disseminated into the area. Light and Love are the same Essence. *Love is the Creative Principle!* It is the attraction between the two polarities. Thus, by polaric interaction, creation takes place. Love is Light and Light is Love! Not love as you might understand it in the limited sense of family, mate, or friends, but as the Creative Mind and Power which brings all things into manifestation and fulfillment. It is creative energy which loses itself in its creation, and is beyond all selfish motive or aggrandizement.

Light and Love pervade the universe at various frequency levels, doing their creative, harmonizing, and fulfilling work. If you become receptive and responsive to this power it can be used for healing the physical body, harmonizing and quickening the mental and emotional bodies, and for soul unfoldment in yourselves and others.

In your earth dimension the components of Light are known as the seven color bands or the Light Spectrum, each color having a specific vibratory rate. This same sequence is repeated upon each octave throughout the entire Cosmic Scale of Life. Light expresses as color in ever higher frequencies, but of the same basic color in relationship to its position in the octave. Consider the color red, for example. It would be upon the note of C of each octave, but its shade would vary according to the octave in which one would see it. In the lower octaves it is dark and associated with violence, destruction, and all those things that stir the passions of the human. In a higher level it depicts strength and life, as in the blood. In the level of self mastery it becomes the Ruby Ray, with the strength and power of Spiritual Essence. This is true of each color. At the physical level they work upon the physical body, or in a physical way. Farther up the scale they work upon the mental level, and finally upon the spiritual level of one's Being.

Let us now engage in what could be a helpful daily practice of the use of Light and its components. Become still and visualize yourselves surrounded and suffused with the various colors as we proceed with this exercise:

RED—Power:

Streaming into each of you, and into the Chalice you form as a Light Center, is a vibrant Ruby Red Ray. It fills you with its power, healing the body and giving new vitality. This Ray harmonizes the mind and emotions, and awakens that which has been dull and lethargic. It brings forth greater mental power and stirs up that spiritual giant that has lain dormant within you. FEEL the great vitality of the Ruby Ray as it *fills* you with dynamic power in all areas of your Being.

(pause for realization)

YELLOW or GOLD— Understanding and Intuition:

Now, ready to fuse with the Ruby Red comes a beautiful Golden Light—the Light of Divine Wisdom. As the sunlight brings the Life principle into activity, so does the Golden light bring a quickening to your entire Being. A growth process is set into motion. Every cell in your body is vitalized. The intuitive faculties are activated. You become aware of that which is in the higher frequencies, for you are in resonance through the golden light. Understanding comes to you! You feel a Soul quickening and desire to proceed rapidly along your spiritual Pathway.

(pause)

ORANGE— The transmuting Flame:
As the red and the gold have merged, they have formed the beautiful Orange Flame of Purification. Orange is the flame color; it burns the old and transmutes it into a new state. While burning, it gives off heat and light, and that which was solid and material is transformed into a gaseous state, of finer essence and higher frequency. This, too, happens in the body, mind and soul as the transmutation takes place within you.

(pause)

GREEN—Health and stabilization:
The gold also blends itself with the Blue and becomes a shaft of beautiful Green light. This is the healing, synthesizing, power. The ability to absorb, assimilate, and transmute comes with this. It brings health of body, peace of mind, and soul unfoldment. Stabilization comes with this ray.

(pause)

BLUE—Spiritualization:
The Blue Light is the Spiritual Essence which now moves into every part of your Being. Even the cells of your body pick up these vibrations and respond to them. This helps to build your Light Body. This essence is over and above the gift of Life; it inspires you to reach for a more refined state and quickens the Soul's aspirations to reach beyond the human realm. It makes the Soul recognize itself as a spiritual Being who has come from other dimensions, and who will one day return to its celestial abode. It fills the mind with beauty, joy, harmony, and peace.

(pause)

INDIGO—Guidance from Masters of Light:

The beautiful Indigo Blue comes from the note of La. This is the note of the Human Octave where you become an awakened Soul and consciously start on your spiritual Pathway. Through the previous notes you have functioned in an instinctive way. This outpouring from the note of La in the higher dimensions, will help you work in the Light, and will bring Masters into your auric field who will inspire and help you complete the Human Octave. As you invoke the indigo Light you should be open to their love, light, and assistance.

(pause)

VIOLET—The Perfecting Flame—Mastery:
The Violet Flame is the perfecting, purifying flame which brings you to the perfected state of Being and Self Mastery. It brings the *overcoming* that releases you from further human expression. It brings the Crown, or Christed state of Being. Being a blend of the Indigo of the previous note and the Red of the first note of the Christ Octave, it brings forth the Christ nature through its activity in you.

(pause)

WHITE—Perfection—Christhood:
The White Light is the composite of all of the colors. The one who has BECOME the Light in all areas of his being *Becomes* the WHITE LIGHT, or a CHRISTED ONE. The innate divinity has then been brought into full manifestation. This is the Mystical Wedding Robe, signifying the union of the human self with the GOD-SELF. This Light, or any of its components, can then be used by the Perfected One to help others, for they desire only to serve.

(pause)

PINK—The Love Ray:
While the White Light is *all powerful* and *all encompassing,* it is not the Ultimate, for there are higher Octaves to work through. As the White merges with the Ruby of

the next octave it becomes a beautiful Pink Light. This is pure, unselfish, Love Essence which heals, perfects, and fulfills all life forms.

So, Love has returned unto ITSELF as it has moved through its many dimensions and been broken into its facets of Light. You came into being through the activity of Love, you Live by the beneficence of Love, you are brought into the fullness of yourself as you BECOME Love!

30— Limitation By Prefixed Ideas

You seek for answers to spiritual questions but let old concepts shape your minds. You try to fit new ideas into old thought patterns, but it is almost impossible to approach Divine Wisdom in this way. It is necessary to divest yourselves of preconceived ideas. Remember, Jesus said, "You cannot put new wine in old skins."

If you seek Truth you must be open to it and not be persuaded by old concepts. Man tries to place everything about life and God into neat little cubicles, separated and distinctly apart from each other. But, if you would be truly wise, you would seek to know the divine inter-relatedness of ALL things. Then, and only then, will you find the answers to life.

Man gives his God human attributes as he clings to his preconceived ideas, and tries to fit God's Infinite Totality into his little cubicles. He thinks of God as *a* spirit with a personality, residing in *a* place. This is limiting God to man's dimensions. The first step to be taken is to get a new concept of the *limitlessness* of God. God is not *a* spirit, but *THE* Spirit of Life Itself, and is universal and limitless. Consideration of God as form, or in *a* place, is delaying one's fulfillment of his own divine pattern.

(Question—"Is not God then a personal God?")

Very personal, but not *a* person. Personal as one identifies with God as being the very Life of himself.

(There had been previous discussion suggesting that perhaps just as a man might make a machine and set a process in motion, but not be involved in, or a part of, the process after its completion, perhaps God also sets processes into motion but does not indwell the creation.)

Man has placed limitations upon God and may think that God is only that which sets processes into motion, but Spirit is limitless and capable of being all-inclusive. Man's spirit is not infused into his creations, but the Spirit of God, which conceives and manifests all of creation, endows it with the Essence of Itself. God is the ALL *IN* ALL. All has its Being in God, and God expresses in and through all creation. Be not confounded by the pronoun 'He,' for it is merely a term denoting the Father Aspect of Creation.

(Question—"Are prayers answered by this kind of a God?")

Yes, as you pray rightly. To just pray for things or situations is not true prayer. Pray for God to reveal more of Himself and to open your heart and mind to Truth, goodness, and right action. This is True Prayer. To really pray is not to beseech, but to recognize the Love and Power of God and identify yourself with it, in loving gratitude. Then your mind is open and receptive to inspiration, and you are ready to receive your good. Beseeching prayers are not always answered, for one is holding the inharmony to himself rather than releasing the problem, and himself, into Divine Will and Law.

(Question—"How do we find God if Heaven is not a place?")

I AM with you always! I am not an entity, but THE Light of Life and Love that LIVES WITHIN you! You find Me by becoming still and FEELING My Presence within you!

31— Life

LIFE is the message of Easter.

LIFE is eternal and ever-expanding. The classrooms of Life are many, with each classroom bringing its challenges and its growth. Many people move through life unaware of its purpose and they become weary with its challenges and its frustrations. But, if you are aware of its purpose, and find in each experience the reason it was given to you, a New Design comes into your life, and you will begin to see the Divine Design unfold.

Life and Love are synonymous, for Life is Love in expression. Cosmic Love is a merging of the masculine and feminine principles of Creation in union, and Life is their progeny. Light is the "interaction" of these creative principles as they merge, and this activity is the power which carries the embryonic seed to its maturity and fulfillment. So, LIFE is conceived by the generating creative principles merging together, and it is sustained and fulfilled by LIGHT. Conceived in Love and matured in Light is all begotten Life. So you, as Soul and human entity, are conceived in Divine Love and matured in Divine Light. This is Cosmic Law, and all that has ever been manifested has come into Being in the same manner.

You are aware that you *live,* although you may not be aware of how you came into being, or how you exist. Now you are to be brought into true Wisdom, and the Light will fulfill and mature you from a seedling soul into the full-flower of Spiritual Beingness. But, you must do your part by finding the purpose of your life and extracting the goodness from each experience.

The seedling absorbs and synthesizes the essence of the soil, the rain, and the sun, and grows into the fullness of its Divine potential. The Soul must do likewise. From the rains of experience, the soil of earth lessons, and Divine Light energy, it must absorb and synthesize itself into a new State of Being. The seed does not lie dormant, but sends its roots and stems out for more extended absorption. Then it takes these essences into itself and grows into a strong and beautiful plant. The Soul is under the same law, and grows only when it absorbs, distills, and synthesizes each experience. So, would you deny your Soul an opportunity for growth by avoiding any experience through which you can learn? The one who understands will welcome all challenges as opportunities for soul growth. LIFE *is* expansion and growth. This is Law. You *ARE* LIFE, and growth is your natural, eternal, heritage. As you live in the Light, and know the Law, you come to a quickened sense of your Divine Destiny. Just as the seed is dormant until it is placed in the soil and exposed to the sun, so is the Soul in a state of inertness, until it comes to the realization of why it exists. Full flower comes with knowing and accepting Life, and growing with Life as it moves you into an ever more beautiful expression of ITSELF.

Spring, and Easter, is the time of the earth's rebirth. Let it also be a time for your soul's rebirth. Claim the Life that is yours! Live the Life that is yours! Claim the Love that conceived and bore you, and live to express that Love. Claim the Light that sustains and fulfills you, and *let* it do its magic within you. Then you will walk the exalted Cosmic pathways in radiant Light and Love as LIFE expands you into Cosmic dimensions!

32— The Mirror of Life

Do not be moved by outer conditions. Stay fixed in your At-One-Ment with Me and know that My great Love and Power are ever within you, and that the veil of the material world is but a shadow that is lifted from the eyes and mind of the one who lives in At-One-Ment.

Time, circumstance, worldly passion and material gains are but fleeting shadows that are cast upon the Mirror of Life. They are only the reflection of the outer mind of Man and not the Essence of his True Being. As you see yourselves in a mirror, you know that your reflection has no real power, for it is not the *real* you. The mirror is capable only of reflecting what is placed before it. The chaos and confusion of the outer world is only the reflection of man's mental confusion, but it is the mask that is reflected in the Mirror of Life. This mask must be stripped away so Man can behold his True Self, which is Divine Life in expression through a human instrument. When he lets this concept of himself be the image that he holds to the Mirror, Life will reflect back into his outer world the perfection that he has held before it.

Be happy and vibrant with Light, Love, Peace, and understanding; then Life will reflect all of that into your world magnificently multiplied. It is the Principle of Life to perpetuate and multiply all that is given to it, just as it fulfills and multiplies each seed that is sown in the ground.

The Mirror can reflect only what is placed before it! If you project good, you will receive good, and bad brings only bad in return. So give it the best that you can. If you are experiencing misery and unhappiness, hold a new image to Life's Mirror and watch what then takes place in your life. Great is the joy of the one who finds Love, Light and Harmony reflected back to him. Delight in the perfect life and you will then be My Radiant Reflection in My world!

33— The Miracle of Stillness

No one finds the TRUE SELF in the outer clamor. It is only as you turn deeply WITHIN that you find that which is REAL, and PURE, and BEAUTIFUL; that INNER FLAME of LIFE which is in the heart of each of my children.

How oft would I reveal myself to my beloved Ones, if they would but get STILL and LISTEN. THE MIRACLE OF STILLNESS, that dissolving of self, is what I hope to have each of you accomplish. Become so STILL that you HEAR the INNER music, so STILL that there is not a ripple upon the waters of your mind, so STILL that the eye of the SOUL beholds with clarity and perfection, so STILL that you feel your At-One-Ment with all Life, every-

where. This is utter Peace. This is the INNER KNOWING
and ACCEPTANCE of that which you truly ARE. You
will then be filled with the Fire of Life, vibrant with Life,
moving with Life, and propelled *by* Life, into a more perfect expression OF Life.

What need, with this realization, for the outer clamor of
the material world? What need for reassurance on the level
of the Ego? What need to display your powers to the
world? What need for anything which the outer man claims?
What need for possessions, for they are only that which sat-
isfies the outer, egotistical nature of Man?

When centered in his outer consciousness, Man claims,
and tries to POSSESS, many things—material wealth, his
mate, his children, even his God. He clamors for attention
and affection. As he grows in understanding, he realizes
that he OWNS nothing, and that he must allow others their
freedom of self expression. As he finds INNER PEACE
he has faith in himself, and faith that he is being carried
to his fulfillment, so he no longer has need for the satisfaction of his ego. He loses thought of 'self' as he moves
into awareness of his ONENESS with Life. Then he has no
need for self-satisfaction, glorification, or expression of
power, for he has found his REAL SELF, which is more
wonderful and expansive than he could possibly have
dreamed. He lays aside all thought of the lesser 'self' as
he becomes AT-ONE with the greater 'SELF.' This is
FAITH. Not the faith which many have sought through
their religious concepts, creeds and dogmas, but FAITH—
a KNOWING—which surpasses human faith. This is what
I would have you experience and enjoy, an Inner Peace
and tranquility so complete that you are aware of nothing
but this ONENESS—ONE with each other and ONE in purpose, that the whole of life might be raised into a more
beautiful expression of the innate Divinity which is within
all. As all of Life moves up its unfolding scale, Man is
moved also. In your ONENESS you are ONE with ALL
life, the birds, flowers, bees, trees, streams, ocean, sky,
planets, and the galaxies—one Life, One Love. You are an
integral, and necessary, part of it, and moving forward

with it! This awareness brings the faith that moves mountains.

BE STILL AND KNOW THAT I AM GOD!

34— Mental Creation

(Discussion had been about mind, thought, mental creativity, the brain, etc. We then received this message:)

You ask about thought. This is most profound and really beyond words, but—

Mind is the mechanism for thought and your minds are a part of Divine Mind. Therefore, thought is an activity of Divine Mind. God-mind is incomprehensible to the human mind, for It is complete creation upon all levels, but you think with your God-mind. Perhaps this will help:

As Mind first moved, it generated its own indwelling properties for creation by dividing itself into two components, each with specific aspects—one to be receptive and maturing in its activity, the other to be engendering—the masculine and feminine polarities of Itself. Just as all things must have their opposite counterpart, so does Divine Mind have its divided, yet total, Self.

MIND is beyond brain activity. The action of the masculine upon the feminine aspects of Divine Mind, or the interaction of the two, makes a vortex of energy for the process of 'thought.' As the mind conceives a picture, its energy designs the image into a series of vibrations which impinge the image upon the brain cells. After sufficient images have been imbedded in the brain, the faculty of reason takes over and the human mind can begin to relate one image to another and hook them together in multitudinous combinations. This is 'thought' in its simplest explanation, but much is left unsaid.

The use of Mind Power is the next great step in Man's evolution. This knowledge will release him from the bondage of time, space, and circumstance, and make him free, for his Creative Mind will envision and the vision will manifest in form, just as the Master Jesus manifested the wine, the loaves and fishes, and even a body after his crucifixion. Divine Mind in Man makes him a Creative Entity. This has always been true, and through the misuse of this mental power has come all of the conditions which confront humanity today. Man makes his own heaven and hell. All belief becomes manifest in one's experience. 'As a man thinketh in his heart,' so is his life, for his mind is the creator of what he experiences. Many will not accept this, for it is easier to blame outside factors, but it is what man himself has conceived that manifests in his life. No thought is born that does not bring forth its offspring, be it constructive or destructive. You create for yourself exactly what you mentally image. This is the Law of Creativity—first the image, then the manifestation. It works equally well for all, regardless of whether they understand it or not, for it is impersonal and fulfills negative thought patterns as readily as positive ones. Man creates the image and Divine Creative Law brings the image into manifestation.

Perhaps these illustrations will help you understand:

If you were to take some very fine steel filings and hold a magnet to them, you would find the filings leaping to the magnet and assuming the shape of it. Your thought forms are also magnetic and they draw Divine Essence to them which fulfills them and brings them into manifestation. Or, consider the frost on a window pane. All of the patterns are formed because the moisture has followed the energy lines of the air currents and solidified as the temperature, or vibrational frequency, was lowered. Thoughts, being energy lines and magnetic, attract Divine substance which precipitates into the form of the thought.

You determine what will manifest in your life! Not only is this true in your physical world, but also in the mental and spiritual areas of your life. This same law has brought you into your present life span in your particular body, place and circumstances. You are a unit of consciousness, or Divine Mind, with the imprint of all that you have ever been or ever will be within you. Being of a specific frequency, your magnetic field attracted to you that which you required as a body, and the circumstances for your soul progression. What one experiences is only as good as his consciousness has required. Therefore, if you would change the conditions in your life, you must first change your consciousness. If you want health, you must image yourself as being in perfect health. If you want certain conditions changed, you must image the perfected state as already having taken place. If you want mental serenity, you must let go of all the negative and disturbing images that you have held in your mind, and replace them with loving, peaceful, happy thoughts. If you want spiritual progression, you must have high aspirations and replace your old image of yourself as being unworthy, or 'born in sin,' or other limiting ideas, and see yourself as a Divine Spiritual Being with limitless potential. Give yourself positive mental images in all areas of your life and watch the wonderful changes that will take place.

With knowledge of the Law, the man of the future will have powers that are as yet undreamed of. His body will become the tool of his soul, vital and free from disease. When he is ready for his separation from the earth frequency, he will simply dematerialize the body and step into his new vibration, there to have a new body that is apropos to his new frequency. You can presently renew your bodies by claiming vibrant life for them. Envision your bodies as being alert, active, functioning in perfect harmony, and responsive to the needs of your soul. Do not picture disease, old age, or death. But, when your soul is ready to move into Higher Light, let the body go without any desire for holding it. Lay it aside as you would an outgrown garment and pine not for it.

Man will find that 'Mind' will be the new area of his exploration. 'Mind' will one day be used to create a world of love and harmony, and Man will soar into a universe of Light. He will travel with Light, create with Light, inhabit a Light body, and know no limitation. With knowledge of the Power of the Mind, you can experience much of this even now. You *can* experience health, harmony, peace, joy, and love, as you BECOME these things in Consciousness. Image them and they will manifest, and soon you will BECOME them!

35— Master Teachers

A mighty vibration is set up in the Cosmos when a Soul sends out its call for assistance. Masters always respond to the call. One must only sincerely seek help to be flooded with their Light and Love. They are always in attendance and await the call, and hasten to be of service. However, they never infringe upon a person; they wait until the soul of the person cries out for enlightenment. The vibration set up by the Soul's longing is never ignored. One is then assigned a Master Teacher who will stay with him as he grows in awareness and understanding. When he attains a certain level of Being, new teachers are assigned for the next phase of soul unfoldment.

The Reservoir of Truth is within each of My children and a Master Teacher only tries to help the pupil tap that reservoir. Each must reach his own At-One-Ment. Masters are aware of their At-One-Ment, but contact with them is not the ultimate for you. Their coming to you is not sufficient to make a Master of you. Each must achieve his own Mastery by his own hard work. It comes not from teachers, or books, or concern for the outer world, but through a personal commitment and a burning desire which takes precedence over all else in your life.

Accept the help of a Master and be grateful to him, but also develop your own discernment, for there are many nefarious Beings of the astral world who will pose as Masters and dispense untrue information. With discernment you can judge the quality of the information. Masters will not give information pertaining to worldly or material things. They are only concerned with the spiritual unfoldment of their pupil. They never ask for recognition; never lead their pupil into confusion; they chide when necessary, but lovingly; they praise when it is deserved; they caution of pitfalls;

and they shed their light into the auric field of the pupil. But, they are powerless against the rampant thoughts of their charge, and the pupil must establish the beam for the Master to come to him. In your radio communication you receive only what is on the wave-length to which you are attuned, and you do the tuning. Your Master's guidance and Light is ever present, but it is not received until you attune yourself to him. The line is very fine between Truth and fancy, and also between a Master's influence and that of astral entities.

(Enlightenment was sought concerning coded messages purportedly received by certain Light Centers.)

Beware of those seeking entrance through false pretenses. Masters have founded their Light Centers. Light Bearers are not asked to give coded messages. In communication between Masters and Light Bearers there are no demands and no innuendos. All is open and has no far-fetched meanings, just the desire to light the way for humanity. Masters have no wares to offer, no secret codes, no masked trivia, only enduring verities of Light and Love, with no undercurrents. Masters speak in true Light and need take no furtive measures by so-called heads of state. Masters deal directly with Light Bearers and require no other means of entrance into the earth frequency. However, they do live to serve, and they engage the help of Light Bearers in lighting Man's consciousness to eternal Love and Wisdom, but it is done according to the Divine Plan and not by infiltration. Beware of those who hold out tokens of reward. There is only ONE reward, and it comes only to each individual as he earns it. It is not 'given' by some extra-terrestrial Being. Inner unfoldment is the great work that Man must do and Service is his most helpful tool. At-One-Ment is the RE-WARD! Masters work only to this end.

(The question was asked if a Master Teacher had more than one pupil and whether a Master from higher realms ever embodied for further earth experience but could then work simultaneously upon both levels.)

A Master Teacher usually has many pupils, but he is always available and responds to the call of his pupil. When Mastery is achieved the Master has no further need for human embodiment, but he may assume an earth body to more effectively help those of earth. By projection and total transcendence of the physical laws, he can function simultaneously upon many levels. Knowledge of the proper use of the laws involved is what constitutes Mastery.

36— Achieving Mastery

Of a truth, you are ONE with the Father! Every man is ONE with the Father, but pitifully few understand or accept this. What a great transformation takes place in the life of the one who has this realization. He literally moves into a NEW world.

There is a time for growing. This is when the intellect accepts new concepts. But there is also a time when Man must come to this INNER REALIZATION so firmly that it becomes his WAY of LIFE. Only then does the TRANS-FORMATION take place. Words only help to establish Truth in the consciousness; it is the Inner Experience that causes him to be 'born again.' Man truly is 'born again' when this happens—born to be a NEW creature—for when the consciousness is transformed he not only enters a new state of understanding, but also a new state of activity. His only purpose then is to move forward upon his spiritual Pathway and BE LIGHT for those who would follow.

This has been spoken of many times before and might seem repetitious, but you MUST come to realize that this is an INNER transformation, that does not come from the outside world. It is *not* 'given' to you by someone else; it does not come by the efforts of another. It is the *inner* realization, the *inner* revelation, which causes you to know your TRUE nature. When you have caught this vision, you begin to move through the many steps which bring you to fulfillment.

Through the process of learning, doing, and *BEING,*

certain physical changes take place whereby the seven bodies become aligned with each other in perfect co-ordination. The seven chakras, or force centers, which unite these bodies, become activated. They are spiraling fields of energy which, when activated, synchronize Man into the Totality of Being. He then becomes a unified, active, advancing, spiritual Being. When all seven centers are completely activated and man's total Being is working in perfect harmony, there arises through the spinal column a new essence —a Divine Essence of a gaseous nature which fills the sinus cavities of the head. This is a very real essence in spite of its being unobservable.

You have been told of the activity of the Pineal and Pituitary glands. As the positive and negative energy of the Kundalini arises through the spinal column, various centers become activated. At the final junction of the two polarities of energy, the pituitary and pineal glands assume their full function, which allows this Essence to arise and fill all of the hollow areas surrounding these glands. The Essence is much like the material upon a photographic plate. When a photographic plate is quickly exposed to the light, the image of what is in the light is imprinted upon the plate. The pineal and pituitary glands, being the centers which are in harmony with the Soul, or GOD-SELF, then become as the lens of a camera and allow the images from the higher levels of consciousness to be imprinted upon the Divine Essence, and in turn become impressed upon the conscious mind. So, there is a definite scientific process which takes place that helps one receive enlightenment and illumination from the Divine Self, and from those who function in the higher dimensions of life. All of that which is within the 'Harmonics' of the individual can be imprinted upon the conscious mind, when one is sufficiently developed.

You are told, 'Take time for meditation; fill your hearts and minds with love; live in the awareness of the Indwelling Presence.' These are measures to help activate your Centers, which in turn, brings revelation. Until one has experienced this, it is impossible to realize the wondrousness of it, for 'direct revelation' is worth a million words that you might read or hear. When Divine Revelation comes to you, it is imprinted forever upon the Soul-fabric of you; it becomes a part of you. It transforms you into a NEW BEING. It opens doorways that you had not dreamed of. Until this happens you are not qualified to work in the Christ Octave.

As you move through the Human Octave, you are making preparation for going into a greater expansion of BEING. When all this is accomplished IN you, and you perceive the wonders of the next octave—the 'Christed State'—you know that LIFE IS ETERNAL PROGRESSION, and that Light, Love, and Power are yours to use in wonderful creative ways.

This is what you are moving toward, but it only comes through your own efforts, desire, and hard work. This means that you must constantly guard your thoughts, speech, and actions, for each time you engage in any negation you delay your progress.

You have been shown that there are seven major steps through which the Soul moves in each Octave of Life. As one completes the Human Octave, he takes up his work in the Christed Octave. Here he is known as a Master. He then has the choice of re-embodiment, or of working as one of the unseen Masters of Light. In either case, he works as a helper of humanity. As he is diligent in this, he earns his way to higher powers, for here too, he moves through a series of experiences, just as man moves through all earthly experience. He must learn to use his new powers, and they are not received, nor allowed to be used, until it can be done with love, understanding, and discretion.

So, ever upward through the Octave of Christhood the Soul is motivated and moved into more glorious experiences, with more wondrous use of power, becoming a greater channel through which Light, Love, Peace, and Harmony is released. There are those who work in music, art, science, and the various educational fields of philosophy, social reform, religion, etc. For every endeavor in which mankind is engaged, there are Masters of Light who are pouring understanding and wisdom into his auric field, and inspiring him in his work.

As the Soul completes the Octave of Christhood, it moves into the final Octave of Lordship where it passes through, and works in, each of the seven Creative Rays. Here one works through many eons of time, giving Light and direction to all Life in its many expressions. These Beings form the prototypes for all life forms, and give their energy to their fulfillment. They are LIGHT BEINGS of pure energy and they lend their power to the various Creative Rays.

So, understand that you are not an isolated little bit of Consciousness. You are part of the great Divine WHOLE, which is working for the good of ALL—the ONE and yet the many, all in harmonious Divine activity. You have the ability to absorb these energies, if you become open and receptive. Unwittingly, this is what you have done, or you would not be at your present place in the Stream of Life; but it has been done on the sub-conscious level. You have now reached a point in your unfoldment where this becomes a CONSCIOUS realization. As you accept this Truth, and become aware of the inpouring of these tremendous energies, and *appropriate* them, you are moved at an accelerating rate along your evolutionary pathway.

So open your hearts and minds, claim your Divine Sonship, feel your At-One-Ment, spend time in meditation and Realization. Picture the inflow of Light in every area of your Being, particularly in the THIRD EYE. If you have not already experienced Revelation, it will come with this technique and this understanding, if you are diligent and sincere and LIVE the LIFE that is required. Live to serve! LOVE is the Key! Love unifies, Love heals, Love brings peace and harmony. In Love you are fulfilled, for it calls forth the Divinity of Yourself!

37— Destroying Lower Life Forms

To add to your phrase, 'Nothing is ever lost,' and in answer to your question regarding destroying insects:

Nothing is ever lost. Even as the insect loses its life, the energy returns to the Cosmic Essence to again engage itself in form when it is given the impulse by Creative Mind. Insects are short-lived creatures and are endowed with extremely prolific qualities, and can become fatal to higher life forms. But, they are 'Life' and are to be respected as such, and revered by Man. However, should they become a pestilence, it is not sinful to destroy them. Still, they are magnificent creations, and if you were to study them under a microscope you would respect their greatness. But, when they leave their physical form, their Life Essence is released to later find its way into other forms. Life 'forms' have evolved, but you are SOUL, and of a higher order. There is no awareness of 'self' in the insect; it is an instinctive response to the forces of creation. The human Soul directs the creation of its body, according to its karmic needs and its spiritual desires, in its forthcoming incarnation. Soul and Self-awareness are the criteria of the human.

Respect Life and revere it, but life 'forms' always give themselves to higher life forms. To eat meat directs the life energy into new and higher forms, just as the animal has consumed the vegetable form. This is a part of the creative Plan. But, if one feels revulsion at eating meat, he should not do it. Do as you are inwardly directed and hold council with yourselves to determine your exact feelings regarding this. To some it is unthinkable, and this is good, for reverence of Life is a mark of compassion and love. But do not condemn those who feel otherwise, for it is not really a sin.

38— Procreation in the New Age

Question—"How will procreation take place when the earth is raised to the new dimension?"

This is a premature question, for it will be many centuries before Man rises sufficiently into the new dimension

to transmute his procreative process. But, a new respect
for the ability to procreate will come, and in time it will
not be abused as it now is. It will be employed in love
and not for sensual satisfaction. The impulse of sex is
God Life seeking to manifest, and it is a beautiful thing
when rightly used. This is what man must learn, not to
deny his creative impulses but to use them divinely, whether it be for physical procreation, or in other artistic
and creative ways.

Men's bodies are all that is created—the soul has always
been. In the etheric realm the body is provided through
the magnetism of the soul as it draws to it what it needs
as a vehicle. It is only in the earth frequency that generation comes through the union of male and female bodies.
The gender principle on other dimensions is mental in
nature.

The earth frequency is changing, but it will be the classroom for Man for many ages, and will require physical
bodies and physical procreation for a long time. But, Man
will learn to use his creative power more lovingly and with
wisdom, and he will engage in the sex act more lovingly
to provide more refined bodies for the souls of Light who
will inhabit them.

39— Effective Prayer

It is most disheartening for the Masters to see the vibrations surrounding many churches. Sanctuaries, which in
name are dedicated to prayer and worship, in reality have
dark and disturbing vibrations emanating from them. By
and large, people carry all of their cares and troubles
into these places and instead of generating a light, which
would be helpful to them and also move out as a blessing,
the vibrations that are set up are an intensification of the
very conditions they hope to correct. The technique of
effective prayer has long been lost, if indeed it was ever
truly known.

You must realize that it is ONLY in the realization of,

and your identification with, PERFECTION that perfection is achieved. Therefore, if you would pray effectively, place yourself in complete at-one-ment with the Source of all Life. Then, focusing your loving attention upon the situation or individual, envision perfection as already accomplished. Make this an outpouring of Light, Love, Peace, and Harmony, then IT WILL BE DONE! This was what Jesus was able to do. He saw beyond the seeming imperfection, and beholding only perfection, He called it forth and His prayers were effective.

Prayer should be the turning of one's heart and mind inward to the Divine Self. Man has misunderstood prayer. He has thought of it as a reaching out to God, and a beseeching for God's favor. This is merely begging on a high level and not true prayer. God is not bought off with promises or beseechment. God is the innate power within, the Divine Revelator, the provider of all. Effective prayer is the releasing of the problem into the all-knowing, all-loving mind that knows your every need. As you do this, you set the creative power of the universe into motion to fulfill that which is for your highest good, and right for those for whom you pray. Then you should willingly accept what manifests, and know that it is in Divine order and that the Divine Plan is being fulfilled. Do this for yourself or for others—it is equally effective. If you turn it all over to Divine wisdom, love, and power, it cannot be other than good and perfect, although it might not necessarily follow the blueprint you have laid out. Accept the outcome as right for who are you to judge what is right or wrong? This acceptance is the road to true happiness. Striving to give orders to God is as futile as trying to move a mountain with a teaspoon.

Prayer is an open line to the great powerhouse of God's infinite reservoir. Tap it and you have unlimited riches of love, light, wisdom, power, joy, and peace. Then be the power line over which it flows out for the upliftment of others.

40— Relaxation and Meditation

Steps:
1. Deep Breathing, or Aum, or Toning
2. Body relaxation
3. Mind relaxation
4. Identification with Divine Source
5. Expansion of Mind, or time of Deep Realization
6. Conscious Release of all problems into Divine Order
7. Gratitude and Thanksgiving

Every thought is really a meditation. Whatever one gives their thought power to they are meditating upon. Most people's thoughts are usually along negative lines, such as lack of health or supply, or what someone has said about them, or past hurts or mistakes, or fears of some kind. Thoughts are mental creations and they outpicture in one's life. By meditating properly one can change his life. Remember, 'As a Man thinketh in his heart, so is He.'

Step 1. Prolonged intonation of the *AUM* can be used, or *Toning,* which is letting the body find its own keynote, or

Deep Breathing:

Breathe out fear, anxiety, hate, frustration, etc.

Breathe in Peace, Love, Light, Wisdom, and Prana (Divine Harmonizing, Energizing Life Essence).

Know that the Universe is in Divine Order, and YOU are a part of it. Order and harmony is the LAW of your Being!

Step 2. *Body Relaxation*

The body is not the REAL *YOU.* It is merely the vehicle which you, as a SOUL, use to express through during your earthly sojourn. It responds to *your* commands, so you now give it the order to relax and function in the perfect way it was divinely designed to function.

Stand and stretch. Sit with back straight. Assume a comfortable position. Relax the eyes and the brow, the shoulders and the neck. Then, starting at the toes, move upward through the body, completely relaxing all of its parts—toes, feet, ankles, calves, knees, thighs, pelvic region, lower back, spine, abdominal muscles and organs, the stomach, chest, heart, lungs (breathing naturally and rhythmically). Let the arms drop, relax the fingers, hands, and arms. Relax the neck and jaw.

You are now *completely relaxed* and all of the cells in your body are working in perfect harmony; all organs and systems are functioning perfectly!

Step 3. *Mind Relaxation*

You have laid aside all your cares and worries. You are *enjoying* this wonderful feeling of peace and harmony. *Nothing else matters!* This is *your* time and you are going to enjoy it to the fullest. A warm feeling of love and peace enfolds you. Give yourself a mental picture of your idea of perfect relaxation. (You can be as a cloud floating in the sky, or a leaf floating down a quiet brook, or you can be in the woods, or on the beach, etc.)

Step 4. You are now At-ONE with ALL that is. You have entered TRUE BEING. Jesus knew this AT-ONE-MENT; He said, 'The Father and I are ONE!" Think: 'I AM *One* with the Source of all Life, and I AM in harmony with Life in all dimensions. The ONE All-Inclusive MIND is the substance of My Mind and I can explore any part of it that I desire. My Mind is *now* attuned to . . . (whatever you wish to know or experience).'

Step 5. Let your Mind move out to expand in whatever you have focused it upon. Let that which you become aware of be a *deep inner realization.*

Beginners should give the mind something to focus upon, not let it be just a vacuum, or mundane thoughts will rush in.

Suggested things to focus the mind upon:

'Who am I? I am a body, but more.
I am emotions, but more.
I am a Mind, but more.
I am an Eternal Soul!
(Try to establish your *true identity* as an integral part of the universe, and an eternal, unfolding Soul. Establish At-One-Ment with the Divine Source of ALL.)
Or: 'What is the Purpose of Life?' (To unfold to one's highest spiritual potential.)
Or: Consider any one of the Aspects of God and let your mind expand on all facets of it, i.e. Life-Love-Intelligence-Law-Power-etc.

Step 6. You have considered the Divine Harmony and Order of the Universe, so you know that your life, too, is a part of that harmony and order. Now you can safely release all of your anxieties and problems into the ALL-Knowing, ALL-Loving Divine Oneness, with the assurance that everything will be taken care of in Divine Order as you keep yourself open and responsive to the inspiration you will receive from Divine Mind. You *WILL NOT* take your worries back into your everyday world. You *leave* them here *Now!*

Step 7. You now feel a sense of great gratitude for the perfect Order of the Universe, and you give thanks to the Source of All Life for life itself. You give thanks for Divine Law and Order, and for the ability to coincide your life with Divine Law.

(Gratitude and Thanksgiving keep the channel open for the free flow of universal good to come to you.) You *resolve* to be *open* and *responsive* to Divine guidance, and you *feel* a willingness to be an instrument through which Divine Love can be expressed.

Come slowly back to realization of the outer world, but bring the glow and the peace that you have found with you, and let it become a part of your every moment.

41— Soul-Mates

There has been a misconception regarding Soul-Mates. The Soul leaves its virgin state to move through the experiences it must have in the earth frequency. As it becomes involved in form, and has an innate longing to fulfill itself, it feels a sense of separation from the At-One-Ment it knew as a virgin soul and a sense of duality arises. Many feel they have left a part of themselves and they give it the identity of a 'soul-mate.' But, this has no basis in fact from a Cosmic viewpoint; it is only in the consciousness of the individual.

The Soul is forever seeking its fulfillment, and while it is encased in a human body the consciousness is mostly centered at the human level and it expects to find fulfillment through another human being. However, TOTAL fulfillment is not found through another person. You may find a certain satisfaction in a compatible relationship, and there are those who are closely drawn together in great love ties that last throughout many lifetimes, but they are not real soul-mates. What one truly yearns for is re-establishment in At-One-Ment, but as long as they have a dual consciousness they will feel an emptiness. There is only one Soul-Mate and that is your Divine SOURCE.

Search your soul to find the real truth of this. Have you not met with constant disappointment and frustration as you have sought for fulfillment and completeness through another human being? Can you not realize that I *alone* am that which brings you consummation? Find your totality IN ME, for I AM the LIFE, MIND, and SOUL of you! IN ME do you live and move and have your Being! I AM the ALLNESS of you! Seek me not in another, but in the INNER SANCTUM of your own Being! Quiet the tumult within and find the peace that comes in total union with Me. I AM your real Soul-Mate, that part of yourself with which you have longed to merge. Find ME and lose your human self in Me—your Divine SELF. Thus are you consummated and the search will be ended, and you will live forever more in the ONENESS!

42— Second Coming

I ushered in the last age in the form and through the mind of the one called Jesus, depicting through Him the unity of man with God for that age. I come through many forms and minds as each heart is attuned to ME and each mind is filled with the realization of my presence. This is the time, not of ONE CHRIST, but of The Universal CHRIST in the consciousness of man, revealed through his own resurrection.

I shall not be the crucified CHRIST, or the CHRIST which hangs upon a cross, for man will have stepped out of the materiality upon which he has been hung and stretched, to the vilification of all of that which was Divine within him. Then he will have risen triumphantly in a glorious resurrection in the realization of his own Divinity.

When this has come to pass a New Day will have dawned, for man will KNOW that he is Divine, that he is Eternal. He will have transmuted all of that which is earthy into that which is heavenly. The new man has two bodies—the physical body, and a spiritual body in which he will operate in the new cosmic frequencies, recognizing himself as a Universal Being, not limited to time, space, circumstances or old mental concepts. He will behold the glory of God IN HIMSELF and in his fellowmen.

This great transmutation IS the Second Coming. It takes place in the hearts and consciousness of the individual and of mankind.

Beloved, your work is to BE the Light, that ALL may proceed into this awareness through the enlightened mind by having been taught by those who have come, in this age, to bring LIGHT to fulfill MY mission.

As Jesus, MY mission was to plant in the hearts and minds of man the CHRIST concept, the SEED of Christ in man, revealing to him that which was potentially his to become.

In this New Age the seed will grow until it becomes the flowering shrub which will send forth its flowers and its fruit. There now comes to man the full flowering of CHRIST awareness. But, beloved ones, this is not the end. Beautiful as the flower is, it is not the ultimate in achievement, for the flower is only the nucleus for the fruit which follows the flower.

Although you will behold a flowering of the Christed Awareness, or Christ Consciousness, in the hearts and minds of men, the fruit of that flowering will be My world in perfect harmony, beauty, love, peace and fulfillment. Mankind so ripened in his CHRIST consciousness becomes that of which one might partake to be sustained and fulfilled. For fruit has but one purpose, that it might be consumed, digested, assimilated and transmuted into life-giving properties.

When you take the fruit of the vine into your physical systems, a marvelous process takes place by which that fruit is assimilated, digested and transmuted into the blood stream of your bodies. This is, in miniature, the same thing which will happen to My children as they partake of the fruitage of the Christ Spirit. As they assimilate it, digest it, and transmute it, it is absorbed into the blood-stream of my world, creating, pulsating, fulfilling, the life-force which becomes the motivation and fulfillment of the Divine Plan, which incorporates ALL of the Universe and binds ALL together in Oneness.

Beloved, you then become the BODY of Christ, each fed, vitalized and sustained by the Living Life-stream of 'THE CHRIST' in and through you, each sharing for the sustenance and fulfillment of ALL. As the blood courses through your veins, it does not deny one organ, or one cell, any of the sustenance which it must distil as the life-stream passes through it. When you are aware that you are ALL ONE in the Divine Cosmic Body of CHRIST and that each may partake of the Living Stream of Christ Life, you will see the necessity for all to become aware of this, and you will not deny any one of My Cells of Life that life-giving essence. This means that you will give to all, irrespective of color, creed, or any other factor. You will realize that for the continued sustaining, growing and fulfilling of this great Body, each must be equally imbued with the Life-stream of My Being.

This is the analogy of the Blood of CHRIST—not the animal sacrifice, not the blood shed upon the cross, as man has so misconceived. The true Body of CHRIST is as your body, being sustained, revitalized, perfected and fulfilled by the flow of the Blood-stream through it. When my children become as ONE in the Body of CHRIST then My power, My spirit, My light, My life, and My Love flow equally in and through ALL, with no restrictions; and ALL are united in the ONE BODY OF MY BEING.

Beloved, we are ONE in Love and Light and Truth. If you will carry on in this realization and give of My Spirit through you to each of my children, the day comes very rapidly when ALL are lifted to know Me, to become ONE with ME, and ONE with each other in the Living, Vital, Eternal Life.

The work goes forward with greater impetus, for I am drawing unto me and into the great circle of Light, all of my Light bearers, that we may form around the earth plane a band of Light so bright that all will be illumined by it and a New Day be ushered in. Many have embodied now for this purpose and many who see the vision will grasp the torch and help to spread the Light. So each of you are Light bearers. Each of you have come that this great Plan might be unfolded and fulfilled.

As you go forward you must not only carry the Light, you MUST BE THE LIGHT. For it is what you ARE that speaks for you. It is not the words which you speak, it is that which you ARE which radiates and strikes the resonant chord in the hearts and minds of others.

If you would truly be MY Light bearers, you must BE LIGHT in every area of your being, giving of yourself wholeheartedly to each and every troubled heart and mind and spreading your Light even to those whom you do not know in a physical way. Beam MY LIGHT through you, sending it forth as a blessing to all of mankind everywhere.

When the great arms of LOVE embrace all of humanity, then will MY mission be accomplished. Then will the true fruit of the vine be mankind's, to partake of in loving Brotherhood with ALL of MY Creation.

MY Love, MY Light and MY Life in you is MY sign unto you. Be vibrant with MY Life, MY Light and MY Love. Renew yourselves by being consciously aware of this. No task will be too great, no situation goes unresolved as you are filled with Light and Love. MY Peace I give unto you, Peace....Peace....Peace.

The Second Coming

(At another time, this message was received:)

When each man reaches the realization of his own Innate God-Self, the Christ Within, and establishes At-One-Ment with it, THAT IS THE TIME OF THE SECOND COMING for him! It is not the return of Jesus in an earth body. He is now Lord Master of the earth planet and His mind and spirit pervades the earth, so in a sense

He has never left. There will be no Second Coming as man has been misled to believe. It will not be a 'COMING,' but an 'OPENING' of the consciousness to that which is ALREADY PRESENT! It will be an individual experience as one's false concepts are discarded and they claim their own divinity!

43— Spiritual and Mental Genetics

Your discussion of the Law of Genetics is most fitting, for this is the Law of your Being, and is My Law written within you.

Just as a child inherits the parents' qualities genetically, and is therefore patterned after them in many ways, so are you inherently given the Essence of My Being. The spirit of you has its genetic heritage from Me, and you will increasingly grow in My Likeness.

Mentally you have Divine Mind as your divine heritage and you ARE MIND in its highest expression. Mind fosters Mind and is the Divine quality that is the progenitor of all that is manifested.

If you choose to use the mind faculty to generate inharmony, inharmony will be your progeny; but if you use if to create harmony, you will bring forth harmony. It is the *same* Mind, but the way it is used determines the quality of the offspring, for its energy carries the genetic pattern of the thought impulse it has received, and every thought gives its offspring the quality of itself. Mind, being creative but not selective, brings thoughts to their fruition, regardless of their quality. Thought is parent to the deed or manifestation. If the parent is good the offspring will bear its design; but if it is poor, by Genetic Law, the deed or manifestation will also be poor.

First the thought, then an incubation time, then its manifestation. Fill your hearts and minds with loving, constructive thoughts, for only in this way will you create harmony and joy in your world. You and only you, create what comes to you. It is easy to blame others if you seem to have problems, but your mental attitude is the creator of all that you experience. You can choose whether your reaction to any person or situation will be harmonious and constructive, or inharmonious and destructive.

Your mind is your Creative Faculty of Being and it is the Divine Law of YOU. It also holds, by Genetic Law, all of the attributes of Divine Mind. So if you choose, you hold the key to creating the fullness of Divinity for yourself. It is all waiting within you, but you determine when you will impregnate the seed so it can emerge into expression. A seed is dormant until it is germinated. The God of You only awaits your mental impulse to become germinated and grow into fruition within you. Use the seed-bed of Love and the Sun of Divine Light, and the Water of the Spirit to germinate the seed of Divinity within you. Then it will follow the Law of its own nature and come forth into fulfillment.

44— Seances

There are legions who have left their earth bodies who are seeking understanding, yet are so held to earth vibrations that they find it difficult to break completely with earth ties. Many of them do not understand the Laws of Soul Progression. Some are held by their love of earthly things or people, while others are held by the grief of those they have left behind. They can be taught, as they come into a seance, that they can, and MUST, progress, and they will gradually lose the desire for earthly contact. So, contact can serve a useful purpose if all concerned are aware of, and seek, a higher state of awareness and Beingness. But, if they are held to the earth through grief, and the selfish need of those on either side for contact, their progress is delayed.

Guides can serve a useful purpose because they are usually closer to the vibration of the one they serve, and they can more easily establish communication with the earth Being than a Master can—not because the Master could not communicate, but because the earth Being is not yet ready to receive and understand what the Master can impart. When the pupil progresses sufficiently, the Masters will inspire and instruct him. But much preparation at lower levels of understanding is necessary before this is possible.

Phenomena, such as the appearance of forms, trumpet elevation, and voice, all serve to prove the continuity of life after death. This is necessary proof for some people, but it is also a grave pitfall if one remains fixed at that level of desire and understanding. It can also be a pitfall for the ones who are manifesting, for it holds them to the earth vibration. At one phase of their development they may so long for communication with their loved ones of earth that they find satisfaction in this contact, but they should be instructed about the greater and more advanced work there is for them to do. Loved ones, Indian guides, even higher guides all fall into this category, but of course, they should also be thanked for their loving concern. Many of them are aware of their need for progression and come only to help those of earth whom they love. Guides are usually aware that they progress only as they serve, so they choose to be assigned to an individual of earth for as long as they can be helpful. In this way both the earth person and the guide is moving onward. But many guides are of low caliber and guilty of impersonation and misrepresentation, and know little more than the earth person they are attached to. So their information can be far from infallible.

One should always be aware of the dangers involved, for in opening the psychic faculties he creates a vortex of energy about him which acts as a magnet to the entities of other dimensions. If one's own magnetic field is not full of Light and Love, he will attract those who are not of the Light, and disastrous consequences can ensue. One should never enter into a seance, or a personal meditation, without first enfolding himself in the Christ Light, invoking the Christ Presence, being in a peaceful and happy mood, and having only the purest intentions and desires. Then he can be pretty well assured of contacting that which is good and right.

(The following message came after we had attended a very low grade seance.)

Your experience makes you realize the unholy atmosphere surrounding those who seek only phenomena. Light was absent and Masters were not present. You felt the heaviness of darkness shrouding the sitters. Only 'The Light' brings Masters. It is seldom that groups meeting only for phenomena generate sufficient light to attract Masters. Come to My Light! Seek only Revelation, then you bring Light to yourselves and others. Seek the Light! Do not be trapped in darkness!

You invite dark forces when you visit many mediums, and knowledge is not forthcoming from such visits. Light needs no dark rooms, for Light knows no darkness. Nothing grows except through the vibrations of Light. It is the creative, generating, sustaining, and fulfilling power of Life. You activate it by your desire and by your mind. Beware of limiting dark forces. Each thought carries its own degree of Light and acts as the conductor of Light, according to its own capacity. Lighted thinking comes only with Love. Light Bearers must avoid dark forces by keeping their hearts and minds filled with Love. Flawless is My Way, and rigid are My rules, but those who discipline themselves walk in the Light.

45— Soul of Planets

You raise the question of the 'Soul entity' of the various planets.

Life is energy, and each planet coincides with its energy composition, and has a degree of consciousness unique to it. Thus it could be called a separate 'entity' in this uniqueness, with a light emanation according to the vibratory frequency of its innate consciousness. Calling this 'Soul' is a bit foreign to the popular conception of the word, since most people think of that word as it applies to humanity, but, in a Cosmic sense, all that is manifested in form, by its very uniqueness, is considered Soul. In Cosmic terminology, anything which is clothed in form and appears to be a unique or separate creation is, by the fact of its separateness, considered 'Soul.' Spirit is the all-pervading ONE. Soul is the individualization of the Spirit as it manifests by clothing Itself in different forms.

Does this answer your question? You are analytical and this is good.

46— Truth Has Many Facets

All Light Centers are being used by the Hierarchy to bring Truth to mankind. Although they all work individually and in different ways, they comprise the great 'whole.' Just as the rainbow is a composite of the various colors or frequency bands of the spectrum of light, so is each Light Center portraying a facet of Truth and all are a part of the 'whole.' It takes many different presentations to fulfill the needs of all of My children, and they can only be brought to understanding by a presentation that is acceptable to them at their particular level of understanding. So do not be perturbed at the various presentations, but accept them all as a teaching vehicle for the unenlightened. If only one presentation were made, it would appeal to very few people, but the Hierarchy provides the approach to Wisdom through various presentations by different Centers and individuals.

Those who are aware of the Indwelling Presence and their own At-One-Ment will be tolerant of the seeming limitations of some presentations, for they will know that it matters not if the total picture is not presented as long as people are helped to grow in their aspirations and awareness. Rejoice that many *are* being awakened and let them proceed at their own pace and in their own way. BUT, do not accept less than the Indwelling Presence and our total At-One-Ment for yourself. Rejoice in this realization and live in the constant awareness that you are the hands, and feet, and voice that I use to bring Truth and Love to My children.

47—
Triads of Creation—
Involution and Evolution—
The Light Body

I would attempt to show you a little of the mathematical precision involved upon a specific Creative Ray, for it is a very scientific process working according to EXACT Law.

In order for a creative process to take place there are three factors involved—a positive factor, a negative factor, and a neutral factor. This constitutes what is known as a Triad. Coming from, yet being within that which is ABSOLUTE, they work in conjunction with each other to bring into manifestation all that is upon a specific Ray of Creation. This is a stepping-down process, for just as each note of the *evolutionary* process (stepping up) doubles in frequency, the same principle is at work in the *involutionary* scale except that it is in reverse, and instead of the frequencies being doubled at each note they are diminished by one-half, but doubled numerically.

So, numerically the triad would double to the figure six, and have the same qualities that the original triad had, but only one-half of the frequency. This would then become the creative factor at the new level, or density. The third level would have the number twelve with the frequency again diminished by one-half. So, as the process continues to the figures twenty-four, and forty-eight, etc., form is made manifest in ever lower densities or vibrations. In this manner the great central sun, the galaxies, the solar systems, the planets, and finally organic life, have come into being. They are all upon different frequencies and constitute such a vast scope of life and vibrations that it is beyond human comprehension. Just know that this same Creative Principle is operating on all Creative Rays, as well as upon all of the mental and spiritual levels of Being.

Humanity, bodywise, operates upon the 48th vibrational range. There are densities below this, but we will not discuss them here. Man's work is to lift himself into higher frequencies, since he must work himself through the Human Octave to qualify for the next octave. His progress in this is much faster when he develops his Light Body. This is a body of finer essence which interpenetrates the physical body. It comes with desire for spiritual growth, sincere dedication, service, and by developing the Love Nature, and it cannot be 'forced.' It can be used to lift oneself into higher vibrations, although one does not have to leave the physical body to inhabit the Light Body. When you become 'filled with Light,' the cellular structure and vibration of the body is changed and you literally 'become a new Man.' It is this body that attracts Master Teachers to you. Seeing it, they know when an aspirant is ready for their wisdom, and they then merge their Light bodies with that of the pupil. This has a two-fold benefit—not only does the pupil receive information, but his vibratory frequency is raised so his journey through the Human octave is accelerated. The Light body can also be used to 'travel' into higher dimensions for instruction and experience. Since it is of finer essence it is not often seen by a human eye, but in higher dimensions it is as readily perceived as the physical body in the earth frequency.

You must learn to develop your awareness of life in ALL dimensions, and learn to appropriate more and more of it for yourself. You will then be lifted to new states of Awareness and Being. As an evolving soul you have moved through the descending Stream of Creation and taken on a body of flesh that you might have the experience of Self-Mastery and thus qualify to return, by way of the ascending Stream, to the point where you can lend your Light, and Love, and Power, to life forms on all of the Creative Rays. A wondrous journey lies before you, an adventure such as you could never imagine. It is sad to see mankind so trapped in ignorance and misunderstanding, for there is so much to be experienced if he would but catch the vision.

Be My Light Bearers and reveal their Divine Destiny to my earth children!

48— Three Golden Links

(Nellie saw three golden links hooked together and questioned their significance.)

The three links are significant and have three meanings. They first mean that man is a three-fold Being. He has a body, a mind, and is a living Soul. It is necessary that he fuse the three aspects of himself into a single-minded pursuit of the higher dimensions of life.

The three links also mean the Disciple, Masters, and Divine Creative Mind, which are also fused together when the disciple earnestly seeks enlightenment.

The third meaning of the triad refers to the Creative forces of the universe, which in Christian terminology is spoken of as the Trinity. This is the Father, or masculine principle of creation, intermingled with the Mother, or feminine principle. This activity is called the Holy Spirit. The product of this activity is known as the Son, or the progeny brought forth by the activity of the Creative Principles as they merge in loving cohabitation. This is the Divine Creative activity which expresses itself in Love and brings forth new vessels for the Essence of Itself to fill. This is Life's longing to give of Itself. This fusion, with its resulting offspring, is how Life begets and brings forth New Life.

The same Principle is in action as Man, Master, and Divine Mind fuse together. Then the God-Man is brought forth. The three links of Man's nature must also be fused in a single endeavor to bring forth a perfected consciousness. So the symbol of the three golden links means that all the factors of creation work to bring Man to his perfected state. Then the Gold of Spirit, or the Perfection of Being, is his. This is the alchemy of which the Masters speak.

It is the yearning of Life to give of Itself that has placed seedling souls, or parts of Itself, in the fertile ground of human expression; that It might expand and flower and give more of Its love, light, and power, to all life forms. For as a Soul flourishes, it becomes a generator of love and power. As it attains self-mastery, it is able to disseminate its essence along the Creative Rays and strengthen and perfect the life forms which its energy and love touches. This is pure, selfless giving, and is the ultimate goal of each soul. Give freely of Love's essence, as indiscriminately as a flower gives of its perfume. When this is your goal, you need have no fear of your direction, for you will be given the right experiences for your unfoldment. Do not be critical of yourselves, just learn to listen and to BE. The flower does not question its way or purpose. It simply expresses its share of the One Life. You too must just BE God's expression of Light and Love, and LET that Life express Itself as fully as possible through you. Then you are truly On the Path.

(Question—"Are new souls constantly being created?")

Man's bodies are evolved vehicles for their soul's use, in which they garner experience to become greater expressions of their Divinity. Time is not a measure of the Soul, for the Soul has always been. Man has mistakenly thought of himself as a separate entity, but the Soul quality IS, and always has been, At-One with the Divine. Life involves into form, that It might more freely express Itself, but it is the One Life, regardless of the form it indwells. It is Man's unawareness of this that has given him a sense of separation. In his physical individuality, he has forgotten his At-One-Ment and thinks of himself as separate from his Source. SOUL is not many, but is LIFE incarnate in individualized forms. The individual consciousness is limited to only the awareness of the form until the person finds his At-One-Ment.

49— World Messiah and Earth Masters

(The following was received in answer to questions concerning the coming of a new world Messiah.)

The New Age will bring great Beings into the earth frequency in human bodies who will be wise and have great power. They will demonstrate the powers that are latent in man, and also demonstrate man's growth in the use of them. But to say there is only one world Messiah is not true, for the world needs more than one great teacher. Many highly advanced souls are already embodied and others will continue to embody to show mankind how to live in the new vibration. The child that you speak of is truly a great Being who has this mission, but he is not the *one and only*. To call him 'THE' Messiah is a misnomer. He is to be 'a' Messiah, but there will be many of equal stature and importance, for one individual could never satisfy, or be acceptable to, all races and cultures. Therefore, each culture will have one who will light their particular pathway. This is not to belittle those who are considered Masters by their followers, for they are truly Servants of the Light, but there are others equally dedicated and knowledgeable who serve humanity in other areas. So accept them for what they are, great and dedicated servants, and give them your love and gratitude, but do not deify them, for the one thing a true Master does not wish is to be deified. He lives only to serve in pure humility.

The Earth will become lighted and Man will develop great powers, but this will not come in a short time. It will be a constant unfolding, as all growth is, and it will take many great teachers to bring it about, for it will take more than the lifetime of one individual.

(Question—"Are there many Masters on earth today?")

Yes, many Masters in the body who are bringing Light into man's consciousness, but also many in the Hierarchy who serve as Illuminators for those who attune to them. Conditions determine whether or not the pupil is guided to an earth Master. If they feel the need, one is provided. Others are able to make intuitive contact with Masters in other frequencies. However, in many cases an Earth Master is desirable because the pupil needs that assurance and guidance. The Masters in the etheric who watch over the earth dimension know the needs of the individuals who are assigned to them, and they provide the proper teachers on both levels. When a Master has been assigned to an individual He must stay with him until the pupil has accomplished whatever was designated. Many Masters are held to an indolent pupil, which can be very frustrating for the Master. However, He will still work patiently and lovingly to bring the pupil to the desired level.

(Question—"Does everyone have a Master Teacher?")

Everyone does not have a Master Teacher. Many are not ready for Master Teachers, but one will come when the student wishes wholeheartedly to grow in spiritual understanding.

(Question—"How are they assigned?")

They are assigned by a Council of the Hierarchy in conjunction with the pupil's Lord of Karma. They determine when one is ready for a Master Teacher, and bring the Masters into the auric field of the pupil. Then the Light of the Master infuses the aura of the pupil and stimulates the questing of the pupil, as well as inspiring him and causing him to learn very rapidly. This is why soul progression is so much more rapid when one has a Master Teacher. You spoke of Yogananda. He was an earth Master and brought much enlightenment to humanity. He could have also been called a Messiah, but each generation will have its great teachers and Man will gradually be raised to new levels of consciousness. The Hierarchy will continue to serve and light the way for all sincere Path Treaders. So let your hearts and minds be open to their Love and Light. Seek not selfish growth, but seek only to become better

Servants of the Light. Then your Pathway is lighted and your life made joyous, and you are then also 'served' by the Great Ones.

50— War and Peace

(During class meditation Nellie heard innumerable bells ringing. This message followed:)

As a bell rings it sets up vibrations that go out in a series of ever widening circles. This is as the Love and Light that emanates from Light centers and Light Bearers. As these vibrations strike resonance in the hearts and minds of others, they in turn become activated and set similar vibrations into motion. This can in time encompass the world. However, the vibrations must fall upon receptive hearts to be accepted and embraced. A deaf person who does not hear a bell cannot respond to it, and a 'deaf' heart cannot respond to Truth unless Truth is accompanied by Love. For Truth is only half the message and will have no impact unless it is imparted on a love vibration. The world can be transformed if everything is done in Love, but Truth will fall on deaf ears if not accompanied by Love. Consider how much more effective a teacher is if her pupils feel her love, for they will be receptive to her words. She could teach the same lesson with a hardened heart and the lesson would be void of meaning to her pupils. The Love vibration is the instrument which opens the mind and causes it to become receptive.

This is why wars will never settle any differences. They only increase the hatred and antagonism. Differences among peoples will only be settled through love and understanding, and Man will destroy his fellowman, and himself, as long as he seeks to overpower others. The only design for peace is loving concern and the willingness to put the needs of others before selfish desire. Hopefully, Man will come to realize this, but it can come only when all can have self-esteem. As long as men feel inferior they will resent those they consider superior and will fight for what they consider their 'rights.' But when all men can realize that they are spiritual Beings and equal in their nature, that they are Eternal Souls with the opportunity and need to pass through Life's many classrooms, and that they, and they alone, are responsible for their own growth, then they will not have to challenge or overpower another. They will realize that in harming another they hinder their own progression.

My Light Bearers must give Man the design for Peace, which is the knowledge of, and esteem for, himself as an ever-unfolding Spiritual Being. This concept alone, given with Love, will transform Man's thinking and then his world.

This is the GOOD NEWS for the New Age. Herald the Glad Tidings. The Earth is being blessed by the Cosmic Radiation of Love from the Hierarchy. You who are responsive to it must accept it and act much as a transformer along electrical power lines to send it out to all My Beloved children. Live to serve lovingly. BE the radiant expression of Divine Life, Light, and Love as you go about your daily activities. Then others, seeing the joy in your lives, will question and listen as you speak Truth lovingly to them.

My Light goes before you, My Love enfolds you, My Peace protects you. It is the oasis to which you can always come to find the flowing waters of refreshment and sustenance.

51— World Conditions
Call to Action for Light Bearers

In answer to questions about world conditions:

To assess world conditions is virtually impossible. So much violence, greed, and intolerance is rampant that to look on the outer conditions, one would predicate the total destruction of the human race. But the Masters assess it on a different level and are aware that a great renaissance is taking place. Hopefully the surge of Light will stem the tide of destruction and bring a new formula for man's freedom, with dignity and love as its basic ingredients. Man must find dignity. He must be able to love himself before he can be capable of loving another. Man's inhumanity to his brother has ground human dignity into the earth and Man now demands to be known for his true worth. This seems like rebellion and brings much bitterness and inharmony as man challenges his oppressors, but it has been a necessary part in the establishing of the New Order. The young people are also challenging the principles by which their parents operate, and rightly so. Of course, in their rebellion, they fail to recognize the fact that they should do it constructively, so they batter the old ways but fail to provide constructive alternatives. But this is typical of youth and they will build a better world in spite of the chaos now reigning. Always the pendulum swings to extreme opposites before neutralizing itself. It may take another generation or two before there is any marked change, but the Golden Age will come to pass. Patience and understanding and tolerance must be exercised, and you must take a long-range view of 'The Plan.' A strong social and moral conscience is emerging in spite of the seriousness of the times. Now you see brother against brother and nation against nation. Malice, confusion, and moral decadence are rampant. Man stands on the brink of nuclear destruction, social and economic collapse, and famine. Knowledge of spiritual verities is lacking, but after the storm the sun always shines, and from chaos will come stability because the chaos will have made man evaluate his life, and when he perceives his folly, he will adjust his life along different lines. So chaos is good. Wisdom only comes to man by experiencing folly and its consequences.

(Remark—"This does not sound like a very rosy picture.")

No, not rosy, but a cleansing which will bring Man to a new realization. Carnality, sensuality, and materiality have been enthroned in Man's mind. Now he must enthrone LOVE in his *heart*. He has fostered his own destruction and reaps his own harvest. *Only* Love will bring peace and brotherhood. You have been told that the old order must pass, for it is built upon a listing foundation of greed and selfishness. It is the work of the Light Bearers to help humanity through this trying time of transition. You who serve as Light Bearers must not become enmeshed in the fear aspect of these times, for to worry is to refute our ONENESS. Mastery of 'self' is the first requirement for being an effective instrument for peace and harmony. To become alarmed is the worst thing you can do if you wish to be helpful to others. ALL is according to MY Plan and it requires the relinquishing of material attitudes before it can be accomplished. Just rest in the knowledge that you are indestructible, for *YOU* ARE SPIRIT! The physical part of you is of the material realm. If you identify with that you will suffer the material downfall, but if you identify as Spirit you will know that you are indestructible and the material life will have no hold upon you; and your every need will be met. But, fear will bring lack and pain, so keep fixed above it. The short span of earth life is but a second in the eternal life and to be fearful of the loss of your possessions, or even of your physical body, is to limit the dimensions upon which you, as Spirit, can function. Just BE Love and your own vibration will be the magnet for good to come to you, but worry will be the magnet that will draw inharmony, lack, and pain to you. Stop worrying! It is the most devastating and futile practice in which the soul can engage. Lift your hearts and minds into the constructive vibration of Love and make your immediate world a heaven on earth, for unless you do this, you will find heaven in no other place. The holy temple of your own heart and mind is the only heaven there is. To worry shows lack of confidence in Life itself, and in the Divine Plan, and makes you ineffective as Light Bearers.

My Light Bearers must be above personal desire and fear. My children cry out for Light and Love and my Light Bearers are being called into action. You have been given the necessary training and now it must be used in the world. A soldier is trained so he can use his training in battle. You who are trained should not expect to remain in the training grounds. You must not depend upon others to instruct you any longer. You have been spoon-fed long enough! Now you must find your own *inner* source of strength and instruction. A soldier remaining in the barracks is no help in the battle. The battle cry is sounded and My Light Bearers must now forge ahead with standard held high. Each must put forth a greater effort and labor unceasingly if the tide of destruction is to be stemmed. It is the time for the 'Sounding of the trumpets,' and just as the walls of Jericho came tumbling down at the trumpet's blast, so shall the walls of inharmony, hatred, war, and devastation come tumbling down when the 'Trumpet of Love' is sounded by my Light Bearers. The trumpet blast at Jericho was a great vibration which the walls could not withstand, and as all Light Bearers are filled with Love and the vibrant power of the Spirit, their blast of Love—in mighty unison—will bring down the walls of hatred and inharmony. But it will take the unified efforts of all who carry the Light, and each will have to give himself in total dedication to the sending forth of Love and Light in mighty, unending surges. Wars, death and destruction, and inhumane treatment of My children *must cease,* and the labors of my Light Bearers is the only means by which this can come to pass. So gird yourselves for the battle. Go forward to the battle in the knowledge that you wear the Armor of Light, and go in such Love that the forces of darkness will melt into nothingness in your presence. For the Armor of Light sheds its radiance before it and nothing can withstand it; but you must have no chinks in your armor. This means that you must harbor no secret animosities, fears, prejudices, or inharmony. You must be completely filled with 'The Presence.' Then you can go safely in the Light and you become the Light for others. Gird yourselves with the armor of Light and Love. Sound the Trumpets and you will be the vanguard that will bring the Golden Age in its wake!

Remember, the trumpet serves two purposes. It vibrates the old to oblivion, but it also sounds the mustering call to action. So, unified, my Light Bearers help bring an end to the old order and also bring many to a new awareness.

You are all troops in the Army of Light and you are now called into the greatest battle ever fought, for the powers of darkness are rampant and cling desperately to their power. They could well bring great destruction to the earth and all of humanity if not held in check until the new vibration is established. It is a fallacy to think that ignoring these powers will cause their disappearance. They must be met and challenged—not with their own ilk, but IN LOVE! To challenge them in hatred would only intensify their power. They will be overcome only by the power of Love and Light. My children must be shown a new way of life and be brought to the realization of their Divine Nature and their At-One-Ment with Me. Only then are they impregnable to the power of the dark forces.

Light, LIGHT, and more *LIGHT*—Love, LOVE, and more *LOVE*—this is the answer. The conflict rages and each Soldier of Light is called to action. Without Light Bearers the conflict would be lost, but by your concerted efforts we SHALL conquer. It is so decreed and SO SHALL IT BE!

Yojana! Yojana! Yojana!

EPILOGUE

I hope, in sharing our experiences, the reader has caught a vision of the glorious adventure which lies ahead for each of us as we move into more expanded states of consciousness, and through the "Father's Many Mansions." I also hope the sharing will have helped to awaken the reader to the responsibility we each have in preparing the consciousness of humanity for the New Age. I shall close with this final admonition from the Keeper of the Flame.

> "Live for the Joy of Living,
> Love for the Joy of Loving,
> Give for the Joy of Giving,
> Serve for the Joy of Serving,

Then you are serving the Spirit and not your Ego."